The Tudor Rose

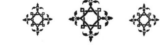

PRINCESS MARY,
HENRY VIII'S SISTER

JENNIFER KEWLEY DRASKAU

The
History
Press

First published 2013

The History Press
The Mill, Brimscombe Port
Stroud, Gloucestershire, GL5 2QG
www.thehistorypress.co.uk

British Library Cataloguing in Publication Data.
A catalogue record for this book is available from the British
Library.

ISBN 978 0 7524 6584 5

Typesetting and origination by The History Press
Printed in Great Britain

Contents

The Young Tudors

A quiver of excitement ran through the chamber. Silken robes rustled as the courtiers craned for a better view. The musicians struck up a merry tune, and out he strode, head high, the personification of England's hopes and dreams, handsome as a young god, the teenage King of England, leading his beautiful younger sister Princess Mary Rose. Dumpy little Queen Katherine looked on, graciously smiling. Marking her approval, the courtiers broke into spontaneous applause.

Katherine, daughter of the 'Catholic kings', Ferdinand of Aragon and Isabella of Castile, knew that even her best features, her long auburn hair, her fair, healthy complexion and cool grey eyes, were outshone by her gorgeous sister-in-law. At 24, Katherine's face retained a child-ish roundness, but her expression was serene and demure. Katherine had long practice of smiling even in adversity. Left an impoverished widow by the death of her first husband Prince Arthur, when her young brother-in-law Prince Henry succeeded to the throne, her own future was still unsure. Now she had achieved her destiny, cherished from childhood: Queen of England, bride of the splendid new 18-year-old king.

Tall and muscular, Henry VIII attacked life like a lion. He moved with the easy swagger of a trained athlete. His auburn hair was cut straight in the French fashion. Despite his aquiline nose, Henry favoured the Yorks, his mother and his handsome maternal grandfather, Edward IV, with his broad face, small, sharp eyes and sensual little mouth. Described in 1516 by a Venetian envoy as 'the handsomest prince ever seen',[1] at this early stage of his career, Henry was also idealistic, liberal and generous. The arrogance and brutality that would tarnish his later years were not apparent. Even his vanity and susceptibility to flattery were masked by his charm and genial manner.

Katherine, by nature more reflective than these flamboyant Tudors, lacked their animation and energy. Indulgently she watched Mary Rose steal the show. Katherine and the princess would remain lifelong friends.

Radiant Mary Rose revelled in the limelight, conscious of her own grace and skill. She had inherited her mother's delicate features, and the passion, wilfulness and charisma of her father's Tudor ancestors.

Glowing with health and high spirits, splendidly clad, jewels flashing, dipping and swaying in the rhythm of the dance, the glamorous Tudor siblings epitomised the new tide of optimism sweeping through England after the horrors of a protracted and bloody civil war. If ever, since the mythical days of King Arthur, the English court recaptured the fabled glory of Camelot, it was for those few glorious years in the early sixteenth century when Henry VIII came to reign.

Thomas More celebrated Henry's coronation:

> Now the nobility long since at the mercy of the dregs of the population, lifts its head ... and rejoices in such a King, and with good reason. Among a thousand noble companions, the King stands out the tallest, and his strength fits his majestic body ... There is fiery power in his eyes, beauty in his face, and the colour of twin roses in his cheeks ...[2]

More's coronation ode contains no portent of his bitter quarrel with the King that would culminate in More's death on the block.

In April 1509, Henry VII, worn beyond his 52 years by his long struggle to hold the throne, succumbed to tuberculosis, the curse of his dynasty. Few mourned his passing. That Henry had brought peace to the land was long forgotten; people chose to remember him as tight-fisted and rapacious.

When his 17-year-old son was proclaimed king on 22 April, a spirit of rejoicing, powered by an outpouring of love for the charismatic young prince, swept through England. The handsome teenager appeared to embody all the knightly virtues. Surely his reign would usher in a 'golden world'.

Beautiful 14-year-old Mary Rose, famed throughout Europe as 'the Rose of Christendom', was the undisputed star of Henry's glittering court.

Nobody watching this radiant pair, brimming with joyous life, could have foretold that Prince Charming would become a diseased tyrannical monster, or that violence and tragedy would stalk the beautiful princess's descendants, chosen by her adoring brother to inherit England should he fail to produce an heir. These dynastic devices would prove a lethal inheritance.

The young Tudors' parents, Henry VII and Elizabeth of York, had embraced the important task of securing the succession and celebrating the reconciliation of their two warring houses by producing several off-spring. Henry, as the first Tudor king, was determined to found a dynasty where the throne of England would be passed from father to son, rather than usurped by a series of random claimants. By the time their third daughter, Princess Mary Rose, was born, the royal couple already had two promising sons, Princes Arthur and Henry.

In an age of widespread infant mortality, even the birth of a princess – a useful political bargaining chip – could invoke celebration. However, this princess was born into a climate of intrigue and suspicion. Establishing a dynasty was a brutal business: visitors gaped at the grisly spectacle of decaying severed heads lopped off traitors and rebels and now adorning London Bridge.

Only Mary Rose's formidable paternal grandmother, Lady Margaret Beaufort, Countess of Richmond, recorded the birth of a new Tudor prin-cess in her exquisite *Book of Hours* on 18 March: '*Hodie nata Maria tertia filia Henricis VII, 1495*'.[3] Not much escaped the extraordinary Lady Margaret. During their formative years, she would be a major influ-ence on her royal grandchildren.

Tall, severe, imposing, Lady Margaret was regarded as a phenom-enon. The Divine Order, the 'Great Chain of Being', the organisational principle of the Tudor world, decreed that women were the weaker sex, inferior not only in physique but in mental ability and moral fibre. Reason and the intellect were the province of the superior male. Females shared Eve's frailty; emotional, irrational creatures, incapable of making decisions. Lady Margaret had escaped the many shortcom-ings of her sex.

Strict, devout and cultured, as Queen Mother she was the principal power at court. She prescribed rules of conduct, and enforced their obser-vance. Margaret let no one forget her exalted descent from Edward III, through the illustrious John of Gaunt, Duke of Lancaster, and his ille-gitimate Beaufort line. Unlike many of her relatives, she had managed to survive, although she had been an inveterate intriguer during the conflict between the houses of York and Lancaster, displaying an unfem-inine flair for Realpolitik.

After a turbulent personal life, her land holdings were second only to those of the King. Her first husband, Edmund Tudor, Earl of Richmond, had died within a year of their marriage, leaving 12-year-old Margaret alone and pregnant. She struggled through the winter storms to Pembroke Castle, where Edmund's brother Jasper Tudor gave her shelter.

Not yet 13, she was married off again. Her second husband, Henry Stafford, second son of the Duke of Buckingham, died a few years after the marriage. After his death, Margaret vowed never to admit another man to her bed. Her third marriage, to Thomas, Lord Stanley, first Earl of Derby, was a marriage of convenience. According to legend it was Stanley who placed the crown on the head of his stepson, Henry Tudor, on Bosworth Field, after it had been retrieved from a thorn bush. Thereafter, Henry was known as King Henry VII. Stanley, who had once been poleaxed by one of Richard III's men, and bore the scars to his dying day, was created Earl of Derby.

Having seen her son established in his divinely ordained place as king, Lady Margaret devoted her remaining years to shoring up the Tudor claim, and supervising the education of her grandchildren. A generous benefactor of scholarship, she founded both Christ's College and St John's College, Cambridge, and became the patroness of the printer William Caxton. Her religious piety bordered on the ascetic. She wore a severe widow's barb up to her chin and, next to her skin, a flesh-mortifying hair shirt.

Nevertheless, on state occasions she donned her gold coronet and, defying her crippling rheumatism, hobbled proudly behind her daughter-in-law, Elizabeth of York, whose gentle personality she overshadowed with her regal presence.

In December 1483, while still in exile in France with his uncle Jasper, Henry had sworn in Rennes Cathedral to marry Elizabeth, recognising that a marriage between himself and the Yorkist Princess would resolve England's political turmoil. Most of his relatives having suffered violent deaths, Henry was the closest legitimate male claimant to the throne on the Lancastrian side.

On the death of Edward IV, his brother, Richard of York (1452–85), appointed Lord Protector of England in 1483 on behalf of his nephew, the 12-year-old Edward V, envisaged consolidating his claim to the throne by marrying his niece Elizabeth himself. Initially prepared to face down the scandal this consanguinity would cause, he eventually dismissed the notion. However, recognising Elizabeth's dangerous potential as the focus of rebellions, he decided to neutralise the threat by marrying her off to someone sufficiently insignificant to preclude any claims on the throne. His choice fell on a young naval officer, a son of his chancellor, Robert Stillington, Bishop of Bath and Wells, whom he owed a huge favour. (The plan miscarried when the prospective bridegroom was captured by the French off the coast of Normandy, later dying in prison in Paris.)

Richard was in Stillington's debt; it was Stillington who had raised the crucial question of the legitimacy of Edward V, on the grounds that Edward IV had been betrothed to another before he married their mother, Elizabeth Woodville. On 25 June, a jury declared the young king illegitimate. Richard promptly had himself proclaimed king and crowned two weeks later, on 6 July. To Lady Margaret, gritting her teeth, fell the honour of bearing the train of the usurper's sickly queen.

Neither the boy Edward V nor his younger brother Richard were ever seen again. As discontent with Richard III's rule grew, sinister rumours that the young princes had been secretly murdered on Richard's orders gained credence. Learning of the darkening popular mood, the exiled Henry Tudor and his allies moved in to strike. In 1485, although outnumbered, Henry, with French support and his superb Welsh archers, triumphed at Bosworth. Richard was the last king of England to die in battle. During the mêlée, Henry reputedly snatched the crown from a thorn bush where he discovered it hanging.

Losses on both sides were heavy; casualties included Henry's faithful standard-bearer, killed in brutal hand-to-hand combat, apparently by Richard himself. This standard-bearer, William Brandon, already a widower, left behind a young son. The orphaned Charles Brandon would rise to unimagined prominence; his close friendship with a monarch would gain him a dukedom. He would also win the love of a queen.

Richard's defeat at Bosworth effectively rang down the curtain on the bloody Wars of the Roses. Henry now implemented his plan of uniting the warring factions through his marriage to Elizabeth of York – hardly an onerous duty. Beautiful blonde, blue-eyed Elizabeth was celebrated as the flower of Yorkist womanhood. The marriage had the full approval of the couple's influential mothers, Elizabeth Woodville, widow of Edward IV, and Lady Margaret. (Popular opinion credited the two mothers-in-law with masterminding the whole arrangement ...)

Henry wanted records to show that he had won the crown by military conquest, not by merely marrying into the Yorkist royal family; he insisted on being crowned before wedding Elizabeth. Their marriage set the seal on the reconciliation between the houses of York and Lancaster. Henry VII commissioned the collar of the Order of the Garter, in which the bride's emblem, the white rose of York, is embedded within his own, the red rose of Lancaster, symbolising their union in the heraldic device of the Tudor rose.

As arranged dynastic marriages went, it was surprisingly successful. Elizabeth, kind and gentle, immersed herself in her charity work and her duties as wife and mother, bearing the King several children, four of whom survived infancy. Worn out by repeated pregnancies, she died six years before her husband.

Mary Rose's baptism in 1495 had been overshadowed by the climate of civil sedition and dissention. But Lady Margaret Beaufort insisted that her grandchildren's christenings should follow traditions observed for Edward IV's ten offspring, including the prescribed height of the dais on which the silver-gilt font was mounted. An impressive circular canopy was erected, but no curtains. Royal babies must be christened in full view of the congregation. Infant princesses were carried by a duchess, another bearing the richly embroidered chrisom cloth. A countess bore the train of cloth of gold furred with ermine. This hung from the infant's shoulders and was so long that the countess needed the assistance of a gentleman usher to hold up the middle section.[4]

Despite the turbulent social and political landscape of the country, Mary's early years were safe and serene. News of local insurrections might create anxieties for the court and the Council, but the reins of the royal household were held by Mary's grandmother, Lady Margaret, whose personal discipline ensured that life in the royal nursery proceeded on an even keel. The thrifty king kept a close eye on household accounts, paying for the children's upkeep from the Great Wardrobe. The queen contributed from her own privy purse. But Henry was a true Tudor: when diplomacy necessitated a splash, he could put on displays of conspicuous extravagance to rival any monarch in Europe.

The young royals wanted for nothing. There were regular consignments of soft furnishings and clothing from the Great Wardrobe, bright silk ribbons for the princesses, new clothes to delight Mary's older sister, vain, tempestuous Margaret. Active children like Mary fretted in the restrictive apparel decreed by the fashions of the day. Royal babies were encased head-to-toe in stiff garments of silk or damask. By the age of 3 or 4, the little princess wore full-skirted, long-sleeved dresses with tight-fitting bodices, miniature versions of the gowns worn by grown women. On formal occasions, both princesses wore close caps, with long gold chain necklaces draped around their chubby little necks. The frequent deaths of members of her family meant that Mary was often in mourning, but black suited her blonde beauty. At 2, she was pictured in gowns of black satin and velvet, trimmed with mink or ermine, and belted with heavy dark ribbon. Her wardrobe included linen smocks, black damask kirtles, hose and a constant supply of soled shoes, testament to her passion for dancing.

At 4, she appeared in purple tinsel satin and blue velvet, crimson, green or tawny kirtles. Kirtles, tunic-like garments worn by both sexes since the Middle Ages, by peasants as well as princesses, had a front-opening bodice and an unlined skirt. At 8, Mary graduated to nightgowns; before then, the list of her clothing includes only night kerchiefs. Children probably slept naked.

When Mary was 2, the Tudors were spending Christmas in one of the King's favourite residences, the delightful old Yorkist palace of Sheen, 9 miles upriver from the Tower. This former hunting lodge, once known as the 'Shining Palace', had undergone frequent refurbishments. Mary's father, enthusiastic about his building projects, had had it repaired and enhanced, adding gardens, warrens and a deer park. Suddenly a mysterious fire broke out and most of the palace burned to the ground.

After the fire, the younger royal children, Margaret, Mary Rose and their brothers, Henry and Edmund, moved more permanently to Eltham, a moated palace in Kent, although they still occasionally stayed in other royal residences. Oarsmen liveried in the Tudor green and white would row the princesses in a state barge between the new palace of Richmond, with its fairy-tale turrets, and Greenwich, where the excited children could watch the bustle as the high-masted sailing vessels put to sea. On summer days the royal party were serenaded by musicians as their barge glided along the Thames. When in London, they were usually based at Baynard's Castle in Blackfriars or the Tower, residences which their mother preferred to the cramped quarters at Westminster.

Eltham, with its royal apartments, chapel, great hall, courtyard and new tilting yard, had been rebuilt by Edward IV. It was an ideal location for the royal nursery, convenient for London, yet set in rural surroundings away from the unhealthy city dirt and the hectic distractions of the court. Discipline here was more relaxed. Mary's grandmother's influence was visible everywhere: Lady Margaret had completed building the chapel started by Edward IV; even the swans on the moat wore enamelled badges bearing the Beaufort insignia, lightly chained about their graceful necks.

Mary's oldest brother, Arthur, Prince of Wales, was universally adored. Meeting him in 1497, the Milanese ambassador noted that Arthur, at 11, was 'taller than his years would warrant, of remarkable beauty and grace, and very ready in speaking Latin'. After Arthur acquired his own household as heir apparent, young Henry became the focus of the nursery establishment. Princes were encouraged to be vigorous and full of bluster, and Henry, an ebullient, forceful lad, needed no urging, lording it over his sisters and attendants by sheer force of personality. Nobody dared rebuke him. His showing-off was regarded with smiling indulgence as a token of manliness.

The princesses were attended by ladies, but shared their brothers' tutors. Like all royal children, Mary was taught French, Latin, music and composition, also dancing and embroidery, at both of which she excelled. Her handwriting was soon better than her sister Margaret's, although when distressed she scribbled. She was given a French companion, Jane Poppincourt, before she was 5, and was soon fluent in French. She was also assigned her own small entourage, including a physician, wardrobe-keeper and gentlewomen of the chamber.

The chatelaine of a great house required a grounding in household administration and, ideally, the skill of an amateur apothecary. Lady Margaret possessed both qualifications and ensured that her granddaughters acquired the same proficiency. A princess also needed to acquire social graces and accomplishments; she must be a competent dancer and able to participate in social activities such as card games and the performance of masques. She must be a good conversationalist, a mistress of table etiquette and manners. Some knowledge of *belles lettres* was desirable, but her sphere was the spiritual rather than the academic. As a mere female, contemporary custom denied her the opportunity to exploit her mental gifts to the full. Greater intellectual accomplishments were not required; her job was to serve her husband and bear his children. Even the enlightened Thomas More, in his *Utopia*, accepted the medieval view that the husband was supreme. In 1595, churchmen in Wittenberg were still debating whether women could be counted as human beings at all.

Although Mary would never receive the same intensive education as her nieces, Mary and Elizabeth, like all the Tudors, she was intelligent and eager to learn.

The natural brilliance of Mary's precocious brothers blossomed under the tutelage of gifted and dedicated teachers. Prince Arthur was conversant with an exhaustive list of works by the classical scholars, and could quote them extensively. Prince Henry showed even greater promise. Besides Latin and French, he displayed a remarkable facility for mathematics.

In the autumn of 1499, 4-year-old Mary and her prodigious siblings encountered a rising star of the humanism of the English Renaissance, the Dutch scholar Erasmus. Erasmus, on sabbatical from his Augustinian monastery, was tutoring young Lord Mountjoy. Mountjoy had been married at 18, in 1497, to the heiress Elizabeth Say, but the bride, considered too young to cohabit, had remained at her father's home in Gloucestershire. Erasmus and Mountjoy had been planning a jaunt to Italy, when the lord's mother, Dame Laura, informed Mountjoy that it was high time his marriage was consummated; he was to forget Italy and get on with it. Mountjoy had also been invited to become what Erasmus called '*socius studiorum*', a study companion, to Prince Henry.

Disappointed to forgo his Italian trip, Erasmus accepted Mountjoy's invitation to stay at his house in Greenwich. Aspects of English manners struck Erasmus as delightful: he enthused to his friend the poet Andrerlini (poet laureate to King Louis XII of France, a future husband of Mary Rose):

> When you arrive anywhere you are received with kisses on all sides, and when you
> take your leave they speed you on your way with kisses. The kisses are renewed when
> you come back. ... If you should happen to meet, then kisses are given profusely. In a word, wherever you turn, the world is full of kisses.[5]

When a visit to the royal nursery at Eltham was suggested by Erasmus's new acquaintance Thomas More, a clever Lincoln's Inn lawyer in his early 20s with impressive connections at court, the Dutch scholar was prepared to be enchanted by a peek into the schoolroom. Aware that Arthur, Prince of Wales, would not be present, Erasmus was not expecting any formal reception. Consequently, when More led the way into the great hall, and he beheld, gathered beneath the splendid hammer-beam roof, the four youngest royals, splendidly attired, posed among their assembled attendants in a reception committee, he was disconcerted. The centrepiece of the impressive tableau was 8-year-old Prince Henry, probably, with his already well-developed notion of his own importance, standing beneath a canopy of state.

On his right stood 10-year-old Margaret. Although golden-haired Margaret was as vain and headstrong as her brother Henry, there was as yet no hint of the outrageous behaviour that would cause notorious scandal. Four-year-old Mary Rose was preoccupied with some childish game. But decades later, Erasmus, in 1523[6], complimented Mary's prospective bridegroom, Prince Charles of Castile, on being 'thrice blessed to acquire such a bride. Nature never formed anything more beautiful, and she exceeds no less in goodness and wisdom.'

England appearing more settled, the Spanish sovereigns felt it was safe to proceed with the plans for their daughter Katherine's marriage to the

English heir apparent. Hoping to engineer a lasting peace between Henry and James IV, they dispatched a new ambassador to Scotland, tasked with progressing the plans for the marriage of Princess Margaret and the King of Scots. This union had been under discussion since Margaret was 6, but negotiations had been intermittently disrupted by various rebellions.

Despite his mission as a peacemaker, the new Spanish ambassador to Scotland, Don Pedro de Ayala, first ingratiated himself with the King of Scots by accompanying him on a border raid against England. Writing to their Catholic majesties, he dismissed this engagement as a skirmish, but noted the warlike spirit of the 25-year-old King of Scots. James, reckless and charismatic, relished hunting, amorous dalliance and combat. Don Pedro had had to drag the King back from the fray by clinging to his skirts.

The Scots pressed to have Margaret sent as a bride without delay, but Margaret, at 9, was small for her age, and delicate. Both her mother and grandmother warned King Henry she should not be forced into a physical union too early. Henry confided their concern to Don Pedro, man to man: 'They fear the King of Scotland would not wait, but injure her and endanger her health.'[7] He spared the ambassador's blushes, and respected his own mother's privacy, by refraining to mention something that was common knowledge, although never openly discussed. Although Lady Margaret had been married three times, Henry VII was her only child. In giving birth to him in extreme youth, she had been 'spoyled' and could have no more children.

Neither Lady Margaret nor the queen would countenance Margaret being sent to Scotland until she was more mature. Their doubts were reinforced by rumours of King James's amours.

All the young Tudors were involved in various matrimonial projects. Formal negotiations for the marriage of Prince Arthur to Katherine of Aragon had been on-going since March 1488. Eleven years later, the proxy marriage finally took place on 19 May at Bewdley in Worcestershire. Henry and Ferdinand spent the next few months haggling over the dowry. Katherine was expected to arrive in England during the summer of 1500, when her bridegroom was almost 14, but various obstacles, notably the bartering between the monarchs, delayed her departure for another year.

Meanwhile, the death of her youngest brother Edmund in 1500 was 5-year-old Mary's first direct experience of death. The Eltham household was plunged into mourning. Even Mary's schoolmaster and Jane Poppincourt had black garments ordered for them.

By early October 1501, the mood lifted when the ships of Mary's long-awaited sister-in-law were sighted off Plymouth Sound. Katherine landed to a thunderous welcome. Her progress was slow:[8] jubilation greeted her at every staging post along her route through the West Country. People thronged the streets, gaping at the foreign dignitaries, the glamorous decorations, quaffing the free wine. At Elthamstead Prince Arthur joined them, heading a procession of splendidly attired noblemen.

There now occurred the first clash between Spanish and English protocol.

Don Pedro de Ayala intercepted the King's procession and explained that both the Archbishop of Santiago and Doña Elvira Manuel, the princess's duenna, insisted that the princess must neither converse with the King nor meet her bridegroom before her wedding day. Such was the old Castilian custom. Henry immediately made it clear that he cared not a fig for the old Castilian custom. Without bothering to dismount from his horse, he held a council on the field. It was decided that, as Katherine was already betrothed to Arthur, she was Henry's subject, so the laws of Castile were irrelevant. Henry pressed on, determined to meet the princess. Informed she was resting, he retorted that he didn't care if she was still in her bed, he had come to see her, and he intended to. Scandalised, Doña Elvira was forced to back down.

Princess Katherine was soon exchanging pleasantries with the King of England. Later, to Doña Elvira's dismay, once the travellers had changed out of their riding clothes, she and her bridegroom met. Both Henry and Arthur were impressed: pretty Katherine appeared well-mannered and biddable. They conversed in a mixture of Spanish and Latin, with a bishop acting as interpreter. Although the queen and Lady Margaret had urged Katherine to learn French, she had found it hard going.

Henry and Arthur rode back to join the queen at Richmond. At St George's Fields Katherine first met her new brother-in-law, Prince Henry. The 10-year-old Prince displayed the self-confidence Erasmus had noted two years earlier, prancing about the town at the head of his own company, 200 men in blue and tawny livery. Katherine was accommodated at the Bishop of London's palace, which had been reglazed in her honour.[9]

Her entry into London was a riot of colourful pageantry. The streets were festooned with draperies of cloth of gold and silver, velvets and gleaming satins. Triumphal arches adorned with the arms of England and the pomegranates of Spain had been erected, and from the fountains red wine flowed. Mary, a wide-eyed child of 6, gazed in wonder at the foreign fashions and the Spanish princess who would become her friend, riding a mule, Spanish style, richly gowned, with a 'little hat fashioned like a cardinal's'.

The young princesses, waiting at Baynard's Castle, had been excitedly trying on their new dresses. Mary had two new velvet gowns for the occasion, one russet, the other crimson, fur-trimmed, with a green satin kirtle and matching sleeves. She chose the crimson one. Margaret, six years Mary's senior, as the betrothed of a king, preened in gorgeous cloth of gold, fully aware that she would be scrutinised by the Scottish ambassadors.

On 14 November the wedding was magnificently solemnised at St Paul's. There was more spectacle to delight a curious child. After the nuptial mass, celebrated by the bishops, trumpets blared and carillons rang out. Enlivened by free wine, Londoners cheered the handsome bridal couple all the way back to Baynard's Castle. The sumptuous wedding banquet was followed by the formal bedding. The Earl of Oxford led the way to the bedchamber. He tried the bed first on the side where the prince would lie, then on the princess's side. The princess was then positioned in the bed, next to the prince, and the bishops blessed both the bed and the anticipated union. The teenage couple were described by an observer as 'both lusty and amorous'.

Many years later, Arthur's gentlemen would swear that the prince emerged next morning from his chamber, flushed with triumph, announcing 'I have been this night in the midst of Spain.'

This adolescent boast would have far-reaching consequences.

The wedding celebrations continued for days. Besides banquets and dancing, there were public games, masques and a grand tournament. The whole affair had cost a fortune; to recoup some of the expenses, seats were offered to the common people at extortionate prices. Princess Mary Rose sat enthralled, with her new sister-in-law, the Spanish princess, along with her mother, grandmother and sister. Hundreds of attendant ladies occupied one whole side of the stands.

The vast processions and the grand tournament created a challenge for the King's new Master of the Horse, Sir Thomas Brandon. Finding stabling in London for so many extra horses was a daunting task. Himself a skilled jouster, Thomas had carved out a successful career at court, serving the King in many capacities, as councillor, naval and military commander, and diplomat. As he watched the grand display, he could congratulate himself on another success: the advancement he had contrived for his teenage nephew, Charles, the son of his disreputable older brother William, a rascal who had redeemed himself by his hero's death at Bosworth Field in 1485, where the Tudor crown was won. The East Anglian estates of Thomas's father, Sir William Brandon, had passed to the second son, Robert, leaving baby Charles and his sister penniless. Now, Thomas, through his contacts, had managed to obtain for young Charles a temporary position in Prince Arthur's household.

On the Friday after the tournament, a 'disguising' took place in Westminster Hall, a versatile building now used to showcase Tudor wealth and status, hung with rich tapestries, sideboards piled high with gold plate. On new mobile stages lavish pageants rolled in, bearing musicians and entertainers.

One highlight of the revels was when young Henry, Duke of York, thoroughly over-excited, dancing with his sister Margaret, threw off his gown and danced in his jacket, to the delighted amusement of his parents.

The final entertainment was calculated to appeal to the youngest princess. A pageant two storeys high appeared, drawn by seahorses and filled with singing children. From the lower storey eight knights leapt down and released baby rabbits, which scattered in panic among the guests. From the upper storey eight ladies released a flock of white doves, which flew around the hall, causing 'great laughter and disport'.[10]

At the end of November the court moved to Windsor. Henry and his Council decided that the prince and princess should leave for Wales. The King, seeing Katherine's distress over bidding farewell to those who were returning to Spain, summoned her to his library, pretending to show her his books. Suddenly a jeweller, until then concealed, stepped forward and spread before Katherine an array of precious jewels. The King invited her to make her selection, and then turned to her ladies, inviting them to choose jewels for themselves.

Henry's ruse cheered Katherine and 'relieved her heaviness somewhat'.[11] Every effort was being made to cherish Katherine. As the bride of the heir apparent, she was precious. It would not always be so.

Lady Margaret Beaufort, deeply affected by Arthur's wedding, wept. John Fisher, Bishop of Rochester, her confessor, fellow humanist and associate in her educational projects, found this show of emotion typical. 'Either she was in sorrow by reason of present adversities, or else when she was in prosperity she was in dread of the adversity to come.'[12]

Lady Margaret's sense of impending doom proved well-founded.

✧ 2 ✧

Princess of Castile

Before the euphoria generated by Arthur's wedding subsided, Henry VII reopened negotiations with the Scottish ambassadors. Despite his reservations about the character of the King of Scotland, Henry had already taken the precaution of procuring a papal dispensation: James IV and Princess Margaret were distant cousins, James I having married Joan Beaufort, whose brother John, Duke of Somerset, was Margaret's great-grandfather.

Rumour (falsely circulated by Don Pedro de Ayala) claimed that James IV had installed Margaret Drummond, his favourite mistress since 1496, at Stirling with her daughter, one of now five acknowledged royal bastards to whom he gave the name 'Stewart'. After each amorous adventure, James, a devout son of the Church, always hastened to the shrine of St Ninian to be shriven. In 1501, Margaret, with her sisters Eupheme and Sybilla, died of food poisoning. Suspicion of murder fell on Scottish courtiers and English agents, who feared James would never marry while she lived and therefore never sire a legitimate heir.

James assured Henry that he now desired 'with a pure mind' to express the affection he felt for the King of England 'by the sacred bond of matrimonial alliance'.[1]

In reality, he desperately needed Margaret's dowry, 30,000 golden nobles.

The marriage treaty was finally signed on 24 January. Little Princess Mary Rose sat through High Mass celebrated by three archbishops and four bishops, and watched Margaret's proxy wedding at Richmond Palace, which Mary would come to know so well.

The ensuing festivities were slightly marred when the realisation dawned upon young Prince Henry that not only was his sister the focus of the celebrations, but that, as a queen, she would henceforth take precedence over him. Henry, bursting into tears of fury, flew into one of his notorious tantrums.

That afternoon his attention was distracted when a recent invention, the hoisting harness to lift fully armed knights onto their chargers, was tested in the celebratory 'notable jousts'. The ladies, snuggling into their fur wraps against the January chill, gasped at the skill of the competitors. The next day Margaret presented the prizes to the victors. In a field of strong contenders, the third prize went to a promising newcomer, Charles Brandon, the dashing young nephew of the Master of the Horse.

Brandon's brilliance in the tiltyard would play a key role in his rise to prominence. The tournament was followed by dancing and feasting. Londoners revelled in the distribution of free wine; celebratory bonfires were lighted throughout the city.

On 14 March there followed more public celebration: it was proclaimed that peace with Scotland had been established 'for ever more'. The thistle and the rose were united at last.

But in April the Tudor roller coaster took another plunge. In the winter of 1501/02, the country had awaited with bated breath the glad tidings from Ludlow proclaiming the pregnancy of the Princess Katherine.

On 4 April 1502, after two days of hard riding, the long-awaited messenger reached Greenwich Palace bearing terrible news. The Prince of Wales, never robust, was dead, apparently having succumbed to the sweating sickness currently ravaging the West Country. The Queen was no stranger to grief, having lost many friends and relatives during the Wars of the Roses. Of the six children she had borne the King, two had died in infancy. The royal couple's sole surviving son, Prince Henry, was now the focus of all their hopes.

Possibly King Henry felt guilty. His Council had warned him that Arthur was not strong. Henry admitted to King Ferdinand that he feared he had risked his son's health because of his love for Katherine. Couples who married very young were sometimes initially kept apart so that the bridegroom might complete his education and the bride mature in readiness for childbearing, or were separated shortly after the wedding, lest the bridegroom in his youthful enthusiasm should overdo things. Ferdinand's son, Katherine's brother, the darkly handsome Infante Juan, had allegedly overexerted himself after his marriage to Margaret of Austria.

But Arthur, at 15, and Katherine, almost 16, were not considered too young.

The question of the consummation of their marriage would become the cornerstone of the most famous divorce in history. Katherine always maintained that consummation never occurred, despite her bridegroom's earthy jests with the young squires of the bedchamber.

The limitations of Tudor medicine failed to explain the exact nature of Arthur's fatal illness. Victorian historians assumed he died of tuberculosis, a disease characterised by night sweats. The herald chronicler's description, when Arthur's body was being prepared for embalming, suggests that the prince may have already been suffering from some malignant disease, possibly affecting his virility.

> The most pitiful disease and sickness that with so sore and great violence had battled and driven in the singular parts of him inward, that cruel and fervent enemy of nature the deadly corruption did utterly vanquish and overcome the pure and frendfull [healthy] blood without all manner of physical help and remedy.[2]

Prince Arthur's body was embalmed at Ludlow. His obsequies were prolonged and costly, amid widespread distress. Even for little Mary Rose, once more dressed in mourning black, Arthur's death cast a pall over the celebrations for her sister Margaret's marriage to the King of Scotland.

It took five weeks for news of Prince Arthur's death to reach Toledo. Ferdinand and Isabella immediately dispatched a special envoy, Hernan Duque de Estrada, to Henry on 12 May with a formal letter of condolence, and a peremptory demand for the return of the money already paid as the first instalment of Katherine's dowry.

The Queen, who had hoped to be equipping her daughter Margaret with a superb trousseau to impress the Scots, instead found herself paying for Margaret's black velvet gown to be relined. For Mary Rose she bought a new black satin gown. Elizabeth also had to finance mourning wardrobes for her nephews and niece, the children of her beloved younger sister Katherine. Their father, Lord William Courtenay, was attainted for treason following yet another Yorkist plot involving her nephews, Edward IV's grandsons, Edward and Richard de la Pole. She had to pay off her debts of £107 10s to Henry Bryan, a London silk merchant, in instalments, after he had presented his bill several times. Elizabeth also came to the aid of Katherine, now penniless. Swallowing her Yorkist pride, Elizabeth resorted to the humiliating measures of pawning her plate and borrowing the sum of £320 from two gentlemen in the City.

The Catholic kings and Henry continued their wrangle about Katherine's dowry for years. Ferdinand needed to keep his alliance with England alive. The French military campaign was storming ahead. By summer 1502, Louis XII had expelled the Sforzas from Milan and set his sights on the Aragonese kingdom of Naples. Victory here would make France the dominant European power, a situation Ferdinand was determined to prevent.

Consequently, Estrada was instructed to arrange a new marriage for Katherine with 11-year-old Prince Henry, who would be heir to the throne, unless Katherine proved to be carrying his brother Arthur's child. In an age of unsophisticated gynaecology, three months was the time traditionally appointed to ascertain pregnancy.

De Puebla, the permanent Spanish envoy in London, anticipated the hopes of the Catholic kings. As a qualified practitioner of canon law, he knew that to render Katherine's second marriage acceptable in the eyes of the Church, a papal dispensation from Rome would be required. According to Leviticus 20, it was forbidden for a man to marry his brother's wife. Their union would be fruitless as an expression of God's displeasure: 'If a man shall take his brother's wife, it is an unclean thing: he hath uncovered his brother's nakedness, they shall be childless.'

De Puebla realised that the question of the consummation of Katherine's marriage to Arthur was key to how easily a dispensation could be obtained. Accordingly, he discreetly enquired of Katherine's chaplain and confessor, her former tutor Don Alessandro Geraldini, whether the marriage was a 'true' one. Don Alessandro replied in the affirmative.

At this point there was an unexpected turn of events. Hearing of the consultation between the two learned men, Katherine's fierce duenna, Doña Elvira Manuel, suddenly fired a broadside. Sexual relations in the traditional sense had never taken place between the young couple, she insisted. No blood-stained sheets had been exhibited to Doña Elvira. Thirty years later, when Henry VIII had set his heart on marrying Anne Boleyn, Doña Elvira's outburst would help change the course of history. The question of the consummation of Katherine's first marriage was the crux on which the English Reformation was based.

Virginity was a serious matter. Although ignorance was rife – a common test for pregnancy or virginity was to wave a chicken wing over the abdomen – an internal examination was also possible. Unless Doña Elvira genuinely believed in Katherine's virginity, it was reckless of her to lie. The marriage of Arthur and Katherine was the culmination of thirteen years of intricate negotiation. To claim non-consummation despite five months of apparently blissful cohabitation was an outrageous admission on Doña Elvira's part, implying gross negligence and failure in her duty to her lady and to both dynasties.

If the couple had never enjoyed full marital relations, a papal dispensation for a second marriage would be more easily obtained. On the other hand, if Katherine were still a virgin, then, on the grounds of non-consummation, she was not legally Princess of Wales – a financial disaster for Katherine personally and for her retainers, since Henry could then claim that he was under no obligation to maintain them.

Henry, grieving for the loss of his eldest son, was affronted by the doubts cast on Arthur's manhood by Doña Elvira's assertion. On 16 June 1502 the rumours reached the Spanish royal household. Katherine's horrified parents pressed Estrada to find out the truth. Ferdinand suspected that Henry feigned to believe the non-consummation story so as to wriggle out of paying Katherine's dower revenues. 'Get to the bottom of it – use all the flattering persuasions you can to prevent them from concealing it from you,' he urged Estrada.[3]

The strongest evidence used to discredit Doña Elvira's declaration was the widely reported boast Prince Arthur made to his gentlemen the morning after his wedding night, where he called for drink, implying that he had had thirsty work of it: 'Gentlemen, I have been this night in the midst of Spain.' Among those who would later claim to remember the teenage bridegroom's bragging was Charles Brandon. Perhaps Brandon and others hoped to ingratiate themselves with Henry VIII, who by then was intent on discarding Katherine in order to marry Anne Boleyn.

Henry, predictably, pointed out that if Katherine were still a virgin, she was not his daughter-in-law; he had therefore no obligation to support her.

Katherine, still in mourning, was excluded from the Christmas celebrations of 1502, and the exciting plans for Margaret's wedding to the King of Scots.

Though distraught over Arthur's death, Elizabeth had comforted the King, assuring him that they could have more sons. She made offerings at various efficacious shrines; by early summer 1503, she was pregnant for the seventh and last time.

As autumn approached, the Queen ordered the finest cock pheasants and venison instead of flowers and cherries; she relaxed, playing and listening to music with her daughters. Mary Rose enjoyed the family Christmas at Richmond, her father's new showpiece, built after the fire at Sheen. Cynics referred to the ambitious new palace as 'Riche mount', a pun on Henry's title, Earl of Richmond, and his skill at heaping up riches. Glazed, paved, lavishly ornamented with gold leaf, the royal apartments exuded luxury. The gardens were embellished with stone statues of heraldic beasts. Henry, unlike his sons, lacked the advantages of cultural education, but he had expensive tastes. Although miserly in other respects, he spent freely on buildings, jewels, ostentatious hospitality and clothes. All these were rapidly becoming Renaissance status symbols, with the new emphasis on culture.

Mary grew up surrounded by fine things. 'There is no country in the world where Queens live with greater pomp than in England,' remarked de Puebla. Calling unexpectedly on Mary's mother, he expressed his surprise at finding thirty-two ladies 'all very magnificent and in splendid style' in attendance. Elizabeth's seamstresses worked tirelessly on the hangings for the Queen's great bed of state, using yards of costly gold twist and silk. At the end of January, Elizabeth was rowed to the Tower for her lying-in. On 2 February, she gave birth to a girl, christened Katherine, after her favourite younger sister, Lady Courtenay. Nine days later, on her 37th birthday, Elizabeth of York died. Her baby daughter did not long survive her.

The King was devastated. All England mourned. In London alone 636 masses were said for the repose of her soul. At Cheapside groups of thirty-seven virgins with chaplets of green and white stood vigil, holding tapers; 3,000 torches burned along the stretch from Mark Lane to Temple Bar; candles burned in all the parish churches. The hearse was emblazoned with the Queen's motto, *humble et reverente*.

Bewildered little Mary donned mourning, like everyone.

Within four months Mary was back in colours, wearing blue damask with velvet edgings, white stockings and tawny silk ribbons. She was nearly 8. Prospective suitors had already been sniffing around for five years. Life had to go on.

Despite his private grief, King Henry's life was dominated by intrigue powered by dynastic ambition. He appreciated the importance of astute alliances and political marriages. The Austrian Habsburgs were reputed to have won more land and power through marriage than through conquest. At 46, despite declining health, Henry felt himself still capable of siring sons. With only one surviving male heir, he briefly considered remarriage, his eye falling first on his daughter-in-law Katherine, now 17. Queen Isabella denounced this notion as barbarous, and suggested Henry transfer his attentions to young Queen Joanna of Naples.

Henry declared that he would consider her only if she was beautiful. De Puebla, through whom negotiations were conducted, told Ferdinand that the English king, although himself advanced in years, was obsessed by physical appearances. Henry dispatched three ambassadors to investigate Joanna's charms, with orders to report back on her age, weight, mannerisms and personality, the colour of her hair and eyebrows, the state of her teeth and skin, the size of her fingers, neck, breasts 'whether they be big or small', 'the favour of her visage, whether she be painted or not, and whether it be fat or lean, sharp or round, and whether her countenance be cheerful and amiable, frowning or melancholy, steadfast or light, or blushing in communication', and, most importantly, her fortune. The ambassadors described Joanna as amiable and presentable, big-busted but sweet-breathed, with passionate lips and a pretty neck, 'having a noble gravity and not too bold, but somewhat shamefacedly womanly, a good feeder, and eateth well her meat twice on a day'.

Henry, still not satisfied, commissioned a portrait of Queen Joanna for his scrutiny. But the young Queen of Naples, irritated, refused to co-operate.

On 30 September 1503 the treaty for a marriage between Katherine and Prince Henry was ratified. It took another year for the dispensation to reach England. Queen Isabella saw a copy a few days before she died, in the great fortress of Medina del Campo in the heart of Castile, where she had reigned as king in her own right.

The succession of Castile passed to Katherine's older sister, the beautiful, fragile Joanna. In the tangled web of European dynastic politics, tragic Joanna's fortunes were to directly influence the fate of Princess Mary Rose.

Joanna had been married at 17 to the Archduke Philip, son of the Emperor Maximilian, in 1496. Although 'Philip the Handsome' was a conceited popinjay, Joanna adored him. Philip had been ordered to remain in Flanders, but he cherished ambitions to control Castile. On 26 November 1504, when Isabella died, Joanna being still in Flanders, her father, King Ferdinand, announced that he intended to represent her as 'Governor and Administrator' of Castile, despite his unpopularity with Castilian separatists. The idea was approved by the Cortes, the region's ancient council, but it enraged Philip. Already Lord of the Netherlands and Burgundy, by virtue of his wife, Philip declared himself King of Castile and prepared to fight his father-in-law. Distress at Philip's incorrigible philandering and the strain of repeated pregnancies had affected Joanna's nerves. As soon as her instability manifested itself, her husband treated her henceforth as an incompetent lunatic. Rumours were spread that Joanna was mad; her husband would rule Castile as her proxy.

Much of what Isabella had achieved began to unravel with her death. Trade treaties favourable to the English were now decreed to have lapsed. In August 1505, 800 English merchants had returned to London from Seville 'lost and ruined'.

Ferdinand had still not sent the next instalment of Katherine's dowry, despite her appeals, describing the humiliation of living on the charity of the King.

Katherine and Prince Henry, six years her junior, were betrothed in 1503, but on 27 June 1505, in a ploy intended to force Ferdinand into paying up, Prince Henry had revoked the contract, it having been made in the time of his minority.

In the autumn of 1505, Ferdinand set the seal on the new hostile relationship with both Archduke Philip and with England by signing the Treaty of Blois with the old enemy, Louis XII. This prevented Philip from crossing through Europe to reach Castile.

In January 1506 Philip set sail with an army, vowing to seize Castile by force of arms. When news of his audacity reached Ferdinand, such was the monarch's fury that he allegedly threatened to throw himself upon Philip with *capa y espada*, the torero's mantle and sword.

Fortunately such dramatic intervention was not required. Philip's Armada was blown off course by a ferocious gale in the English Channel. His ships were tossed for forty-eight hours and then scattered; Philip himself landed at Melcombe Regis in Dorset on 13 January 1506. He immediately sent a plaintive message to Henry.

King Henry welcomed Philip's fortuitous stranding on his shores as a god-given opportunity to revive the old Anglo-Burgundian alliance. Sir Thomas Brandon was dispatched to conduct the royal guests to Windsor. Queen Joanna, shaken by her ordeal, rested until Henry, now Prince of Wales and in his 14th year, arrived accompanied by gorgeously dressed nobles, to extend an official welcome. The King, with a huge procession, rode out to greet his guests personally on 31 January. As they trotted into the castle through the main gate side-by-side, so neither should assume precedence, trumpeters sounded a rousing fanfare. King Henry lacked a natural talent for convivial hospitality, but he had a gift for the spectacular.

There followed weeks of bargaining. Philip, despite his impatience to get his ships repaired and proceed to Castile, was seduced by Henry's lavish welcome. On 1 February, the princesses Katherine and Mary Rose arrived, thrilled by the prospect of enjoying the 'great cheer' brought by the influx of distinguished guests. Captivated, Philip kissed the royal ladies and all their gentlewomen. Entertainments were held in the King's dining chamber; Katherine and her ladies performed Spanish dances; Mary Rose danced, displayed her skill on the lute and clavicle, and was rewarded with an extra kiss from the Archduke. She was not quite 11 years old, golden-haired, exquisite, a competent musician; above all, she behaved like a princess, enchanting everyone, including Philip.

Despite the ten years' age difference, Katherine and Mary had grown close; their mutual affection would last a lifetime. Katherine, at 21, widowed, prematurely grave, kindly and dignified, found a foil in young Mary's light-hearted spontaneity.

Servants were sent to fetch Mary Rose to Croydon, where some of Philip's suite were accommodated at the Archbishop of Canterbury's palace, so that she might be serenaded by the Flemish musicians. Again, her beauty, sweetness and poise won all hearts. With her irresistible charm, Mary was launched on her long career in subtle state diplomacy.

The two sovereigns hunted in the park and played tennis. On 9 February Henry made Philip a member of the Order of the Garter. Philip bestowed on the new Prince of Wales the illustrious Golden Fleece, an ancient Burgundian order of knighthood. They signed a treaty according to which Henry would provide military assistance in Castile if required; Philip would offer support against French incursions. Both would renounce any rebels who sought refuge in their domains. This promise was especially relevant from Henry's point of view, because Philip promised to hand over the last Yorkist White Rose pretender, Edmund de la Pole, the self-styled Duke of Suffolk, who had sought asylum in the Netherlands and had been prowling around Europe since 1498 soliciting support for his dynastic ambitions. After eliciting the promise, Henry detained the Archduke with relentless hospitality until Edmund de la Pole had been duly handed over and deposited in the Tower.

De la Pole's cousin, the unfortunate Earl of Warwick, had been executed just before Katherine's arrival, to secure the safety of the realm.

The next week Queen Joanna, much restored, arrived at Windsor, where she was welcomed by Henry, Mary and her own sister, Katherine. Windsor was the ancient seat of the English kings, but Henry was determined that his royal guests should also admire his own crowning architectural achievement, Richmond, where more hawking, hunting, feasting and dancing were planned. Katherine and Mary were sent on ahead to prepare for the royal visitors. Even Philip, who prided himself on his own showpiece, the palace of Beau Regard, declared himself impressed by Richmond. On the Saturday before Philip departed, perhaps much later than he had hoped, after 97 days as Henry's guest, Henry took him to Eton, where the schoolboys lined the churchyard, waving and cheering.

Henry knew he had made good use of the Archduke's visit. In their discussions, Henry had laid out the foundations of his dynastic masterplan: he would marry Philip's sister, Margaret. Prince Henry was loosely promised to Philip and Joanna's daughter Eleanor; Mary Rose would marry their son, Prince Charles of Castile, also heir to the Burgundian lands.

Then, that very autumn, 1506, Philip died. The European political landscape changed again. To safeguard his plan for Mary's marriage, Henry now needed the co-operation of Charles's grandfather, the slippery Emperor Maximilian.

The deaths of Philip and of her older siblings had left 25-year-old Joanna Europe's most eligible widow, heiress to the entire Spanish empire. Her reputation as a madwoman had allowed her father Ferdinand to step in as Regent of Castile in the name of her son Charles. At 54, and an unwelcome Regent in Castile, Ferdinand knew an energetic son-in-law could be crucial. For Henry, this represented a great opportunity to ensure that Mary Rose and Charles would certainly marry, and that Prince Henry and Katherine were more likely to.

Known to her contemporaries, as to history, as Juana la Loca, the severity of Joanna's condition was almost certainly exaggerated by her family for political reasons. But the death of her beloved husband cast Joanna into a morbid depression. She refused to allow his burial to proceed. Instead, persuading herself that his resurrection was imminent, she dragged his corpse about with her in a leaden coffin wherever she went, in case she missed this glorious event.

For Henry, Joanna's madness was irrelevant: he aimed to gain control of her kingdom, and hoped she was still capable of bearing children. He directed Katherine to write to her father in support of his suit, stressing his affection for her sister. De Puebla, acting for both parties, told Ferdinand in the spring of 1507 that Joanna would soon recover her reason if she were wedded to the King of England, because nobody in the world would make her such a good husband. He added that it wouldn't much matter if she was mad, if she lived in England. Nobody there would care, as long as she could breed.

Joanna's condition deteriorated, however, and English diplomacy embraced closer links with Germany and the Low Countries. Negotiations with Spain collapsed in favour of a general European coalition, the Treaty of Cambrai.

Even while courting Joanna, Henry had continued to toy with his long-held notion of a double wedding with the Burgundians. Impecunious Maximilian and mercenary Henry, despite their mutual distrust, recognised the advantages of such an alliance. The stumbling block to the male rulers' ambitions was the Archduchess Margaret. Twice widowed, Regent of the Netherlands in her own right, Margaret had no intention of becoming a pawn in her father's political games again. Motherless, she had been betrothed at three to Charles, Dauphin of France. Her father Maximilian, delighted with the connection, dispatched his little daughter to Amboise to spend her childhood being groomed to become Queen of France.

Ten years later, she was ignominiously repudiated in favour of 'la petite Brette', Anne of Brittany, who at 14 had been briefly married by proxy to Margaret's own father, Maximilian. Margaret was sent home in disgrace. She did, however, acquire a throne, for she was quickly

married off to the priapic Infante Juan, Prince of Castile, whose unre-
strained enjoyment of his marital rights reputedly hastened his demise.
Despite warnings, his mother Queen Isabella refused to intervene,
declaring it was God's will. Evil tongues whispered that the Queen of
Castile's desire for an heir outweighed her concern for her son's health.
So debilitated was his constitution by this lack of moderation that Juan
was unable to resist the pestilence a few months later, and succumbed.

The baby Margaret carried did not survive. In 1501 she married
Philibert II Duke of Savoy. At 24 she was widowed again, and returned
to Brabant, establishing a distinguished court at Malines, where she
devoted herself to ruling the Low Countries and bringing up her nephew
Charles and his three sisters.

Margaret resisted pressure from her father Maximilian and from Henry.

Henry sent two embassies to the Netherlands in 1508. In the first of
these, Thomas Wolsey excelled himself, accomplishing the whole mission there and back in less than seventy hours, displaying the ruthless
efficiency which would be his ground-note. His first foray into diplomacy
was an eye-opener for Wolsey; he noted the inconstancy, mutability and
total disregard of promises.

Henry, impatient for an answer, commanded Thomas Wolsey, his
royal chaplain, to obtain one. But Margaret was adamant in her refusal.

Henry's prime objective was not so much his own marriage as ensuring fulfilment of the long-standing agreement for the marriage of Charles
and Mary Rose. Maximilian was desperate to stop England forming an
alliance with France or Spain. A treaty was signed at Calais in December
1507. This provided for mutual aid in the event of war, and clinched
Mary's betrothal, scheduled for the following Easter, and the solemnisa-
tion of her marriage forty days after Prince Charles's 14th birthday.

Henry greeted the news of the signing of the marriage contract with
'great contentment'. On Christmas Day he ordered general celebrations –
bells, bonfires and free hogsheads of wine. The citizens, encouraged by the
prospect of free drink and cheered by the news that the old trading links
with the Low Countries were restored, joined in the general rejoicing.

At last this 'great and honourable marriage' now appeared imminent.
So confident was Henry of its success that he announced that he had
built a 'wall of brass' around his kingdom, with on every side 'mighty
princes our good sons, friends, confederates and allies'.

But Maximilian continued to flirt with the French; the treaty remained
unconfirmed. Henry grew impatient. However, he knew Maximilian. As
a sweetener he loaned the chronically impecunious Emperor 100,000
crowns. This tipped the balance in England's favour and in December

1508, after years of negotiations, the Emperor's ambassadors finally arrived for Mary's betrothal.

The distinguished emissaries were led by the Sieur de Berghes, one of the great lords of Northern Brabant and the Emperor's chamberlain, who was to act as proxy for 8-year-old Prince Charles. Underlining the significance of the occasion, the Governor of Bresse came in person, as did the president of the Council of Flanders. King Henry's Latin secretary, Pietro Carmeliano, and the London printer Pynson were stumped by the difficult name of Dr Pflug, the legal expert, recorded in the printed souvenir record of the event as 'Dr Splonke'.

The imperial party were overwhelmed by their rapturous welcome; they were showered with generous gifts. The King received them at Greenwich seated under a golden canopy of state, flanked by the Archbishop of Canterbury and Prince Henry.

Next day, the legalities were completed. Mary's dowry was set at 250,000 gold crowns. Her jointure would include all the lands that had once belonged to her great-aunt Margaret of Austria.

The formalities completed, the ambassadors were welcomed to Richmond. In view of the couple's youth, heavy bonds were exchanged and penalty clauses inserted to guarantee the fulfilment of the contract. Consummation of the union was to be postponed for another four years, when the princess was to be taken to her husband at the court of his aunt Margaret, Regent of the Netherlands. Mary would spend the next four years preparing for her new life.

The espousal contract used in the ceremony was a covenant of betrothal, with marriage to follow. Recognised by both church and state, it took the form of a public exchange of vows known as 'hand-fasting', in which the couple joined hands and sealed the contract with a kiss. In the case of royal marriages, it was quite usual to employ a proxy. Two types of contract were recognised, *per verb de futuro* and *per verba de praesenti*. In the first case, wedlock was pledged by saying 'I will' or 'I shall take thee to be my wedded wife or husband', but fulfilment of these vows was not obligatory.

Such an announcement made in public was a statement of future intent.

This form was used when the parties concerned were so young that the date of consummation could not be definitively established. But the *de praesenti* contract was more binding. In both cases, cohabitation sealed the union.

The initial suspicion of the English court, after the many vicissitudes of the negotiations, had been replaced by enthusiasm. In the streets of London preparations went ahead for the popular celebrations.

Ten days later, Mary Rose took her place on a high dais beneath a glittering canopy of cloth of gold at Richmond for her betrothal to Prince Charles. Slender Mary appeared young and vulnerable for her 13 years, but she displayed extraordinary poise and dignity. The Archbishop of Canterbury delivered a solemn discourse in Latin on the dignity of holy matrimony and the significance of this promising union. The President of Flanders, Jean de Sauvaige, responded. The Sieur de Berghes, acting as proxy for the prince, took Mary's hand, and recited the words of matrimony, promising the loyalty and undying affection of the absent bridegroom, and formally reciting his authority to represent the prince in the marriage vows. He repeated the formula, *per verba de praesenti.*

Mary unhesitatingly took his hand and declared her vows, giving a long speech in French. Her delivery never faltered. Carmelianius observed that some of the audience were moved to tears by their young princess's grace and composure.

The proxy then placed a gold ring on Mary's middle finger and kissed her respectfully. The trumpets sounded a fanfare; the minstrels struck up; Mary was now married, to a child she had never seen. The company proceeded to the royal chapel to hear mass said by the Bishop of London, followed by a banquet and three days of feasting, music, dancing and jousting. From a richly appointed gallery, the new bride and her companions could admire, criticise or laugh at the feats and outfits of the contestants. The highlight of the event was a grand tournament on the third day, celebrated with bonfires and bell-ringing.

At the Emperor's request, the absent Prince Charles was honoured by membership of the Order of the Garter, as his father had been, as a gesture of Henry's good will. Early sixteenth-century diplomacy was becoming a game in which the rules increased in formality as Renaissance ceremonial intensified. From the Netherlands came a stilted letter in Charles's name, formally expressing his satisfaction with his new bride, accompanied by three jewels, presented to Mary Rose in the course of a formal banquet: a balas ruby, pale rose red and set among pearls, from Margaret; a brooch containing one large diamond and an oriental ruby surmounted by pearls from Maximilian. From Charles, a more personal ornament, a ring bearing the monogram 'K' for 'Karolus' surrounded by diamonds and pearls, with the Biblical Latin inscription: '*Maria optimum partem elegit que non auferetur ab ea*' ('Mary hath chosen that good part which shall not be taken away from her' – Gospel of St Luke 10:42).

Pynson's record of the occasion featured a Latin poem by a dazzled Carmelianus: '… what delicate and sumptuous meals, what diversity of pleasant wines, what plate of gold and silver-gilt the King had, no dish or saucer but it was gilded, and as bright as gold.'

Carmelianus's account was circulated in 1508 in Latin and reprinted in English the following year. A copy, translated into Castilian Spanish, reached Charles's other grandfather, the King of Aragon; the English ambassador to Spain reported that Ferdinand was 'sore displeased' by the marriage.

Their mission accomplished, laden with gifts, the imperial ambassadors departed. Maximilian had secured his loan; Henry had engineered the Habsburg alliance he had long desired. Carmelianus regarded the outcome as a triumph of English diplomacy: 'Rejoice, England, and to thy most noble victorious and fortunate sovereign lord and King give honour, praise and thanks ... all Christian regions shall hereafter be united and allied unto thee, which honour till now thou never couldst attain.'[4]

Now, as Princess of Castile, Mary took precedence over her friend and sister-in-law, the Dowager Princess of Wales, but Mary loved Katherine, and was not one to flaunt her advantage. Nonetheless, writing again to beseech her father for money to pay her household, the humiliated Katherine of Aragon wept for shame.

Mary Rose's betrothal to Charles of Castile did not last. Over the next twenty years, Charles would woo and jilt ten different women, before finally wedding Isabella of Portugal.

❖ 3 ❖

Charles Brandon

Mary Rose, as Princess of Castile, had acquired a new significance in court society. The situation of the Dowager Princess of Wales, her friend and future sister-in-law, also improved dramatically. Although Katherine and Henry had been betrothed since 1503, Henry VII had treated Katherine shabbily, keeping her in penury and refusing to allow the marriage to take place, piqued at King Ferdinand's non-payment of the remainder of her dowry, and hoping for a more prestigious match for his last surviving son. Katherine, a 16-year-old widow in a strange land, had endured a difficult few years with limited resources and an uncertain future. Once Henry VII was finally laid to rest in 1509, the young royals were able to enjoy their privileged positions to the full in a court newly fired with *joie de vivre* and devoted to the pursuit of pleasure.

For Henry, his father's death meant liberty from oppression. For the past year, Henry VII had kept his son under such close supervision that, people remarked, he might have been a young girl. Henry, unlike his late brother Arthur, was given neither royal responsibilities nor training in kingship, apart from the odd history lesson when his father could spare the time from his political intrigues and architectural ambitions.

Henry was forbidden to leave the palace except by a private door leading into the park, and even then only in the company of specially appointed companions. He was surrounded by an almost superstitious cloud of anxiety. Henry VII's motives for his tyrannical treatment of his son during this last year of his life appear complex. Possibly, having lost his other three sons, the King, obsessed by the fear that some catastrophe might befall his only surviving male heir, scarcely dared to believe the succession was secure and that the prince, apparently so indestructible, would really live to succeed him as monarch. Preparing young Henry for his future role might be tempting fate.

Or perhaps the King had detected in his son's character potentially dangerous flaws: the Tudor tendency to tantrums, excessive cravings, obsessional competitiveness. He banned from his son's environment anything likely to encourage depravity: all the talk in Henry's presence was of 'virtue, honour, cunning, wisdom and deeds of worship, of nothing that shall move him to vice'.[1] Under the vigilant surveillance of his father and his faithful retainers, the prince had little chance to explore the seamy side of life. His cousin, Richard Pole, seeing how strict Henry VII was with Henry, alleged that the King hated his son, 'having no affection or fancy unto him'.[2] During the year which preceded his death, the King once quarrelled so violently with the young prince that it appeared to horrified observers 'as if he sought to kill him.'[3] Nobody dared approach Henry or instigate a conversation with him. He spent most of his time in a room leading off his father's bedchamber. When he did appear, he seemed 'so subjected that he does not speak a word except in response to what the king asks him'.[4]

This is not the usual view of Henry VIII. But it is small wonder that, released from his father's repressive regime, the young prince threw himself into living with furious zest.

Notwithstanding, during the last weeks of the old King's life, Henry played the part of the dutiful son, remaining at his father's bedside at Richmond. Henry would later claim that his father had reiterated to him on his deathbed his last wish: Henry was to wed Katherine of Aragon and found a line of male heirs.

Whatever his personal feelings for his father, Henry VIII gave him a worthy send-off, digging deep into the apparently bottomless coffers he had inherited to provide a magnificent funeral. Mary Rose received four new mantelets from Paris. Her saddle, pillion and the coverings of her horse required 17s worth of black velvet. The palfreys ridden by Princess Katherine and her ladies in the cortège were similarly caparisoned.

On the evening of 8 May 1509, the King's body was brought to the City from Richmond where it had lain in state, for the formal services and burial. At London Bridge a great crowd gathered excitedly. They were not disappointed: the funeral cortège was magnificent. Torches and lighted candles flickered on the canopy of cloth of gold beneath which the King's effigy, in full regalia, with sceptre and crown, reposed upon the coffin. Five horses decked in black velvet drew the chariot. Behind it rode the Master of the Horse, noblemenè and the whole Guard.

Finally, on 10 May, the staves of the household were ceremoniously broken and the King was laid to rest in the splendid chapel at Westminster Abbey, where his Queen, Elizabeth of York, already lay entombed. Here, in the imposing tomb designed by Pietro Torrigiano, Henry VII was said to dwell more richly dead in his monument than he had done in life, in Richmond or any of his palaces.

Two weeks after the King's death, there was a sense of relief when the long vigil was brought to a close. A month later, on 11 June, two weeks before the date set for Henry VIII's coronation, he and Princess Katherine would be married quietly at the Franciscan oratory near Greenwich.

As the funeral cortège clattered through the streets of London, many eyes lingered upon a large athletic figure riding among the ninety-three esquires of the body. Men regarded him with envy, women sighed. He was strikingly handsome, his bearing impressive; but few of those who rode alongside him or watched awestruck from the sidelines could imagine that within five years royal favour would elevate the dashing young esquire to a dukedom.

There were four Esquires of the Body, proficient knights who guarded and attended the king night and day, helped him dress and informed the Lord Chamberlain 'if anything lack for his person or pleasaunce'.[5] Their business was confidential. Charles Brandon was the ideal companion for the King. Such was their resemblance that he was sometimes taken for the King's bastard brother. Handsome, brave, charming and extrovert, he shared Henry's love of competitive sports. Brandon was the most successful courtier of the Tudor age. After his meteoric rise, he would successfully survive another thirty-one years at Henry VIII's court. At his death he would leave his family among the greatest in the realm, with claims on the throne.

This latter distinction would prove a poisoned chalice.

More remarkably still, Brandon owed his success neither to exceptional talent nor ruthless ambition, but to his personal charm, loyalty and superb physical prowess, in the service of a monarch who valued these qualities above all. Brandon was instinctive: though not skilled in the subtleties of high-level diplomacy, the law and economics or arcane mysteries of strategy and military tactics, he achieved success in both diplomacy and generalship thanks to his common sense and ability to work with people.

Brandon's elevation to prominence was so rapid that it stunned his contemporaries, and later writers devised romantic fables to account for it; in these Brandon saved the King's life, or the two young men, so similar in many respects, squabbled over a maiden, who made them swear eternal friendship. These preposterous fictions captured some aspects of the bond that bound Henry VIII and Charles Brandon – chivalrous rivalry, courtly love, brotherhood in arms, a passion for sport and for the chase. But Brandon's success owed less to random happenstance than might appear. He was reaping the rewards of two generations who had possessed the foresight and good fortune to throw in their lot with the winning side, and had in consequence won honourable places at court.

Nonetheless, at the time of Henry VII's funeral, there was little to suggest that the lives of Charles Brandon, Esquire of the Body, and the dead king's beautiful younger daughter would be inexorably intertwined. Princess Mary Rose was betrothed to Prince Charles of Castile. Brandon, already the veteran of complex and unsavoury matrimonial entanglements, was married to his long-suffering wife, Anne Browne.

Henry VII's will had stipulated that Mary Rose was to have £50,000 for her dowry and marriage, over and above her plate and wardrobe, jewels and accoutrements, and the cost of transporting her to Flanders to take up life as the bride of Prince Charles. Canny to the end, the old King, conscious of the pitfalls of dynastic marriage contracts, determined that, should the Habsburg alliance founder, the money was to be used to finance an alternative marriage, to a bridegroom selected by Henry VIII and his Council. He expressed the hope that she might be married abroad, 'to some noble Prince out of this our realm'.[6]

An English marriage was not envisaged, and certainly not a union with Charles Brandon. Brandon, although a close companion and confidant of Mary's brother, the new King, had no immediate prospect of advancement which would make him a suitable applicant for the hand of a princess. He belonged to the large, ill-defined class of the gentry – some 1,500–2,000 families – but not to the more exclusive, tightly knit superior circle of the nobility. He was a familiar figure at court, having since 1503 been a 'sewer for the board's end',[7] one of those who served Henry VII at table. Between 1505 and 1509, when he was appointed an Esquire of the Body, Brandon had served as Master of the Horse to the Earl of Essex, a leading courtier and a renowned military leader. In this post, Brandon gained invaluable experience which would stand him in good stead when he was appointed Master of the King's Horse.

The King had precocious mental gifts, fostered by a rigorous education from an early age by skilled and scholarly tutors. Charles Brandon could not pretend to equal him intellectually. The foundations of their friendship lay elsewhere. Brandon was a valiant partner in the lists, one of the few who could give the physically brave and superbly athletic king a run for his money. He became a successful military leader, courtier and diplomat thanks to his personal charisma, amiability and candour, rather than bullishness or guile.

Most importantly, he was the King's man, so loyal that he would not shrink from mildly compromising his own integrity if it were in his master's interests. Along with the King's other closest friends, he was a gentleman of the Privy Chamber, a group of dashing gallants with whom the King enjoyed jousting, hunting, play-acting, gambling and making merry. The King delighted in their company and showered them with gifts. As his favourite, Brandon was rewarded for his service with lucrative appointments – stewardships, receiverships, wardships and licences. In 1513, Henry VIII made him a Knight of the Garter.

Even after he had quarrelled disastrously with many former friends and allies, Henry remained conscious of Brandon's qualities. Unlike many of his contemporaries, Brandon retained Henry's affection until the day of his death. It could have been very different: Brandon's antecedents, and some aspects of his own life, were in many respects, highly dubious.

Brandon's father had had a sleazy reputation. Writing in 1478, Sir John Paston, a Norfolk neighbour of the Brandons, recorded how young William Brandon had 'by force ravished and swived an old gentlewoman, and yet was not therewith satisfied, but swived her oldest daughter, and then would have swived the other sister both; wherefore men say foul of him, declaring that he would have not only the hen but all her chickens as well.'[8]

William, a ward of the king, added to his iniquities by marrying a widow without paying the accustomed fee. At the time, people said he was lucky to escape the hangman's noose.

Charles Brandon himself was a bon viveur rather than a villain, but he too boasted a lively reputation with the ladies. He had already left a trail of complicated marriage contracts behind him. Around 1503, while still in his teens, he had become precontracted per *verba de praesenti* to one of Elizabeth of York's ladies-in-waiting, Anne Browne, daughter to Sir Anthony Browne, later Governor of Calais. Brandon admitted to Walter Devereux that he was 'in love and resorted muche to the company of … Anne Browne'.[9] Fond of Anne he probably was, but she was also quite a catch: her mother was the well-connected Lady Lucy Neville, daughter of John Neville, Marquis of Montagu and Earl of Northumberland.

De praesenti contracts were recognised by canon law in England, but a formal church ceremony was supposed to follow. Often, however, this never happened, making it possible for men to wriggle out of their obligations. Since English practice accepted the husband's testimony rather than the wife's, a man could easily repudiate his publicly acknowledged spouse without fear of reprisals or disgrace.

In 1506, Brandon rather callously abandoned the pregnant Anne in order to enter a more advantageous marriage with her wealthy widowed aunt, Dame Margaret Mortimer. At 43, more than twenty years his senior, Dame Margaret was well-born, the third daughter of John Neville. Margaret was a considerable heiress; she had inherited a fortune, and was childless.

Brandon's grandmother had been the sister of John Mortimer's father; thus he was a cousin of Margaret's former husband, placing Brandon and Margaret within the second and third degrees of relationship prohibited by canon law. The marriage therefore required a papal dispensation.

Shortly after Brandon's desertion, in 1506 Anne bore him a daughter, Anne, the future Lady Powis. (Since Brandon's bigamous alliance would have rendered Lady Powis illegitimate, her friends would later claim that Anne Browne had miscarried her first child from shock at Brandon's betrayal, and that Lady Powis was not born until several years later.)

Within two years, possibly because Brandon suffered pangs of conscience about Anne, Brandon and Dame Margaret were divorced on the grounds of consanguinity – the dispensation was revoked and the marriage declared null and void by the Archdeacon's court in London. While he was still in negotiations with Dame Margaret's representatives, Brandon and his mates galloped off into Essex, where they abducted the long-suffering Anne Browne, whom Brandon then married in secret in Stepney Church in early 1508. Brandon's employer, the Earl of Essex, and Anne's family, 'fearing that the said Charles wold use her as he dyd before', insisted that Brandon make a proper job of it this time and so the couple underwent a public ceremony in St Michael's, Cornhill, in the presence of 'a great nombre of worshypfull people'.[10] Brandon put a good face on it, appearing resplendent in a russet velvet gown faced with martens and joined with beaver, alongside Anne, once again heavily pregnant. She would not long survive the birth of her second daughter, dying in 1510.

At the time, Brandon's scandalous marital history had little effect on his career. It would, however, come back to haunt his descendants.

The congregation at Brandon's marriage to Anne included members of the exclusive group who would become the intimates of Henry VIII during the first years of his reign, Edward Howard and Edward Guildford, son of Sir Richard, who also stood as godfathers to Brandon's first two daughters by Anne. The circle was close-knit. Thomas Knyvet and Brandon owed money together to Henry VII in 1508, Brandon and Howard were granted a joint wardship in 1509, and early in the reign of Henry VIII Brandon, Knyvet and Howard twice joined Edward Guildford in trading ventures.[11] Henry had enjoyed the jousts organised by these friends in May and June 1507. Now, as monarch, he showed his appreciation by showering them with favours and lucrative patronage. Brandon and Henry Guildford, in particular, often received gifts of clothing. Over the next two years, Brandon, Knyvet and Howard would take part in more jousts, masques, pageants and tourneys than any other courtiers except Edward Neville.

Brandon was living with Anne in that heady summer of 1509, when he excelled in the jousts and tourneys which celebrated the coronation of his friend and patron, Henry VIII. On 24 June, Midsummer's Day, two weeks after their quiet wedding and six weeks after the funeral of Henry VII, Henry VIII and Katherine of Aragon were crowned. The day before, Princess Mary Rose had watched the traditional procession through the streets of London with her grandmother from the window of a house in Cheapside.[12] Lady Margaret, overcome, again burst into tears.

Henry left the Tower, escorted by his knights, dressed in white damask and cloth of gold. Katherine followed in a litter reclining on white damask cushions under a canopy lined with white silk and adorned with golden ribbons. She wore a kirtle of white damask and cloth of gold, furred with miniver – fine squirrel pelts, exclusively worn by the nobility. Her auburn hair hung down her back beneath a golden circlet set with pearls and gems. Her attendants followed, resplendent in doublets of crimson satin and gowns of blue velvet. Her ladies, in blue velvet trimmed with crimson, followed, riding matching palfreys.

Sir Andrew Windsor, Master of the Great Wardrobe, and Sir Thomas Lovell, Keeper of the Great Wardrobe of the Household, had sent their staff out to scour London and Flanders for 1,641 yards of scarlet cloth and 2,040 yards of crimson cloth to deck the streets and dress the courtiers. When the cost of the Queen's 'silks and necessaries' for herself and her household, and those of the 14-year-old Princess of Castile and her ladies were added, the total expenditure came to £4,748 6s 3d.[13] Tailors, embroiderers and goldsmiths earned a fortune creating the coronation robes of the nobility. On Midsummer's Day, the court in their fur-trimmed scarlet robes processed from the Palace of Westminster to the Abbey along a striped carpet. As soon as Henry entered the church, the crowd surged forward and chopped up the carpet he had trodden on for souvenirs.

In a lengthy, dignified ceremony, Archbishop William Warham blessed the crown of St Edward. The King and Queen prostrated themselves before the high altar, and were then crowned and anointed with holy oil. Warham asked the congregation whether they took Henry for their King. The congregation shouted their assent. The massed choir burst into the *Te Deum*. The crowds cheered, the organ thundered, trumpets blared, bells pealed, all signifying that Henry VIII had been 'gloriously crowned to the comfort of all the land'.[14] Henry thus began his reign on a tide of euphoria.

Thomas More's coronation ode echoes the Easter hymns of joy:

This happy day consecrates a young man who is the everlasting glory of our age, a king worthy to rule the entire world, who will wipe the tears from every eye and banish our long distress with joy. Now the people, liberated, run before their king with bright faces.[15]

The King and Queen then returned to Westminster Hall for a magnificent banquet 'greater than any Caesar had known'.[16] The Duke of Buckingham and the Earl of Shrewsbury entered on horseback to lead in the succession of dishes of 'sumptuous, fine and delicate meats [in] plentiful abundance'.[17] After the guests had finished the second course, they watched the traditional ritual challenge of the King's Champion. Riding up and down the hall in full armour on his courser, the champion, Sir Robert Dymmocke, threw down his gauntlet in challenge to any who questioned Henry's right to rule, proclaiming that he was willing to defend it. No such challenge being forthcoming from the assembled persons, he then approached Henry, claiming a drink. He was offered wine in a golden goblet, which he drained, and with which he then rode off as reward for his services. Originally a simple medieval expression of homage and fealty by a knight to his liege lord, this ritual was now a symbol of the nation's acknowledgement of their sovereign.

When the company had feasted to repletion, a tournament was held, lasting until midnight. The celebrations continued for several days and were only brought to an abrupt end on 29 June, the day before the King attained his majority, by the death of the King's grandmother, Lady Margaret Beaufort. The King ordered the church bells to toll her passing for six days.

The loss of Lady Margaret was a grave blow. But the celebrations had been unparalleled. Mary Rose and other royal spectators had watched the jousting in the grounds of the Palace of Westminster from a specially constructed pavilion hung with tapestries and rich Arras cloth. Heralded by fanfares, young gallants and noblemen took the field, all splendidly attired and accoutred.[18] The tournament played a crucial role in Henry's ambition to be what he regarded as a real king. It was the ultimate theatre of chivalry, attended by lavish pageantry and allegory. Jousts were held in honour of the ladies, who presented favours such as scarves or handkerchiefs to their chosen knights. The champion of the day received his accolade from the Queen or the highest-ranking lady present.

Achieving honour in the joust was almost as prestigious as winning glory on the battlefield. Tournaments were a dangerous business; men were injured and occasionally killed. In 'barriers', the challengers ran at each other down opposite sides of a wooden barrier, aiming to shatter their lance on their opponent or, if they were really lucky, tip him up. The tourney was fought on horseback with swords; in the dramatic tilt or joust, mounted knights with lances thundered towards each other at the lumbering gallop of chargers strong enough to transport a large man in full armour, with the aim of unhorsing the opponent. In the tilt, competitors fought in pairs. In the joust, each man competed alone. The lances, although solid, could be splintered fairly easily by a robust strike at full tilt against a fully armoured breastplate. Hitting the target required a good eye; often knights missed one another completely.

Besides an opportunity to demonstrate courage and prowess, tournaments served a useful purpose, intended to keep fighting men in shape. The King was 'not minded to see young gentlemen inexpert in martial feats'.[19] This meant, on the domestic scene, excelling in the knightly pastime of jousting. Internationally, it meant military victories. The nobility played a key role in these ambitions. They furnished the King with the worthiest challengers in the lists, and, without a standing army, they provided both the military leadership and the troops for warfare.

Henry's coronation tourney was organised by Lord Thomas Howard, heir to the Earl of Surrey; his brother, Admiral Sir Edward Howard; Lord Richard Grey; Sir Edmund Howard; Sir Thomas Knyvet[t], and the only esquire among them owing his position to his skill at jousting, Charles Brandon. Brandon, wearing a complete gilt armour, relished the opportunity to display his skill. The young Princess of Castile could not fail to notice him. Brandon was pitted at barriers against a massive German challenger, whom he 'so pummelled about the head' that his nose bled and he was led away defeated.[20]

The reign of Henry VIII had now been formally launched on its glorious way, and with it the flourishing careers of his most notable servants, the Howards, born into the nobility, and the parvenu Charles Brandon.

✤ 4 ✤

From Esquire to Duke

The riotous self-indulgence of the new reign continued relentlessly for the next couple of years. The King indulged his boyish delight in impromptu disguisings. In January 1510 he and eleven companions, dressed as Robin Hood and his Merry Men, in short green coats, hoods concealing their features, burst into the Queen's chamber, brandishing bows and arrows and swords. Queen Katherine, heavily pregnant, and her ladies, although much 'abashed', consented to dance with the intruding ruffians. Afterwards the King threw back his hood and revealed his identity, to the great 'astonishment' of the ladies. Katherine smilingly indulged the childish fantasies of her young husband.

The headstrong young monarch's next prank, a few days later, on 12 January, horrified court and Council. Desperate to put into practice his years of training, Henry made the first-ever public appearance in tilting by an English monarch. He later pursued a glorious jousting career, impervious to the dismal mutterings of the 'ancient fathers' about the risks. As a token effort to allay their fears, Henry consented to use hollow lances to reduce impact, but he still courted danger, 'having no respect or fear of anyone in the world',[1] and on at least two occasions narrowly escaped death. But his obsession with jousting persisted. His favourite opponent was Charles Brandon, the only man with a physique and courage to equal his own. Brandon soon became his regular sparring partner; they wore matching jousting outfits.

The only cloud on the horizon was Queen Katherine's failure to deliver a living heir. In January 1510, during the Robin Hood episode, the King was exultant, eagerly anticipating the birth of a son. He had ordered a magnificent cradle of estate padded with crimson cloth of gold embroidered with the royal arms, and a 'groaning chair' for the birth, with a cut-away seat, upholstered in cloth of gold, and a copper-gilt bowl intended to receive the blood and placenta. But all was in vain. After hours of agony, during which Katherine vowed to send her richest head-dress to the shrine of St Peter the Martyr in Spain, she was delivered of a stillborn daughter. Katherine was distraught; four months would pass before she could bring herself to inform her father King Ferdinand of her 'failure'.

Henry put a brave face on his disappointment. On Shrove Tuesday he set another new precedent, astounding his court by personally taking part in a revel: at a banquet for foreign ambassadors Henry and his cour-tiers dressed up as scimitar-wielding Turks, attended by blacked-up torch-bearers. Henry later reappeared wearing a short doublet of blue and crimson slashed with cloth of gold, and led the dancing, partnered once again by his sister, Mary Rose.

By September the Queen was pregnant again. Her confinement fol-lowed the rules established by Lady Margaret Beaufort. Throughout her grandson's reign these would be strictly adhered to. The delivery chamber was shrouded in rich cloth of Arras except for one window. The tapestries adorning the chamber portrayed suitably innocuous images, lest the Queen or the infant should be 'affrighted by figures which gloomily stare'.[2] The chamber contained an altar and a cupboard for the birthing equipment. In case the child was weakly and immediate bap-tism was necessary, the 'rich font of Canterbury' stood ready. To this chamber Katherine retired about six weeks before her time, after mass and a banquet. During the weeks of her lying-in, she would see no man, not even the King.

On New Year's Day 1511, to great jubilation, Katherine was delivered of a prince. The King, overjoyed, lavished gifts on Katherine's attendants. After general celebrations, Henry appointed forty attendants for the prince, and embarked on a pilgrimage to the Priory of Our Lady of Walsingham in Norfolk to give thanks. He dismounted a mile from the priory, in the Slipper Chapel, removed his shoes and walked barefoot to the Virgin's shrine, where he lit a candle and offered an expensive necklace.

In February, the King staged a dazzling tournament at Westminster in honour of the Queen. That night, at a banquet in the White Hall, the revels featured a pageant, the Garden of Pleasure, in which the King appeared as 'Coeur Loyal', Sir Loyal Heart, in purple satin adorned with gold Hs and Ks. When guests, including the Spanish ambassador, refused to believe that Henry's ornaments were real gold, Henry invited them to tug them off and prove it. Unfortunately, the common people, admit-ted to gape at their glorious monarch, took this as an open invitation to strip the King and his courtiers of their finery as a form of largesse.

They surged forward, grabbing whatever they could. Even the King was stripped down to his doublet and hose, while poor Sir Thomas Knyvet was stripped naked and had to shin up a pillar to escape. When the mob started on the ladies, the King's guard intervened, driving them back. Henry passed the whole thing off as a huge joke; the evening concluded with a banquet in the Presence Chamber, guests clutching their tattered finery around them.

In future, security surrounding public events would be tightened up.

On 23 February 1511, the baby prince died. Henry, again suppressing his own disappointment, comforted the distressed Katherine.

At Easter, Pope Julius II bestowed on Henry a Golden Rose personally blessed by himself, a sign of high favour. In 1512, this was followed by a Sword and Cap of Maintenance. These were inducements for Henry to join the so-called Holy League, an alliance between the Papacy, Spain and Venice against Louis of France and his aggressive ambitions in Italy. Henry joined the Holy League in October; he briefly abandoned outward show for austerity, urging the court to curb their extravagance, himself donning plainer garments, including a long grey cloth gown cut in the Hungarian fashion.

Henry's ascetic phase was short-lived. By Christmas, he again sought distractions. On Twelfth Night 1513, the court were startled by an outrageous continental innovation: the Italian masque. The King and his gentlemen, disguised, invited ladies they fancied to dance. Many refused, scandalised by the breach of etiquette, but Mary Rose cheerfully joined in. She shared her brother's delight in the novel and the bizarre, participating enthusiastically in his conceits, happy to dress up as a rustic maiden or an African princess.

Henry's feasts were gargantuan gastronomic extravaganzas: one meal might comprise 240 dishes, including: beef, pork, veal, venison, mutton, game, fish, cheese, jellies, fruit, nuts, pastries and sweets, accompanied by wines from all over Europe. Servants staggered under heaped solid gold platters. Before retiring, the overfed guests might be offered a cup of spiced wine. Those accustomed to the restraint of Henry VII's court were appalled by the extravagance. But senior courtiers welcomed it as a return to the grand old days of Yorkist rule.

Meanwhile, still with no sign of a viable heir, Henry indulged his young sister, 'our well-beloved sister the Lady Mary', showering her with new apparel and insisting on her presence at court. Mary shared his love of music, and delighted in the dancing, pageants and disguisings. The two were rarely apart. When Mary was away at one of the royal manors, Henry constantly sent her little gifts, entreating her to return to court, where she was automatically drawn into his intimate circle, and the company of his favourite, Charles Brandon.

The surface of domestic affairs was unruffled. The major threat was the plague, which periodically swept in from the Continent, spreading terror and death. Henry, Mary and their companions fled to the country until the danger had passed.

Although Mary's marriage to Prince Charles of Castile was not due for consummation for five years, plans for her wedding were reviewed annually. In 1510, Henry had sent an embassy to the Emperor Maximilian in an attempt to progress matters. Henry was discovering for himself an unpleasant truth apparent to everyone else: Maximilian's promises were worthless. In 1512, alarmed by reports that Maximilian was dallying with 'amity' with the King of France, Henry again dispatched special envoys to Germany, hoping for a definite response that would bring the marriage forward or at least reconfirm the imperial intent. Since the Emperor was not only shifty by nature but was constantly on the move, Henry's ambassadors had to work mostly through Maximilian's daughter Margaret, now Archduchess and Regent of the Netherlands. Margaret was making every effort to advance the marriage between her nephew Charles and Mary Rose.

Before the end of 1509, there had been plans for Mary to visit the Low Countries and become acquainted with their fashions and lifestyle. The Emperor had appointed her a gentleman-in-waiting in 1512, and the next autumn, Margaret sent a Fleming to attend on her. Mary had been sent patterns showing the style of dress fashionable at the court of the Netherlands. Thanking her *'bonne tante'*, Mary wrote in French that she hoped to introduce Flemish fashions to the English court. No firm date was set for her visit, though there was some suggestion that Henry would deliver his sister personally when he launched his French campaigns.

Henry took the contract seriously; he supported the Archduchess in her war with the Duke of Guelders, sending 1,500 soldiers, thus placing Burgundy in his debt, and also demonstrating English military power. The Archduchess was embarrassed by her father's shilly-shallying. Soon, Henry and his favourite, Brandon, would cause poor Margaret greater agonies of embarrassment.

Brandon's wife Anne died in the summer of 1510, within a fortnight of the birth of their second daughter, Mary. He had obtained the lucrative offices of Chamberlain of the Principality of Wales and Marshal of the King's Bench, a position formerly held by his uncle. In November 1511, Brandon was granted, with Sir John Carew, the marshalship of the King's household. This entailed keeping the Southwark prison, an influential post with little work but the potential for profit, and close involvement with the King's safety. He was created ranger of the New Forest, an appointment he would retain all his life, entitling him to take a number of bucks and fell a quota of forest trees annually. Craftily, he appointed as his deputy a local man, Robert Hussey, who had often been in trouble for felling trees in the royal forest, and would henceforth have to pay handsomely for the right to do so legally.

In March 1512, Pope Julius II withdrew from Louis XII the title of 'Most Christian King' and declared that France belonged to Henry, if he could win it back. A campaign was mounted in June under the Marquis of Dorset. Henry's favourite courtiers all stepped forward to assume military commands. The war would cost Brandon the loss of good friends, yet their deaths would open the door to dramatic advancement. With Sir Henry Guildford, he was given the command of elite troops aboard a large, newly refitted vessel.

Their first taste of real warfare that summer was bitter. In the naval campaign, through either misfortune or misjudgement, they failed to support Sir Thomas Knyvet as he grappled with a French warship. The French vessel exploded; both ships burned to the waterline before their horrified eyes. Knyvet died, along with most of his crew. This tragedy put Brandon off maritime campaigns forever. He never went to sea again. Sir Edward Howard, appalled by Knyvet's terrible fate, swore that he would never again look the King in the face until he had avenged Knyvet. Howard sought battle with the French until, in a fit of foolhardy heroism, he was killed in April 1513.

With Knyvet and Howard dead, of the leaders of the King's intimate circle Brandon alone survived. From 1512 to 1514, he played an increasingly important part in the King's life. Often, they wore identical outfits, different from those worn by other courtiers. In the short term, the death of Edward Howard, Brandon's closest friend, the only man who consistently outshone him, opened up new military opportunities for Brandon; the long-term effects were even more important. Howard bequeathed to Brandon, 'his special trusty friend', the chain on which his admiral's whistle hung, and also the wardship of whichever of his two illegitimate sons the King did not choose to raise.

Brandon and Howard were elected to the Garter on 23 April 1513, but Howard was dead before the ceremony itself. In October 1512, Brandon assumed his uncle's old office as Master of the King's Horse, gaining complete control over the royal stable, the travelling arrangements of the royal household, and the King's own hunters and warhorses. The King's horses played a huge part in his life, dedicated as he was to hunting, jousting, processions and dreams of military triumph. Under Edward IV, annual expenditure on the stables had been less than £380, with forty-five staff employed. Under Brandon, annual expenditure grew to £1,500, and 137 personnel were employed.

Brandon had long been dominant in the jousts, but on 1 June 1512 he and the King challenged alone together for the first time, and this set the pattern for the next two years. Brandon had the good sense never to outperform the monarch, while succeeding against every other opponent, thus highlighting the King's own skill. As Master of the Horse, Brandon was also the King's esquire. When the King rode out to meet his ally, the Emperor Maximilian, and again to meet his grandson, Prince Charles, Brandon rode immediately behind him, leading the spare horse. On these occasions Brandon was attired in great splendour.

Brandon enjoyed the King's favour and his finances had improved; but his status needed enhancement. Even before the death of Thomas Knyvet's widow, Muriel, Lady Lisle, in December 1512, Brandon had acquired the wardship of the Knyvets' 8-year-old daughter Elizabeth. Aristocratic families customarily sent a child to live with a well-connected family. This tradition linked the parents as political allies and the children as friends. The resultant contacts were often useful in the arrangement of future marriages. Little Elizabeth, Baroness Lisle in her own right, was the heiress to substantial estates. Brandon obtained her wardship on very easy terms – £1,400 over seven years. As her lands brought in almost £800 a year, and Brandon could expect to hold them for at least six years, this was a sound investment.

On Lady Muriel's death, Brandon contracted to marry Elizabeth when she came of age. This enabled the King to create him Viscount Lisle in virtue of his wife on 15 May, granting him an annuity of 40 marks. The new title meant a slight increase in income and rank.

His first major command was in the raid conceived by the King in May 1513 to avenge the death of Sir Edward Howard. Edward's elder brother, Sir Thomas Howard, was appointed admiral in his dead brother's place, while Brandon was to lead a landing party in a co-ordinated operation, intended to destroy the French fleet in its Breton ports. The King was very enthusiastic about the raid, planning to travel secretly to observe its execution. But experienced officers warned that Brandon's force of 4,000 was inadequate, the timescale was unrealistic, and would seriously disrupt Henry's main project, the invasion he planned to lead in person. Nevertheless, arrangements went ahead. German mercenaries arrived in Southampton and artillery was sent from London. But the logistics were disastrous: victualling remained problematic, despite the best efforts of Brandon's servants. The diversion of troops from the Kent ports to Southampton caused chaos, and time was running out. By 21 May most of the invading force was assembled two days' march from the port, to avoid pressure on the food supplies. Brandon had arrived, but Howard was still detained in Portsmouth by unfavourable winds. The victuallers' ships from London and Sandwich were nowhere to be seen. Now reports were coming in that their quarry, the French fleet, had dispersed from Brest.

The enterprise was doomed to failure. Brandon and Howard quarrelled. The raid never took place. But for Brandon, the affair had important consequences. It initiated a decade of difficult relations with Howard, soon to be Earl of Surrey. On the other hand, Brandon's appointment to such a significant command, to which he was entitled neither by rank nor experience, clearly demonstrated the high favour he enjoyed with the King. He was to lead men who outranked him; however, most had participated in the previous summer's disastrous expedition to Guyenne. Brandon, untried but with an untarnished reputation, was appointed High Marshal of the Army for Henry's invasion of France.

Henry had been itching for action ever since the League of Cambrai gave way to the Holy League in October 1511, but had heeded his advisers' counsels to withhold English support and continue his father's policy of peace, avoiding the waste and expense of belligerence. But the papal prompting, the Spanish connection and, above all, his own hankering after military glory tipped the scales. Henry ached for a victory to rival Agincourt. Of the great Plantagenet empire, only Calais and its Pale remained. By the spring of 1513, Henry, in a ferment of excitement, prepared a huge invasion force against France.

The Emperor Maximilian had at last concluded a treaty, Henry advancing him 25,000 crowns, most of which was to be used to bribe the Swiss. Henry promised to invade France with a force of 30,000 men. The Emperor, sweetened by English gold, graciously offered to lead a division under Henry's command. England, Germany, Spain and the Papacy were pledged to declare war on France within thirty days, and attack a month later.

Thousands of suits of armour had been ordered from Italy and Spain; a dozen new cannon, nicknamed the 'twelve apostles', from Germany. Henry hastened to the docks every day to inspect his navy. Transport vessels were being equipped to convey a force of 40,000 men across the Channel. The pride of his navy, the 1,500 ton *Great Harry*, was almost ready for launching. The young men of the King's Chamber enthusiastically supported the King's new venture, fired by notions of chivalry, valour and glorious military pageantry; his new efficient servant, the upstart Thomas Wolsey, was proving invaluable in matters of administration and organisation.

In 1508, the last year of Henry VII's reign, Wolsey, newly returned from an embassy to Scotland, was dispatched by the King on a mission to Flanders. Wolsey left Richmond at noon, took a barge from London to Gravesend, travelled on by post horse to Dover, sailed for Calais within three hours and by the next day had reached the Emperor's court and completed his mission. Returning immediately to Richmond by the same route, he encountered the King on his way to early mass only three days after he had been sent out. The King, supposing he had tarried, reproved him sharply for delaying on his errand. Learning to his astonishment that Wolsey already been and come back, he created him Dean of Lincoln on the spot.

By the beginning of Henry VIII's reign, Wolsey had advanced to the post of Royal Almoner. Henry was young and too self-indulgent for the serious work of government. Wolsey, noting this, 'took upon him therefore to disburden the King of so weighty a charge and troublesome business',[3] so that he was not forced to 'spare any time from his pleasure'. The young royals trusted him. To Mary, only 14 when her father died, Wolsey became virtually a father figure.

Henry left Greenwich for Dover, accompanied by the Queen, who was to act as Regent in his absence, and an entourage of 21 peers, the Duke of Buckingham, Bishop Foxe, Wolsey, heralds, musicians, trumpeters, the choir of the Chapel Royal, 600 archers of the Yeomen of the Guard and 300 household servants. He also took his bed of estate, several suits of armour and numerous gaudy tents and pavilions. On 30 June, the King, his great army and his copious impedimenta set sail for France.

On 24 July, Henry and his ally Emperor Maximilian laid siege to the town of Thérouanne. On 16 August the French were routed at the Battle of the Spurs – so called because of the haste with which the French cavalry, arriving to relieve the town, retreated, overawed by the sight of the allied forces encamped around. Thérouanne fell. It was England's first victory in France since 1453.

Brandon commanded the vanguard of the King's ward, some 3,000 men. Though he took little part in the military decisions of the campaign, and at first saw little action, as High Marshal, and especially since the King had commissioned him lieutenant of the whole army, he commanded dukes, earls and veteran warriors. Although the effective victualling of the army was in reality Wolsey's achievement, Brandon acquitted himself honourably of his command, earning great recognition.

After their triumphal entry into Thérouanne, Henry and his entourage made a 40-mile detour to Lille, where they were lavishly entertained by Maximilian's daughter, the Archduchess Margaret. Margaret's agent at the siege of Thérouanne had described Brandon to her as 'a second King'. The Burgundian nobility flocked to her court to be presented to Henry, whom they were pleased to find 'merry, handsome, well-spoken, popular and intelligent'.[4] Officially enjoying rest and recuperation, his energy astonished everyone. In a hastily assembled tiltyard constructed from planks, he displayed his skill before the Archduchess and her nephew, Prince Charles, his sister's young fiancé, running numerous courses against Brandon and against the Emperor's champion.

The Milanese ambassador, amazed at his stamina, reported: 'He was fresher after this exertion than before. I do not know how he can stand it.'[5]

One tournament was held indoors in a hall with a black marble floor. The horses wore felt shoes to prevent damage to the floor. The King demonstrated his skill at archery, and in the evenings entertained the company by playing various musical instruments and as the night wore on dancing 'magnificently in the French style'[6] with Margaret and her ladies, at one point becoming so hot he had to discard his doublet and hose.

After three days of feasting, the English proceeded to besiege the wealthy town of Tournai. On 25 September, the King was handed the keys of the city, and also a great quantity of *vin de Beaune*. Tournai became his headquarters throughout October. While Henry and his nobles were celebrating their triumphs, the Emperor Maximilian, the Archduchess Margaret and Prince Charles of Castile arrived in person to discuss the prince's forthcoming marriage with Princess Mary Rose.

Henry found Charles delightful, while the Emperor, still grateful for English gold and military assistance, declared that he loved Henry more than a son. The two exchanged gifts, a jewel and a great ox. By 15 October, they had signed two treaties: a military one, for a joint invasion of France with Spanish support, by June 1514; and another, for the consummation of the marriage between Mary and Charles by mid-May 1514.

One secret clause in the marriage treaty reflects the cunning of its chief author, the Archduchess. She extracted an oral promise from Henry that,

lacking male heirs, he would settle the succession on his sister Mary
and her descendants. Margaret would later remind Henry of this pledge,
urging him to obtain Parliamentary sanction, but no action was taken
until the third Succession Act of 1543, which empowered the King to
dispose of the crown at will. Henry's will would be publicised a decade
later, in the summer of 1553, in connection with Northumberland's plot
to secure the throne for his family. It would reveal the King's clear preference for the descendants of his sister Mary Rose, thus placing them in
mortal danger, costing some their freedom and others their lives.

The campaigning season was ending. His triumphs and celebrations on
the Continent completed, and the treaties signed, Henry was now keen
to consolidate his alliance with the Emperor, and return home to devote
himself to his next exciting project: organising the grandest of weddings
for his beloved sister – a marriage he knew would bring him massive prestige in Europe, equalling his recent triumphs on the battlefield.

When the army reached Calais, there was a shortage of hay for the
horses. Henry noted that this must be corrected next spring, when Charles
and Mary were to meet there, and he would be there with his army. He
envisaged a stunning double event comprising nuptials and military campaign. On 22 October, Henry returned to England in triumph.

Between Henry's accession in 1509 and June 1513, more than £1 million had flowed out of the treasury, two-thirds of it having been used to
finance the war with France. Ten years later, Wolsey's protégé Thomas
Cromwell would remark that the winning of Thérouanne cost his
Highness 'more than twenty such ungracious dog-holes could be worth
to him'.[7] The whole campaign had in fact been quite unnecessary, since
the French king had already made peace with the new Pope, Leo X, even
before Henry and his forces embarked. But Henry, flushed with conquest, rewarded those who had served him well during the campaigns
of 1513. At Candlemas 1514, while still convalescing from small pox, in
a move deplored by many members of his court, he elevated his faithful
commander and companion, the charming upstart Charles Brandon, to
a dukedom.

Duke of Suffolk

Henry VIII rewarded his faithful servants. On 2 February 1514, Thomas Howard, Earl of Surrey, was restored to the Dukedom of Norfolk in recognition of his defeat of the Scots at Flodden. (A permanent, if gory, inset into the earl's family coat of arms was an image of the Scottish lion, chopped in two, with an arrow down its throat.)

The King's cousin and Lord Chamberlain, Charles Somerset, Lord Herbert, was created Earl of Worcester. Charles, the bastard son of the last Beaufort Earl of Somerset, had acquitted himself valiantly in the French campaign.

The elevation of Charles Brandon to the Dukedom of Suffolk caused the greatest upset among Henry's courtiers. Brandon's rise to prominence had been spectacular: knighted on 30 March 1512, within fourteen months he was a viscount, a mere nine months later a duke. The Dukes of Norfolk and Suffolk had to be created separately, there being insufficient peers of comparable status to accompany them both at once. The Marquis of Dorset obliged; the Duke of Buckingham sulked. The ceremony of ennoblement, which took place after high mass in the great chamber at Lambeth Palace, followed the procedure established in the fourteenth century when Edward III had raised his sons to the peerage. Each Duke received a crimson robe and cap of estate, a coronet and sword, and a golden rod. Henceforth, Brandon had the right to be styled 'the right high and mighty Prince'; he was usually more simply addressed as 'Your Grace'.

The ceremony was watched by the Queen and her ladies, a crowd of peers up in London for the parliament sittings, and also by Louis d'Orléans, the Duc de Longueville, the most prominent of the noble hostages taken in accordance with the rules of medieval warfare, to ensure that the defeated government honoured the terms of the truce.

During their time in France and the Low Countries, Henry had been impressed by the sophisticated culture of the Franco-Flemish Renaissance. The cessation of hostilities heralded a new craze for French style, etiquette, fashion, food and art, architecture and entertainment. The King himself initiated the trend, which would last for most of his reign. The French language, banned during the war, now once again became the fashionable mode of communication among the upper classes.

The Duc de Longueville was lodged comfortably in the Tower with six attendants. He and Henry had become so friendly that Henry offered to pay half of the Duc's ransom out of his own pocket. The Duc became a popular figure at court, and, although he had a wife back in France, embarked upon a prolonged romance with one of Mary's ladies, the Frenchwoman Jane Poppincourt.

The Duc would also soon come to play a brief but memorable role in Princess Mary's life.

The elevation of Brandon infuriated the older nobility, resentful of Brandon's influence over the King, and suspicious of his ambition. The family of the Duke of Norfolk were waiting for the opportunity to destroy him. Buckingham, who since 1503 had been the only Duke in England, was so outraged by Henry's ennoblement of Brandon that he boycotted the ceremony. It was Buckingham's rival, Wolsey, who had recommended that the King should raise his friend to the peerage, perhaps with the intention of reducing the influence on the Council of the new Duke of Norfolk.

Henry's reasons for elevating Brandon were complex. He wanted to honour those who had contributed to his own modest success in France, signalling that this victory, bought at such enormous cost, was truly momentous. But bestowing on Brandon the title of Suffolk, formerly held by the royal Yorkist de la Pole family, fulfilled Henry's political agenda. Divesting them of the title deprived the last major Yorkist claimants to the throne of their final chance of restoration. Edmund, the last Earl in the de la Pole line of Dukes and Earls of Suffolk, which stretched back to 1385, had fled England in 1501. Five years later, he was forcibly repatriated, attainted and executed in 1513 by Henry. This left at large on the Continent his brother Richard, who styled himself Duke of Suffolk, served the French as a general and canvassed French support to claim the throne of England.

In Europe Brandon's new dukedom kindled immediate speculation; it fed the rumour, current by early 1514, that Brandon and the King had hatched some plot to marry Brandon off to the Archduchess Margaret, and that Henry had ennobled Brandon to facilitate such a union.

In early 1514, Henry had half-jokingly envisaged this unlikely fairy-tale romance between lowly esquire and Emperor's daughter as one pillar of his triple marital edifice designed to cement European alliances. Three marriages would bolster this structure: the far-fetched notion of a marriage between Archduchess Margaret and the new Duke of Suffolk; the already-contracted dynastic marriage between Mary and Charles of Castile; and a possible marriage between Henry's older sister Margaret, recently widowed by the death of James IV of Scotland at the Battle of Flodden, and the Emperor Maximilian himself. But Maximilian, at 54, fancied Mary, confiding to his daughter Archduchess Margaret his intention of forcing Charles to repudiate her so he could marry her himself. Six months later he abandoned the notion, announcing that he would never go near a woman again as long as he lived.

The gossiping about a possible romance between herself and Brandon would upset Archduchess Margaret, and offend her father, Emperor Maximilian, but Margaret retained a soft spot for Brandon. Brandon had rescued little Magdalen Rochester, the 8-year-old daughter of an English resident of Calais, from drowning and subsequently adopted her. He entrusted Magdalen to Margaret's care, and later sent his older daughter Anne Brandon to be educated at the court at Malines on the Dyle, at the palace built for the Archduchess. Both girls remained under Margaret's tutelage for two years. This great concession by the Archduchess Margaret fired more speculation about a potential match. The rumour that Brandon had one or more wives living added spice to the gossip. Writing to Venice from London, at the end of July 1514, Andrea Badoer spoke of it as a fact, adding 'The Duke is a very handsome man, may have had more than three wives and she more than one husband.'[1]

Elevating Brandon to a dukedom was certainly a radical step. When Henry granted Brandon the former de la Pole estates, this made him immediately wealthier and therefore more powerful than most of the landed aristocracy. The former Master of the Horse took it all in his stride. A Venetian observer assured the Senate that 'no one ever bore so vast a rise with so easy a dignity'.[2] Brandon was now 'the chief nobleman in England, a liberal and magnificent Lord'.

Brandon was not the only man of humble origins to be honoured. On 6 February 1514, Wolsey, the Ipswich butcher's son, who had worked so hard to ensure the success of the French campaign, was created Bishop of Lincoln. The base-born cleric had been plucked from obscurity when his brilliance was recognised by Richard Foxe, Bishop of Winchester, the ablest of the councillors whom Henry had inherited from his father. Wolsey's career was already set on its remarkable trajectory as one promotion succeeded the next: in quick succession he was made Archbishop of York, Chancellor of England, and Cardinal. Wolsey was to prove his worth yet again when in March Henry, still a political innocent, received a nasty shock.

Preparations for the wedding between Mary Rose and Charles of Castile, scheduled, according to the terms of the contract, to take place at Calais before 15 May, were already far advanced. Charles would be 14, the age of majority for boys. Mary had already approved the list submitted to her of temporary attendants for her Flemish household; her betrothed had sent her a pompous letter from Mechlin, addressing her as 'my good wife'. The letter was signed, in a childish hand, '*votre bon mari*' (your good husband), but had been written by a secretary. Charles was a cold fish. Even his grandfather, the Emperor Maximilian, admitted the lad was 'as cold and immovable as an idol'.

England was in the throes of wedding fever. Henry, still fretfully convalescing from smallpox at Lambeth Palace, Westminster having been damaged by fire, energetically dictated memoranda planning next season's military campaign and also sent envoys to the Netherlands, bombarding Archduchess Margaret with queries about his sister's wedding: the precise number of riders in the three cavalcades that would escort the Emperor, the Prince and the Archduchess. Would there be enough hay for his horses this time? Was the provision of hangings and furniture for the Burgundian contingent his responsibility? Would the marriage be solemnised in a private chapel or a parish church? He assumed that the principal royal visitors would bring their own beds with them, but he needed a detailed guest list. As he proposed to march off to war immediately after the wedding, he needed to know which VIPs would be staying on in Calais and what provision he would need to make for their accommodation in England's last continental possession.

At home, proud of his sister's beauty, celebrated throughout Europe, he personally supervised her trousseau. Erasmus had told the Abbot of St Berthin that Prince Charles was blessed with his bride's beauty, goodness and wisdom; Peter Martyr wrote, 'Her deportment in dancing and conversation is as pleasing as you would desire.'[3] He added approvingly that her legendary complexion was achieved without the help of cosmetics. Henry wanted to ensure that such beauty was worthily set off. Impressed with Archduchess Margaret's taste, he sent her swatches of fabric by royal courier, asking Margaret to 'devise all things so that Mary's apparel would be Queenly and honourable'.⁴ The King wanted his sister to honour the Burgundian fashion, but, knowing her tastes and her colouring, he wished to select the materials himself. Margaret received a complete list of the princess's retinue of 101 persons, which included 2 ladies in waiting, 5 gentlewomen, 12 gentlemen of the chamber, chamberers, chaplains, an almoner, several grooms and yeomen. Her officers included a tall, sturdy doorkeeper whose job was to drive beggars away from her door.

For travelling Mary had a rich litter of cloth of gold lined with satin or damask, chariots, three wardrobe cars to transport her clothing and splendid caparisons for her palfreys and horses. The Archduchess's advice was solicited on everything.

In the ferment of preparation, the teenage bride allegedly carried about with her a miniature of her unknown bridegroom, 'sighing dutifully', as required.⁵ But Mary's time was chiefly taken up with assembling her trousseau. The inventory of her plate and jewels ran to eleven pages, every item meticulously selected, down to the tiny silver-plated scales for weighing spices and a little pot for ginger, with a fork.⁶ Henry intended no expense to be spared. Besides jewels, Mary had dresses and robes, bonnets, mirrors, gold necklaces and chains, ornate girdles. For her wedding day she had a golden gem-studded coronet. Her chambers and stables were expensively equipped. Her gold and silver plate filled four coffers. The two gentlewomen who were to sleep in her chamber would have pallet beds and fustian sheets; Mary was to have a featherbed of fine down, with linen sheets, a bolster and two pillows. Her chapel was to have a silver crucifix, a private pew, vestments of purple and crimson, candlesticks and a missal of fair print. Her household larder, buttery, almonry, scullery, chandlery, spicery, bakehouse and pantry were all set up. Hundreds of people, including the whole court, were involved. Everyone awaited the summons to the Netherlands for the ceremony.

It never came.

The groom's government prevaricated, issuing one excuse after the other. Charles was ill; he was feeble, unfit to enter an early marriage; there was an outbreak of plague in Calais; Mary was too old for Charles, he needed a wife, not a mother (in England the 19-year-old princess was officially being passed off as 16, perhaps anticipating this objection). The seamstresses were still finishing Mary's gowns, when international politics intervened.

Henry's trusted ally, his father-in-law Ferdinand of Aragon, joined forces with Maximilian behind his back and signed another pact with Louis XII. Ferdinand, who, according to the English ambassador in Spain, was working against the marriage of Charles and Mary, announced a year's truce with France, while still protesting his good faith to England.

Louis seized on this as the thin end of the wedge leading to peace, and quickly capitalised on it in hopes of breaking up the Holy League. He was confident that Spain would make a defensive alliance with France, offered the right lure, and he had just the right inducement: the hand of his 3-year-old daughter Renée, for the 10-year-old Infante Ferdinand. Renée would bring as her dowry Milan, Genoa and the other territories Louis and his armies had conquered. Little Renée was to become the most frequently engaged princess in Europe.

Louis then turned the pressure on Maximilian, who was caught in a dilemma, urged by France and Spain to join their alliance, and on the other hand, by Henry to continue the war and proceed with the marriage of Mary and Charles. Louis, with two marriageable daughters and now the backing of Spain, pressed his negotiations hard. Charles could have his pick of the two French princesses, little Renée or her older sister Claude, who, according to the Spanish ambassador, was lame and deformed. Mary, fêted as the fairest princess in Europe, her splendid trousseau poised for transport to the Continent, had been betrothed to Charles for six years. The Archduchess Margaret wrote to her father the Emperor, stressing the importance of the English marriage for the safety of the Low Countries and pointing out that the treaty he had signed the previous year contained heavy penalty clauses. Towns, nobles and burgesses would have to foot the bill, if the nuptials were not celebrated before the end of May. Aware of the Emperor's cupidity, she also reminded her father that Henry was to pay £100,000 of Mary's dowry at Bruges. Henry sent to Flanders urging them to get a move on with the nuptials, but again was fobbed off. He was becoming angry and disillusioned. Mary felt humiliated.

When Ferdinand deserted the Holy League to make peace with Louis XII, Maximilian quickly followed suit. Henry, outraged by this betrayal, rose from his sickbed, fired with rage against Louis and disappointed and furious with Ferdinand. Peter Martyr wrote: 'The King of England bites his lips.'[7] Henry was now spoiling for another fight. His appetite for military campaigns had replaced his obsession with jousting; war was the real thing, and he wanted more of it. He had planned to arrive in Calais with his sister, see her wed to the Prince of Castile in a blaze of glory, and then continue his own valiant deeds against the French. Now, the wedding with Maximilian's grandson was clearly off.

Young and hot-headed, Henry cast around for a scapegoat. Poor Queen Katherine bore the brunt of his rage. Had Katherine not failed to provide him with an heir? Was she not the daughter of the treacherous Ferdinand? This sowed the seeds of discord between them. Suddenly, Katherine's success in rallying the troops during Henry's absence and achieving victory at Flodden against the Scots – a feat of greater significance than any of Henry's much-trumpeted triumphs in France – faded into insignificance. The Queen was no longer his most trusted adviser. There were even rumours in Rome that year that divorce was on the cards.

The worst aspect of the betrayal by Ferdinand and Maximilian was that Mary was betrothed to the Prince of Castile, heir to both monarchs. Henry, outraged by their duplicity, declared he would attack France, even if the only support he could look for came from the Swiss. From this rash enterprise he was dissuaded by Pope Leo X, and by the combined efforts of Foxe and Wolsey. Wolsey, who had lived in Calais and remained strongly pro-French, advocated making peace with France. As he came to deal with increasingly complex matters of national importance, the King had begun to rely on Wolsey's judgement and advice even more than on Brandon's. While relations between Brandon and Wolsey remained superficially cordial, lacking the open animosity displayed by the Howards and Buckingham for the King's new Councillor, privately Brandon was discomfited by Wolsey's growing influence over the King. But Brandon would soon have cause to be eternally grateful to Wolsey.

While Wolsey negotiated peace with France, Henry concentrated on another of his interests. He began building the first of his recreational complexes at Greenwich. The new, larger tiltyard may have been completed in time for the tournament held in May 1514, when the King and Brandon appeared disguised as hermits, Henry in a white velvet habit with a cloak of overlapping pieces of leather and a hat of cloth of silver, Brandon in black velvet. Before the violent joust began, both champions threw off their disguises and tossed them to the Queen and their ladies as largesse, as modern sporting celebrities throw their shirts. Now Henry was seen to be dressed all in black and Brandon in white. Both bore pennants with the motto: 'Who can hold that will away?' This was interpreted as a reference to the notional romance between the Archduchess Margaret and Brandon.

Erasmus, who besides being a great thinker was an incorrigible gossip, wrote to his friend Gonnell: 'Rumour has it that Maximilian's daughter Margaret is to marry that new Duke, whom the King has recently turned from a stable-boy into a nobleman.'[8] This incautious remark was expurgated from the published edition of Erasmus's Letters printed in Basel five years later.

The story had to be squashed. Despite his feigned ignorance, Henry was well aware of the particular incident that had generated it; he also knew that it was largely his own fault. During his French campaign, he and Brandon had been frequent guests at the court of the Archduchess. As early as October 1513, Brandon's supposed flirtation with the Archduchess had set tongues wagging. Margaret was highly eligible. Having buried two young husbands, she was intelligent and attractive, and only a little older than Brandon himself. Brandon was already contracted to his child ward, Elizabeth Grey, Baroness Lisle, now aged 10, and bore his title of Viscount Lisle by virtue of her right to it. Margaret feasted the King and his company lavishly, and Henry spent a fortune on gifts for her.

There prevailed an air of celebratory informality at the Archduchess's court; it was a hotbed of courtly love, where amorous dalliance was an acceptable part of the tradition. Henry himself indulged in a courtly romance with a Flemish lady-in-waiting, Etienne de la Baume. According to a letter she wrote to him later, they laughed and joked together, and he called her 'his page'. Henry promised her a dowry of 10,000 crowns if she found a husband. Gallant after-dinner flirtations were nothing out of the ordinary in that highly charged atmosphere.

But matters got out of hand: Henry's half-jocular suggestion of a possible marriage between the Archduchess and Brandon caused major embarrassment. Marshal of the Army and celebrated throughout England as a star of the tournament though he was, in the eyes of continental aristocracy Brandon was merely a jumped-up East Anglian squire, certainly no match for the daughter of an Emperor. Later, Margaret reminded Henry exactly how the 'misunderstanding', as Henry and Margaret hastened to describe it when others began to take it seriously, arose. At Tournai Brandon had knelt before her, drawn a ring from her finger and tried it on his own; his clowning had made her fall about laughing. Brandon 'put hymselfe opon hys knees befor me, and in speking and hyme playng, he drew fro my finger the rynge, and put yt upon hys, and sythe schewde yt me, and I took to lawhe'.[9] Margaret spoke no English, and Brandon was pretending not to speak French. When Margaret could not get him to return her ring, after trying in French and then in Flemish, Henry stepped in as interpreter. Up till then, everything had been perfectly acceptable, Brandon promising to be her 'rygthe humble servant', Margaret swearing 'to do unto hym alle honneur and plesure'.

But Henry then urged her to take Brandon as a husband. It being common knowledge that Margaret had sworn never to remarry, Henry, with his laddish sense of humour, doubtless thought his suggestion hilarious. Margaret later tactfully noted that Henry, probably in his fondness for Brandon, overinterpreted his desires. Henry and Brandon were probably flushed with wine and military conquest, relaxing in an atmosphere of mirth and conviviality, and showing off before the attractive Archduchess and her ladies.

But the tale of a budding romance spread until bets were being taken in London on the likelihood of a marriage; Margaret's enemies began to promote discreditable rumours. Crucially, the story reached the ears of Margaret's father, the Emperor Maximilian. Things had gone too far. Margaret assured her shocked father that it was a fabrication; she would rather die than entertain notions of such a union. Henry, knowing he was to blame, overreacted, setting in motion a major investigation into the source of the rumours, and threatening with death the rumour-mongers themselves. He fired off disingenuous letters of apology to Margaret and Maximilian, wondering how such an idea could ever have got into people's heads.

Margaret asked him not to send Brandon back to Flanders to raise troops for next year's war, and Henry meekly agreed. He did, however, draw the line at commanding Brandon to marry little Lady Lisle, which would have redeemed Margaret's reputation. Henry was not willing to sacrifice his friend's happiness on the altar of Anglo-imperial amity.

Anyway, as Wolsey's efforts had borne fruit and the possibility of peace with France was becoming a reality, Anglo-imperial alliance was less urgent. Henry demanded Thérouanne, Boulogne and St Quentin, plus 1½ million gold crowns, this sum to include arrears of pensions due from the kings of France to the kings of England since the fifteenth century. Wolsey had avenged the King's honour by out-tricking the tricksters.

As a final incentive in the peace negotiations, Henry threw into the deal the hand of one or other of his sisters as a bride for the ageing Louis XII. If the king agreed to accept Margaret, the widowed Queen of Scots, Henry declared that he was prepared to settle for a lower annual payment of 100,000 crowns. But Louis had already seen Mary's portrait. Although the bride-price was higher, it was beautiful Mary the French King wanted.

Mary was informed that, instead of being sent to the Netherlands as the bride of a teenager, she would be dispatched to Paris to become the queen of an old man.

✤ 6 ✤

Queen of France

Pock-marked, ailing and no spring chicken, King Louis XII, unabashed by his own lack of personal attractions, was convinced that he could marry any lady he chose. Accordingly, drawing up a shortlist of five potential candidates, he made a cool appraisal of their qualifications: the Archduchess Margaret, her two nieces Eleanor, 16, and Isabella, 13, and Henry VIII's sisters, Margaret and Mary Rose. It was rumoured that the Archduchess could not produce a live heir; Isabella was too young and her older sister too slight and, more importantly, unattractive. King Ferdinand attempted to reassure Louis, telling him thin women got pregnant more easily and were better breeders. But the king found Eleanor unappealing. Although the widowed Margaret had recently produced a male heir, thereby proving her fertility, France had no need to woo Scotland; their help against England could always be depended upon. Besides, reports claimed 25-year-old Margaret was growing stout and beginning to lose her bloom. Tempted by stories of Mary's legendary beauty, Louis listened attentively to accounts of her grace and vivacity. Crucially, she appeared healthy enough to breed successfully. Louis decided young Mary might suit him very well.

Peace negotiations between France and England had been encouraged by the papal nuncio, who had arrived in London in January 1514, and further advanced behind the scenes by the Duc de Longueville, who, although officially a hostage, was unofficially an envoy of the French king. By June, it was becoming clear that peace would soon be sealed. Ferdinand made a last-ditch effort to salvage what he could. His envoy was instructed, if it were true that Louis was contractually bound to Mary, to press for the marriage of Princess Renée to the Infante Ferdinand; if Louis were not yet committed to Mary, then he must be persuaded to choose Eleanor instead.

On 30 July 1514, in a formal ceremony at Wanstead in Essex, Mary repudiated her contract to marry Charles of Castile. In a rehearsed speech, she renounced her marriage vows, charging her fiancé with breach of faith, and declaring that malicious gossip and evil counsel had turned him against her. Thus humiliated, she was no longer willing to keep her part of the bargain, so the contract was null and void. Disclaiming any wifely affection for the prince, she swore before Wolsey, Norfolk and Suffolk that she was acting of her own volition, and was 'in all things ever ready to obey the King's good pleasure'.[1]

One week later, on 7 August, the treaty of peace and friendship with France was signed. But its public proclamation a few days later prompted no general rejoicing. Londoners received the news in glum silence. There were no celebratory fanfares or ringing of bells. The mood in England was far from conciliatory; the memory of recent hostile exchanges was too raw. Prior John, the freebooting French admiral from Rhodes, discovering that his Levantine galleys could out manoeuvre any other vessel in the Mediterranean, had used them to harry British vessels at every opportunity. In May 1514 he went even further, landing at Brighton, then a small hamlet on the Sussex coast. Before the watch were alerted, he and his men set fire to the town and made off with 'such poor goods as he found'.[2] When the alarm sounded, six battle-ready English archers chased the invaders back to their boat, wounding several, their arrows flying so thick and fast that they grazed Prior John's face. When Edward Howard, the commander of Henry's fleet, heard of the outrage, he sent Sir John Wallop to Normandy where the English perpetrated fierce reprisals, burning twenty-one small towns and villages. Henry sent Sir Thomas Lovell to strengthen the defences at Calais.

Despite the resentment in both countries about armistice with the traditional enemy, the peace would be sealed by the projected marriage between the two royal families. Louis, having selected his bride, was now determined to secure her hand without delay. On 12 August Henry VIII wrote to inform the Pope of the change of plan. His sister, he explained, had been engaged to Prince Charles of Castile for six years. During this time, the Emperor and his government had prevaricated, reneged on their word and made specious excuses, until the situation had become both humiliating and untenable. In consequence, to seal the new peace, the Princess Mary would now marry the King of France.

The negotiations were supposed to be secret, but news of the betrothal soon spread like wildfire. Horrified, the Archduchess Margaret, who had worked for so long to bring about the marriage between Mary and her nephew, sent envoys to London to find out if it were true. When she learned that it was, she burst into tears. Prince Charles, when informed by his councillors, bitterly accused everyone of breaking their promises and disrespecting him because of his youth. In an unpleasant episode which indicates something of the character of Prince Charles, and suggests Mary may have had a lucky escape, he gave a cruel and graphic symbolic response when his councillors told him that he was young, whereas the King of France, as the first King in Christendom, had the pick of princesses. Thrown into a furious sulk, the prince turned to stare out of his window. His eye fell upon a man with a hawk on his wrist. He sent one of his courtiers to buy the bird. The courtier reported back that, apparently, the hawk was young and not fully trained, so not a sporting bird fit for a prince. Charles stormed out, thrust some coins at the man and seized the unfortunate bird himself. Returning to his council chamber with the hawk perched on his fist, he began before their startled eyes to pluck out its feathers one by one. To their appalled murmurs, he announced: 'You asked me why I plucked this hawk; he is young, you see, and because he is young he is held in small account, and because I am young, you have plucked me at your good pleasure; and because I was young, I knew not how to complain.' He added with scorn 'Bear in mind that for the future I shall pluck you.'[3]

While England's former European allies speculated wildly, the proxy wedding of the French king and the English princess was set for Sunday 13 August. Mary set about learning more about her prospective bridegroom.

Louis XII, third Duc d'Orléans, born around 1462, was the son and heir of Charles d'Orléans, the poet prince captured at the Battle of Agincourt, who spent 25 years in England. His mother was the delightful Mary of Cleves who presided over the lively and cultured court of Blois, which throughout Louis's life became his favourite bolt-hole, where he relaxed from the stresses of kingship. In his youth, Louis was athletic and physically impressive, excelling at various sports. This 'lusty and beautiful' young man was forced at the age of 14, for dynastic reasons, into a marriage with his unfortunate cousin Princess Jeanne. Jeanne's congenital deformity was such that her own father, 'Spider Louis', King Louis XI, vilified her as the most hideous thing imaginable. She was feeble, hunchbacked and lame, and suffered from a number of incurable conditions. She had little hope of ever bearing children. Poor little Jeanne was only 8 when the travesty of a marriage was celebrated and the cousins were pronounced man and wife. Jeanne bore her afflictions patiently and even grew to care for her husband, although Louis made no secret of his disgust at being tied to this pathetic figure. He could hardly swallow his revolt at her presence and for most of the twenty-two years of their grotesque marriage they lived apart. Louis, angry and frustrated, sought adventure, both romantic and political, wherever he could.

His father-in-law, Spider Louis, died in 1483 and was succeeded by Jeanne's 13-year-old brother Charles VIII, who was as deformed in body as his sister, and much less intelligent. Louis made a bid for the Regency, leading to the 'Foolish War'; he spent three years in prison for his reck- lessness. When, in 1498, he finally inherited the throne of France at the age of 36, the former sportsman was a broken-down old man. He imme- diately sought annulment of his marriage on the grounds that Jeanne was infertile, despite her insistence to the contrary. The current Pope was the accommodating and politically astute Alexander VII. Alexander needed French military aid in Italy; in return for this, plus a title, a fief and a French bride for his son, the infamous Cesare Borgia, he granted the annulment. Tragic Jeanne, 'given to God because she was not good enough for man,' retired to a convent, where she died six years later.

Louis had already set his sights on a new bride more to his taste, a lady with excellent prospects, capable of bearing him an heir. This was Dowager Queen Anne of Brittany, who had for six years been the devoted wife of his brother-in-law, Charles VIII. As heiress to the rich feuda- tory province of Brittany, the one large quasi-independent state Louis XI had failed to integrate into his empire, ambitious suitors had com- peted for Anne's hand since her early childhood. At the age of 5 she had been betrothed to the Emperor Maximilian. When her father Francis II of Brittany died in 1488 without male issue the pledge was reinforced by a proxy marriage which was never consummated (the couple never met). Anne was married off to Charles VIII in 1491. This marriage could have been as disastrous as that of Louis XII and Jeanne, but it turned out well. France acquired Brittany, and Charles got a wife who accepted his physical and mental challenges. Anne bore and buried four children before Louis XII married her in 1499. Anne was a fairly small woman with a limp, but, although Louis had reacted with queasy inhumanity to his first wife's disabilities, despite her imperfect physique, he adored 'his Breton'. Anne was a helpful queen and a pleasant companion. Her court at Blois retained its reputation for culture and education. In only one respect did she fail, but that failure was crucial. Providing a male heir was a wife's first duty. Lack of heirs was always blamed on the woman. Anne gave Louis four children, two stillborn sons and two surviving children who were mere girls. Under Salic law, Claude, the first-born, could not inherit the throne of France, but she would have Brittany. Anne had insisted in her marriage contract that the duchy should revert to the second son or failing male issue to the eldest daughter. She knew in her heart that betrothing Claude to Francis d'Angoulême was the sensible thing to do, but she fought against it tooth and nail. Louis, conscious of his own failing health, pushed for the match to ensure France's continued possession of Brittany. The last year of their marriage was not harmonious. Louis got his way over the betrothal, but he was embittered over his queen's determined opposition to it. Nor did he forget that, when she thought he was on his deathbed, Anne attempted to salvage whatever she could by sending boatloads of plate, jewels and the best of the royal furniture to her own château at Nantes.

However, Louis outlived her by almost a year. Anne died on 9 January 1514, 'wonderfully lamented'. She was accorded a royal burial in Paris and entombed in the church of Saint-Denis.

Now in his 50s, Louis's health was far from robust, yet he proposed to embark on matrimony for this third time from dynastic as well as diplomatic motives. He had been plagued by premonitions of death since the demise of his beloved Anne. 'Before the year is out, I shall be with her, to keep her company,' he had sobbed over her coffin. Having only daughters, he desperately needed a son and heir, otherwise his throne would pass to his son-in-law Francis d'Angoulême, whose betrothal to Claude when she was 7 was consummated with their marriage in May 1514. Louis dreaded that Francis, with his extravagant Renaissance ideas, would ruin France.

Louis, formerly rash and improvident, had grown cautious and thrifty. He was paying the physical price for his years of prodigality and over-indulgence, and for the debilitation exacerbated by his spell in prison. He suffered from gout and a skin condition. People who saw him in later years referred to him as infirm and diseased. He had been given up for dead on at least two occasions. The previous summer, in 1513, when he led his troops against Henry's English forces, it was commented that his heart was stronger than his legs. That autumn he had to be carried to the battlefield in a carriage. In the English Parliament the following January, his increasing infirmities were contrasted with the robust vigour of Henry VIII, 'who is like the rising sun, that grows brighter and stronger each day'.[4]

France, on the other hand, was thriving under his governance. Even the Italian wars, fostering the Valois dream of an empire beyond the Alps, did not affect growing domestic prosperity or hold back the administrative reforms that were improving conditions. His chief minister, Cardinal d'Amboise, was responsible for the financial measures, but Louis got both the credit and the blame. He settled down to become a good and caring king, earning the epithet 'the father of his people'. Life at the French court, previously brimming with gaiety and over-indulgence, was quieter. When courtiers grumbled at the frugality of the royal household, Louis replied that he preferred listening to their sneers at his parsimoniousness to hearing the groans of the people labouring under the yoke of their sovereign's extravagance.

Now a royal wedding to a beautiful princess, with attendant extravagant festivities and lavish feasting, raised everyone's spirits. An official at the Venetian Embassy, Nicolo di Favri, joined the guests as the court foregathered in the great banqueting hall at Greenwich in a ferment of excitement to witness Princess Mary's ceremony of betrothal to the King of France, with the Duc de Longueville standing as proxy for Louis. Resplendent in cloth of gold and rich silks, wearing heavy gold chains about their necks, the Dukes of Norfolk and Suffolk, Dorset and Buckingham, and the principal nobles assembled early in the morning in the hall, which had been decked with arras of cloth of gold, bordered with an embroidered frieze emblazoned with the royal arms of France and England.

The buzz of pleasantries was hushed when, three hours later, the King and Queen arrived – Katherine, in silvery satin with a little gold Venetian cap on her head, visibly and joyfully pregnant again, closely followed by Mary, bedecked with jewels, wearing a kirtle of silver-grey satin under a purple and gold chequered gown which matched, as French tradition demanded, the robes of the French king's representative, the Duc de Longueville. Mary looked stunning and appeared composed. Such was her innocent radiance that di Favri thought she looked 16, not 19. After a Latin sermon by Archbishop Warham, Archbishop of Canterbury, vows in French, rings and a kiss were exchanged. After the nuptial mass, there followed a banquet. Two hours of energetic dancing were led by the King and Buckingham, who removed their long gowns and danced informally in their doublets; even older dignitaries following suit.

The dancing concluded, a frisson of anticipation ran through the company as they proceeded to the official bedding, a symbolic act which supposedly represented consummation and thereby rendered the union irrevocable. In an adjacent chamber a great bed had been prepared for the bridal couple. Mary, who had now changed from her wedding gown into a magnificent déshabillé, lay down on the bed, with one leg bared to the thigh. The Duc de Longueville, having removed his red hose, also bared a leg, with which he touched the bride. Warham then declared the marriage consummated, at which the 'King of England made much rejoicing'.[5] Later the legal documents were drawn up and signed in de Longueville's chamber. His ransom paid, the noble hostage returned home next day with ten horses and a cart carrying £2,000-worth of gifts, one of which was the splendid gown worn by the King the previous evening. This garment alone was valued at 300 ducats.

In some quarters the marriage caused outrage. Resentful that Mary was not, after all, to come to the Netherlands, the Dutch 'spake shamefully of this marriage, that a feeble, old and pocky man should marry so fair a lady'.[6] From Valladolid, Peter Martyr expressed the Spanish view that 'an old valetudinarian' should not consort with a handsome girl of 18.[7] She would be the death of him. To Katherine's chagrin, the Spanish ambassador boycotted the wedding and left London.

Yet if Mary herself had objections, she kept them to herself. There has been some speculation that Mary, wearied and humiliated by the Charles of Castile fiasco, almost welcomed the prospect of becoming Queen of France, preferring to marry an aged monarch than a shilly-shallying adolescent with a Habsburg lantern jaw and jutting lip. Marrying Louis was a matter of politics; Mary had little choice. Her own motto, 'To do God's will is enough for me', was an ironic summary of her position. Her brother had appealed to her sense of patriotism and duty, mentioning 'the peace of Christendom'. The French king had no male heir. If Mary could manage to put aside her personal feelings and revulsion inspired by his geriatric fumblings and eventually produce the longed-for dauphin, ousting Francis d'Angoulême from the succession, she would establish herself and her brother at the head of the most powerful alliance in Europe.

What puzzled the Venetian ambassador Badoer was the air of exultation the princess radiated as she stepped down the aisle. Surely mere satisfaction that she was fulfilling a patriotic and dynastic duty could not account for it. He could only assume she was dazzled by the realisation of her august new status. In his report to the Signory, he commented: 'The Queen [princess Mary] does not mind that the King [of France] is a gouty old man ... and she herself a young and beautiful damsel ... so great is her satisfaction at being Queen of France.'[8]

Few realised that Mary owed her serene and blissful aspect to very different reasons. What buoyed Mary's spirits on her wedding day and throughout the remainder of 1514 was the knowledge of her secret bargain with her brother the King. Between her repudiation of Charles on 30 July and the drafting of the meticulous French marriage treaty, signed in its final form on 14 September, she had somehow managed to extract from Henry a promise which he probably had little intention of fulfilling, his sole aim being to get the French marriage accomplished quickly, with as little protest from the bride as possible.

Mary was quietly determined to hold Henry to his word.

Historians have suggested that Mary was crafty and calculating. But women had few options. In the Tudor taxonomy of world order, woman was an inferior creature, in thrall to man. Even a princess was relatively powerless, a mere pawn in the political game, with few options other than to manipulate men and exploit every twist of fate. This required a measure of cunning, even in women not naturally scheming or underhand. Mary, already deeply in love, found the courage to force Henry into striking a deal. She certainly must have been reluctant to be married off to an ailing monarch thirty-four years her senior; she was already infatuated with Charles Brandon. The letters that passed between Mary, Brandon and Wolsey in 1515 reveal that not only was the King aware of his sister's feelings, but that she had only 'consented to his request, and for the peace of Christendom, to marry Louis of France, though he was very aged and sickly',[9] on condition that if she survived him she should marry whom she liked. Mary played her trump card skilfully.

In the light of that bargain, the more ailing and sickly her husband appeared, the better, for the sooner would she be united with the man she loved.

Hugging this secret knowledge, Mary appeared overjoyed.

❖ 7 ❖

La Rose Vermeille

After the betrothal ceremony, Louis dispatched to England the French portrait painter Jehan Perréal, with orders to capture a good likeness of his bride and to help design a trousseau in keeping with the latest Paris fashions. Clearly, the splendid wardrobe prepared for Mary's planned marriage to the Prince of Castile would not suffice for a Queen of France. Some gowns were remodelled. The insignia of Castile was speedily unpicked from more valuable items and embroidered over with the fleur-de-lis. Henry again emptied his coffers to send his sister off sumptuously attired, with gowns in the English and Milanese styles, matching hats, in cloth of gold, silks, rich brocades and crimson velvet. He supplemented her already considerable store of jewellery with sapphires, rubies and diamonds in settings representing the Tudor rose and the fleur-de-lis, and extended her inventory of luxurious furnishings. The magnificent trousseau was loaded on elegant closed carts, emblazoned with Mary's coat of arms and with her new rightful emblem, the fleur-de-lis. Goldsmiths' work embellished her saddlecloths, chapel hangings and bed curtains.

Perhaps with a touch of irony, Henry added to Mary's massive impedimenta a set of seven superb tapestries depicting the labours of Hercules.

In contrast to the wavering indifference and stilted formality displayed by her youthful Habsburg suitor, Mary now found herself an old man's darling; her elderly bridegroom showered her with letters and gifts. The Sieur de Marigny, who accompanied Perréal to London, brought along two coffers crammed with jewellery, so heavy that they had to be carried into the Presence Chamber on a white horse. With a flourish, de Marigny presented Mary with the legendary 'Mirror of Naples', which had belonged to the father of Anne of Brittany. Henry, impressed, sent the pendant off to be valued by the 'jewellers of the Row'. Awestruck, Lorenzo Pasqualio, an Italian merchant resident in London, described it as a diamond as big as a finger, surmounting a pearl the size of a pigeon's egg. He estimated its worth at 60,000 crowns.

Henry sent the Earl of Worcester to France to finalise the paperwork for both the peace treaty and the marriage. Worcester reported that the marriage was proving very popular. Mary's jointure was to comprise the traditional lands and revenues enjoyed by a Queen of France. Like her predecessor, Anne of Brittany, she was to have the town of la Rochelle, the county of Saintonge, Chinon with its fine castle, and the revenues from Rochefort, Pezenas, Montigny, Cessenon and Cabrières, in addition to dues from Montpellier, and rents and taxes from other estates scattered all over France, to the tune of 10,000 'livres tournois'. According to the Venetians, Henry also hoped she would be granted the Duchy of Milan. Louis was to pay Henry the million crowns stipulated in the peace treaty.

Mary's dowry would be 40,000 gold crowns, including her plate and jewellery. However, the English, mindful of Louis's poor health, ensured that the contract included a proviso guaranteeing the return of Mary's personal property if the King should die. Once the contracts were signed and sealed, Louis underwent a proxy betrothal ceremony. Mary was represented by the Earl of Worcester. The French, bamboozled by his name, recorded it as 'Nonshere'.

Thankfully, this ceremony, unlike that held in England, dispensed with the symbolic 'bedding'.

Mary's retinue would include, as Mother of the Maids, Lady Guildford, the widow of Sir Richard Guildford, Controller of the Household to Henry VII; she had been a lady-in-waiting to both Mary's grandmothers. She would be Lady of the Bedchamber, chaperone and mentor, guiding the young Queen and the younger, dizzier members of her suite. She had been chosen for this delicate appointment by Henry, Wolsey and Katherine. Of unimpeachable English descent and forthright character, she spoke French well. Despite Perréal's interference, she ensured that English milliners received their share of the lucrative orders for the princess's trousseau and the apparel of her entourage. By 12 September, more than £76 had been spent in London on hats alone.[1] The wedding had benefited the London garment trade; before Mary left for France, drapers, mercers and haberdashers foregathered to bid her godspeed. Mary graciously gave her hand to each, and delighted everyone by making a brief speech of thanks in French, which she had been practising with her tutor, John Palsgrave. Everyone hoping for a place in Mary's entourage had been polishing their language skills. Pasqualigo noted that 'the whole court now speaks both French and English, as in the time of the late King'.[2]

Golden-haired Mary was now a major celebrity. Her appearance and demeanour were scrutinised and analysed by commentators both at home and abroad.³ Peter Martyr praised her dancing and conversation. Pasqualigo described Mary as 'very beautiful, tall, fair, of a light complexion with a colour, and most affable and graceful. She wore a gown in the French fashion, of wove gold, very costly.' The Mirror of Naples gleamed against her fair skin. Mesmerised by Mary's beauty, Pasqualigo called her 'a nymph from heaven, a paradise'.⁴

The agents of the Archduchess Margaret, aunt of Charles, Mary's former betrothed, reported that Mary was lovely and, contrary to rumour, not oversized.

Philip Sieur de Brégilles wrote in March 1514: 'I think never man saw a more beautiful creature, nor one having so much grace and sweetness, in public and in private. There are not any so small or so sweet as she.' Ambassador Gerard de Pleine, after studying Mary carefully, informed the Archduchess: 'I think I never saw a more charming creature. She is very graceful. Her deportment in dancing and conversation is as pleasing as you could desire. There is nothing gloomy or melancholy about her ... I assure you she has been very well educated.'⁵ He noted her good figure and outstanding beauty. She was less tall than he had believed, and would have been a much better match for Prince Charles than he had imagined before seeing her.

But Charles was the past. Now Mary was to be a queen.

Her final preparations for the move to France complete, in August 1514, Mary joined King Henry on his summer progress. In the royal cavalcade, sister and brother rode side by side, followed by a great procession of nobles glittering in cloth of gold, golden chains jingling. Katherine, well advanced in her fourth pregnancy, travelled in a litter. She had suffered a miscarriage the previous September. During the New Year revels of 1514 Henry embarked on an affair with Bessie Blount, Lord Mountjoy's charming teenage cousin, an interlude interrupted by Henry's attack of smallpox. No sooner had he recovered than Katherine was pregnant again.

King Louis, too, was hoping his marriage to a young, healthy and desirable princess would produce the longed-for heir who would displace as dauphin his daughter Princess Claude's husband, Francis. Francis had been brought up by his clever, fiercely ambitious mother, Louise of Savoy. Louise, widowed at 19, had focused her whole life on her son; she deplored the thought that her ambitions would be dashed if this English princess provided Louis with an heir. When Louis left Paris on 22 September to meet Mary at Abbeville, Louise balefully recorded in her journal: 'The King, *very antique and feeble*, has gone to meet his *young* bride'[6] – representing Louis as a lustful old rake drooling at the prospect of a smooth-limbed maiden.

Louis, rackety in youth, had grown moralistic. When the names of Mary's permanent attendants were submitted for his approval, Louis raised only one only objection, to Mary's childhood companion Jane Poppincourt. The King had learned – probably from the Earl of Worcester – of Jane's liaison with de Longueville. The Duc was married to a princess who would be among the guests at the royal wedding; Louis struck Jane's name off the list, declaring that he would rather see such an immoral woman burned alive than have her anywhere near his new wife.

Mary's departure was delayed by foul weather. At last, on 2 October, she was able to take ship. At the waterside in Dover, Henry embraced her and gave her his blessing, saying: 'I betoken you to God and the fortunes of the sea, and the government of the King your husband.'[7] Mary took advantage of his evident emotion to remind Henry of his promise. Escorted by the Duke of Norfolk, she then embarked for France with a fleet of fourteen ships. The plan had been for de Longueville to welcome her at Boulogne with a retinue of 200 French ladies, but the autumn storms continued to disrupt arrangements. On 4 October, ten days later than expected, the new Queen of France, pale, dishevelled and soaked to the skin, was borne through the waves by Sir Christopher Garnyshe and deposited on dry land, where she was received by the Duke of Vendôme and the Cardinal of Amboise.

She travelled on to the village of Montreil, where she rested while her servants unpacked the dress she had selected for her first meeting with her bridegroom. At 2 in the afternoon on 8 October, messengers rode post-haste to inform the King that Mary was on her way to Abbeville. Louis sent the Dauphin Francis, accompanied by the royal dukes, to escort her procession. This was part of an elaborate romantic stratagem: Renaissance custom demanded that their meeting should have the character of a chance encounter. Francis detained Mary's party at a prearranged rendezvous about 2 miles from Abbeville. Suddenly, Louis appeared, dressed for hawking. Louis was, nonetheless, accompanied by 200 gentlemen, a guard of mounted archers and the Swiss foot guards, and by the Cardinals of Auch and Bayeux, and the Duke of Albany, who, as the heir to Mary's infant nephew, James V of Scotland, was such a thorn in the flesh of her older sister, Margaret.

Louis, although showing his age, cut a fine figure in a short riding dress of cloth of gold on crimson, mounted on his splendid Andalusian horse, Bayart, caparisoned in cloth of gold chequered with black satin.

According to the Dauphin's best friend, the young Sieur de Fleuranges, the elderly, gout-ridden King made Bayart caracole. However well-trained the horse, this sideways dressage manoeuvre requires good balance and a strong seat and legs on the part of the rider. It must have delighted the crowd, who had braved the persistent Normandy drizzle to watch the royal couple meet.

There followed a romantic pantomime in which Mary blew Louis a kiss – scandalising the Venetian observers – and he gamely blew one back, then rode up and embraced her properly from the saddle. One Venetian noted that the King kissed his bride 'as kindly as if he had been five and twenty and came in this dress and on horseback the more to prove his vigour'.[8] Mary sportingly pretended to be astonished by this apparently unscheduled meeting. However, her gown of cloth of gold on crimson matched Louis's outfit perfectly, thus rather giving the game away.

The royal couple exchanged pleasantries; the King greeted Norfolk and the English lords, and then continued with his hawking expedition, while Mary made her grand entry into Abbeville, accompanied by princes and nobles in a spectacular piece of theatre. The Swiss Guard marched first, followed by the French gentlemen and then, skilfully matched and choreographed by the Master of the Horse, the French princes and English lords in pairs, in gorgeous brocades, their signature gold chains looped about their necks and shoulders up to six times; one wit joked that the English milords looked like prisoners, weighed down by the shackles of their wealth.

The Papal, Venetian and Florentine ambassadors followed in the procession. Fleuranges later estimated Mary's escort at 2,000 *chevaliers*. Mary, mounted on a white horse, was preceded by her squires dressed in silk with heavy gold collars. Four footmen held over her a canopy of white satin, embroidered with the roses of England and two bristling porcupines, the heraldic beasts which traditionally supported the arms of France. Her hair was dressed 'in the English fashion' with gold and pearl ornaments; she wore a gown with tight-fitting sleeves, also considered to be an English fashion, but changed en route. When she arrived at Abbeville to a civic welcome by the dignitaries and the deafening roar of a salute from the cannon, she wore white and gold brocade, embroidered with jewels. She wore her crimson silk hat throughout, jauntily cocked over her left eye. Two running footmen in velvet caps and black-and-gold chequered doublets kept pace with her palfrey. The Dauphin Francis rode at her side in a surcoat of silver and gold, remaining outside the canopy in order not to usurp Mary's place as the centrepiece of the glorious cavalcade.

Three carriages had been shipped over from England for the procession. The first two were covered in cloth of gold, drawn by horses wearing golden bridles. Each carriage transported four sumptuously attired ladies, probably including the Duchess of Norfolk, her daughter the Countess of Oxford and Lady Guildford. Then came six ladies mounted on palfreys caparisoned in cloth of gold and purple velvet. Another carriage, decked in crimson velvet, was occupied by four more ladies. More ladies followed the carriages, their mounts decked in mulberry-coloured velvet, edged with silk fringing in white and light blue. After the ladies, 200 archers marched in pairs, the first row wearing the Tudor livery of green and white. Their precision deeply impressed Fleuranges, himself a seasoned soldier, affectionately nicknamed by Louis 'the Young Adventurer'.

Among the Queen's ladies rode Henry VIII's future mistress Mary Boleyn, the older daughter of Sir Thomas Boleyn, Henry's semi-permanent ambassador in the Low Countries. The younger Boleyn sister, 13-year-old Anne, had been sent the previous year to the court of the Archduchess Margaret, regarded as one of the finest finishing schools in Europe. Anne was said to have taken to French like a duck to water; Mary Rose had requested her by name as one of her *demoiselles d'honneur*. Reluctantly, Margaret allowed Anne to leave. But she did not join Mary's retinue in time for the grand entry into Abbeville.

When the procession reached the town centre, Mary attended a mass of thanksgiving at the Church of St Vulfran before rejoining the King for a state reception. She was welcomed in the main city square by the King's elder daughter, the unattractive but worthy Claude, wife of the Dauphin Francis. Princess Claude conducted her new stepmother to her apartments in the palace, the ancient Hôtel de Gruthuse, separated by an attractive garden from the King's apartments.

That evening a grand ball was hosted by Claude and Francis, who had a talent for organising spectacular entertainments. The night could easily have ended in disaster. A fire broke out in a quarter where many of the Venetians were lodging, and four houses burned down. The Venetians were saved by the river that flowed between their lodgings and the fire. The blaze could have been controlled earlier had it been permitted to ring the bells, but this was forbidden to avoid disturbing the King at his amusements.

The Venetians reported back from the French court so assiduously, because the Venetian Signory desperately needed to know whether Louis intended to try to recapture Milan. After losing their greatest general, the brilliant Gaston de Foix, at the Battle of Ravenna two years previously, the French had been forced to retreat from Milan, leaving the Sforzas back in power. Shortly after Mary arrived in France, the Venetian ambassador, Marco Dandolo, managed to broach the subject. The King, who but a few months previously had publicly declared that his days were numbered, and his sole desire was to join his late wife Anne of Brittany in her coffin, was now fired with renewed optimism. He announced that not only did he intend another Italian expedition, but that Mary had begged him to show her Venice, and he intended to do so.

The morning after the ball, the Venetian informant reported that Mary, with the Duke of Norfolk and other lords in her entourage, had risen before daybreak. The wedding procession formed up outside the Queen's apartments in the cold October dawn; the English knights wore sumptuous, sable-lined damask, velvet, satin and cloth of gold. Mary walked through the garden preceded by 236 knights, two heralds and the royal mace-bearers, the Duke of Norfolk, as her brother's representative, at her side, her ladies following, each walking between two gentlemen, holding their caps in their hands. There was a great crush inside the palace, where the Bishops of Auch and Bayeux were to perform the marriage in a great hall hung with cloth of gold. Mary entered to a fanfare of trumpets. Her golden hair flowed about her shoulders, crowned with a coronet of precious stones. Her gown was of gold brocade edged with ermine and ablaze with diamonds (the Venetians preferred this French design to her English gowns). Louis, also in ermine-trimmed gold brocade, swept off his hat and bowed. Mary curtsied. The King raised her to her feet, kissed her, and then, taking from his Treasurer Robertet a superb necklace of rubies and pearls, he fastened it about her neck. After the nuptial mass, Mary curtsied again gracefully and retired to her own apartments to dine with her ladies.

That evening the royal couple co-hosted a three-day feast and ball at the Hôtel de Gruthuse. At 8 o'clock the pregnant Dauphine led her stepmother to her bridal bed, already blessed by the bishops. The Dauphin's circle, led by his mother Louise of Savoy, feigned detachment but were in reality agog. Louise recorded scathingly: 'On 9 October took place the *amorous* marriage of Louis XII, King of France, and Mary of England. They were married at 10 in the morning and in the evening they went to bed together.' To his intimates, Francis declared that his father-in-law's marriage had 'pierced his heart'. Privately, he muttered to Fleuranges that the King was incapable of begetting a son.[9]

However, next day, the King triumphantly asserted that he had 'crossed the river three times that night and would have done more had he chosen'.[10] Courtiers greeted this boast with amazement, incredulity and lewd giggles. Fleuranges was in no doubt: 'In the morning the

King said he had performed marvels.' He added sardonically: 'I certainly believe this was true, for he was most uncomfortable.'[11] Louis appeared remarkably rejuvenated. The French were euphoric, the Venetians fretful. The Venetian ambassador wrote:

> Everything is held up, politics like the rest. No one speaks of anything but fêtes. There you have the French. They always believe that what they wish for will be successful. This marriage has been a success; they see themselves already installed in Milan. They feared only England; this phantom has vanished. The King says everywhere that he will take Milan or die … no one thinks of an obstacle, which terrifies me. To amuse himself with a wife of 18 is very dangerous at his age.[12]

Perhaps Louis had indeed overdone things; he promptly suffered a new attack of gout. Consequently, the state entry into Paris was postponed. The court remained at Abbeville. Francis spent his time planning grand tournaments to celebrate Mary's coronation.

Perhaps illness made Louis irritable. Mary had been upset when he had objected to the appointment of Jane Poppincourt, because of her 'evil life'. Now Louis once again threw his weight about, causing the only known rift during their brief marriage. Louis, reflecting that Mary's large entourage would represent a drain on the French exchequer, remembered how his last queen had undermined his authority by filling her household with Bretons. He summarily dismissed many of Mary's suite, including Lady Guildford. Mary was dismayed. 'Mother Guildford', her former governess, known since childhood, had been a tower of strength. Some authorities, noting the Venetian ambassador's observation that the day after his wedding the elderly King of France seemed 'very jovial, gay and in love', conjecture that the wedding night had been an unexpected ordeal for the 'nymph from heaven',[13] and that the bride had confided in the experienced Lady Guildford. Mary dreaded the prospect of staying in France without Lady Guildford's reassuring presence. She had been deprived even of her secretary Palsgrave, her former tutor. She dictated an appeal to her 'kind and loving brother' on 12 October:

> My Good Brother,
> As heartily as I can I recommend me to your Grace. I marvel much that I have [not] heard from you since my departing, so often as I have sent and written to you. Now I am left post alone, in effect, for on the morn next after my marriage my Chamberlain and all other menservants were discharged and in likewise my mother Guildford, with other my

women and maidens except such as never had experience nor knowledge how to advise or give me counsel in any time of need, which is
to be feared more shortly than your Grace thought at the time of my
departing as my mother Guildford can more plainly show your Grace
than I can write, to whom I beseech you give credence, and if it may
be by any means possible, I humbly request you to cause my mother
Guildford to repair hither to me again. For if any chance happen other
than well, I shall not know where nor of whom to ask my good counsel
to your pleasure nor yet to mine own profit.
I marvel much that my good Lord of Norfolk would at all times so
lightly grant everything at their requests here. I am well assured that
when ye know the truth of anything as my mother Guildford can show
you, ye would full little have thought I should have been thus treated.
Would God my Lord of York had come with me in the room [in place of]
my Lord of Norfolk. For I am sure I should have been left much more at
my heartsease than I am now, and thus I bid your Grace farewell.

She signed with an urgent plea in her own hand:

Give credence to my mother Guildford
By your loving sister, Mary Queen of France.[14]

Conscious that Henry would be reluctant to compromise his new
cordial relationship with the King of France, Mary sent an even more
urgently worded letter to Wolsey, pointing out that she had been specifically told always to consult Lady Guildford; she found the Duke of
Norfolk unsympathetic, and entreated Wolsey to find some way to have
Guildford reinstated:

I have not seen in France any lady or gentlewoman so necessary for
me as she is, nor yet so meet to do the King my brother service as she
is. And for my part, my lord, as you love the King, my brother, and
me, find the means that she may in all haste come hither again, for
I had as life lose the winning I shall have in France to lose her counsel
when I shall lack it, which is not like long to be required as I am sure
the noblemen and gentlemen can shew you more than becometh me to
write in this matter.[15]

Mary may have found her marital duties distasteful. Lady Guildford
knew everything; she would tell both the King and Wolsey how
Mary felt. Perhaps Louis's doctors had also hinted that his days were

numbered. While his death could open the door to freedom – Mary believed her brother would honour their bargain and allow her to marry the man of her choice – she realised with alarm that as a widow, she could find herself stranded in France at the mercy of the scheming Louise of Savoy and her son the Dauphin.

Her comments about the Duke of Norfolk's callousness are the first suggestion that Norfolk had ulterior motives for supporting Louis, and that he was working at cross-purposes with Wolsey, whose increasing influence at court, in politics and over the King, Norfolk resented. Norfolk had not been consulted over the selection of Mary's attendants, many of whom had been suggested by Wolsey.

Wolsey tried to help. He wrote tactfully to Louis from Eltham on 23 October, explaining in excellent French that Lady Guildford, wise, discreet and respectable, had been specially selected. He humbly requested that she be reinstated, pointing out that she had come out of honourable retirement to serve Mary, and assuring Louis that when he got to know Lady Guildford, he would esteem her for her excellent qualities.

Louis remained adamant. Eventually, the reason for his aversion to Lady Guildford emerged. Louis had found Guildford over-protective of the young Queen, and her forbidding presence inhibiting. Her interference in the relationship between man and wife was intolerable. He did not want 'when he would be merry with his wife to have any strange woman with her, but one that he is well acquainted withal, afore whom he durst be merry,'[16] wrote Worcester, Henry's ambassador to France, adding that Louis swore that no husband ever doted on his wife more than he did, but rather than have a woman like that around her, he would be without her altogether.

Mary now accepted that wifely duty meant obedience and resigned herself. Louis allowed her to retain the services of several attendants and six ladies of the bedchamber, one of whom was Anne Boleyn. Apart from this one spat over Mary's household, the relations between the newly-weds appeared cordial. When Louis's health delayed the court's progress to Paris, courtiers suspected that Louis so delighted in Mary's company that he was using his illness as an excuse to linger in dalliance before confronting more formal occasions – the coronation and the return to Paris. As Louis reclined on his chaise longue, Mary, seated at his side, played her lute and sang, causing him such pleasure that his physicians considered it health-giving. He could not bear her to leave his side. It was a fortnight before the royal party made it to Saint-Denis.

Mary's state entry into the capital would be followed by the jousts the Dauphin was busily organising. Throughout Europe the prospect of this grand tournament had created a flurry of excitement. The English nobles who had attended the wedding took a proclamation back to England, inviting challengers. Henry, predictably, fielded a formidable team, including the Marquis of Dorset, his four brothers, all champions, and Charles Brandon, Duke of Suffolk, the greatest champion of all. Brandon, granted £1,000, brought his own horses and equipment.

In late October, Brandon, Neville and Sir William Sidney crossed the Channel, travelling incognito in grey hooded coats. Brandon caught up with the royal party at Beauvais on 25 October. Intelligence he had received at Canterbury made him suspect that the dismissal of Mary's attendants had been part of a malicious attempt by Norfolk to sabotage Wolsey's policy of peace with France by causing trouble. Brandon urged Wolsey to work for the reinstatement of Lady Guildford, and also wrote to Henry from Beauvais, reporting that he had found the King lying in bed, Mary in attendance. Louis had embraced Brandon, clutching him warmly as an expression of the love he bore Henry, who had given him 'the greatest jewel ever one prince had of another'. Louis instructed Brandon to inform Henry that 'never Queen behaved herself more wisely and honourably';[17] Brandon added that this opinion was shared by all the French aristocracy. Brandon also repeated, man to man, a coarse jest Louis had made. Louis promised to send Henry a destrier and a set of saddlery, 'for he says your Grace has mounted him so well'.[18]

Louis revelled in displaying his delight in his physical passion for his young Queen, hinting lewdly at its reinvigorating effects, especially in the hearing of the Dauphin, whom it was calculated to annoy. Doubtless it had reached the King's ear that Francis was putting it about that Louis was incapable. Otherwise, Brandon made no mention of Mary. The rest of his letter dealt with sport and the grand tournament, his main reason for being in France.

Louis introduced Brandon to Francis, suggesting that Dorset and Brandon should be his aides at the tournament; Francis invited them to dinner and declared they should be not aides but brethren, and assist in the organisation. Travelling to Paris ahead of the King and Queen, they paused for a boar hunt in which Francis courteously allowed Brandon the kill. Brandon slew one boar with such a powerful thrust that he bent the sword, a portent of the remarkable prowess he would exhibit in the tourney.

An arch was erected in front of the Bastille bearing four shields, upon which contestants could register their names. Challengers wishing to fight on foot or in the mêlée signed up on the black-and-tawny shield, those intending to 'run at the tilt' inscribed their names on a silver shield, but major stars like Brandon and Dorset wrote their names on the gold shield. They would 'run with the sharp spears and fight with the sharp swords'.[19]

The day before Mary arrived in France, Louis had taken Worcester aside and shown him the collection of jewellery he intended to bestow upon her. Dazzled, Worcester wrote to Wolsey that he had never seen such opulence; at least 55 pieces of superb quality, 'diamonds and rubies and seven of the greatest pearls that I have seen'. The cheapest stones were worth 2,000 ducats, the dearest more than 100,000. But Louis said slyly that Mary would not receive them all at once; he intended to dole them out piecemeal, and 'have many kisses and thanks for them'. The court understood: when, on the day after the marriage, he gave her a 'marvellous great pointed diamond with a ruby about two inches long', the next day another ruby even larger, valued at 10,000 marks, and on the third day a 'great diamond with a great round pearl hanging by it', there was sniggering; Mary had clearly earned her baubles.[20]

In late October, Louis having recovered, they resumed their journey, pausing at each town so that, as tradition dictated, all prisoners could be released on the Queen's command. As they travelled, Louis discussed his projected Italian campaign. Mary listened, enthralled; Louis promised to take her to Venice after her coronation. The Venetian Signory's informant revealed that Louis, apparently enjoying a temporary relief from his gout, had slept with his wife two nights on the journey.

On 5 November, Mary's coronation at the abbey church was witnessed by a large crowd of nobles who had ridden out from the court. The Bishop of Bayeux officiated at the simple ceremony. The Dauphin led Mary to the altar, where, after anointing her, the bishop invested her with the ring, sceptre and rod of justice. The crown was then placed on her head and she was conducted to a throne erected in the sanctuary, where she heard high mass and received the sacrament. During the mass Francis held the heavy matrimonial crown above her head to relieve her of its weight. The Queen and the Dauphin then joined the King for dinner. Louis ignored the regime recommended by his doctors and dined at noon.

Louis left Saint-Denis early the next morning to ensure that all was ready for his bride's triumphant entry into his capital. Sixteenth-century Paris was Europe's chief city, a sprawling metropolis, five times bigger than London, seductive, dangerous, a nest of robbers, a haunt of assassins, a by-word for wickedness. Every echelon of late medieval society thronged the dog-leg alleyways; nobles and artisans rubbed shoulders with merchants, vagabonds, hustlers, hawkers, monks and students. At the heart of a city where thousands of paupers eked out a subsistence-level existence, the French court feasted, each banquet featuring two to four dozen meat courses. Outside the sheltered court, in a dog-eat-dog society where so many were scraping a living by fair means or foul, there was constant threat of violence. Murder was commonplace. Organised gangs like the *mauvais garçons* systematically looted and terrorised more law-abiding inhabitants. In its filthy glamour, the great city fascinated and repelled in equal measure. The Venetian Contarini wrote 'it stinks of mud. There is much silk; the whole court dresses in silk; even the pages trail it on the ground.'[21]

On 6 November, despite the chilly late autumn weather, Paris excelled herself to welcome the beautiful new Queen. The city was adorned with lilies and roses, some fashioned from silk, others painted on arras or on giant scaffolds lining the processional route. A large contingent of prominent merchants, dignitaries and 3,000 members of the French clergy welcomed Mary at Porte Saint-Denis, still the main gate of the walled medieval city, and conducted her to the Palais Royal where Louis awaited her. Arrayed in gold brocade, crowned with a diadem of diamonds and pearls, and riding in an open litter draped with white cloth of gold, Mary was the star of yet another magnificent procession. The Dauphin, also clad in gold studded with diamonds, escorted her, along with the French dukes. Mary smiled: in place of the insensitive Duke of Norfolk, rode Dorset – and Brandon, the charismatic Duke of Suffolk.

Passing through the gate, she saw the second in a series of seven *tableaux vivants*, an imaginative blend of heraldry, allegory and pantomime verse, designed to surpass even those that had celebrated Anne of Brittany's entry into the city in 1504. Three of the tableaux were sponsored by the municipality and the other four by private organisations. The first, presented at Saint-Denis, comprised a giant ship bearing figures of Ceres, Bacchus and, at the helm, Paris herself, symbolising the corn, wine and commerce of the city. Real matelots dressed the rigging, choirs sang songs of welcome, and the four winds of classical antiquity filled the sails. The leitmotif was peace. The mariners sang:

Noble Lady, welcome to France,
Through you we now shall live in joy and pleasure,
Frenchmen and Englishmen live at their ease,
Praise to God, who gives us such a blessing.

An orator addressed Mary as 'most illustrious, magnanimous Princess'.[22] Mary was the symbol that war had been replaced by peace, alliance and friendship. The humanist and court poet Pierre Gringoire recorded that

Mary's entry into the city was magnificent – perhaps with a hint of self-congratulation, since he himself had composed the celebratory anthems. He presented Mary with a handwritten souvenir programme, illuminated with gold leaf.

In the second tableau a marble fountain, bright with lilies and roses, played against a background of celestial blue, while three Graces danced in a garden. The third showed Solomon and the Queen of Sheba, a flattering allusion to Louis's popular title of 'Father of his People'. In the fourth, a scaffold erected before the Church of the Holy Innocents featured God the Father, robed as in the medieval mystery plays, holding a huge pasteboard heart and a bouquet of red roses above the heads of figures representing the royal couple, wearing gold and ermine. The fifth pageant impressed even the illiterate, familiar with the tradition of the French courtly romances of Guillaume de Loris. The imaginative staging introduced a walled city enclosing a rose garden; a huge rosebud, raised by concealed machinery, approached a lily growing on a balcony, beneath a luxurious pavilion before a golden throne. When the rose reached the balcony, onlookers gasped when its petals opened, disclosing the figure of a living maiden, who now recited Gringoire's fulsome odes. Mary was identified with the fabulous '*rose vermeille*', the symbol of peace that had bloomed in the gardens of Jericho and adorned the margins of a thousand romances. The Parisians declared her a goddess of love and an emblem of peace.

At the Chastellet de Paris, another lengthy ode was recited, in which Louis was compared to the sun and Mary to the moon. By the time the procession reached the Palais Royal at 5.30, the young Queen had been on show since early morning. If she was flagging, she hid it well, continuing to enchant spectators and welcoming committees by her beauty and grace.

Her long day culminated in a reception by the dignitaries of the Sorbonne at Notre Dame de Paris, where, after high mass, she was welcomed by the Archbishop of Paris. She then returned to the Palais Royal for a state banquet. Louis, no longer young, healthy or used to late nights, retired long before the feast was finished. Several reports claimed that Mary, too, collapsed from exhaustion and was carried sleeping to her chambers.

Next day the royal couple proceeded to the Hôtel des Tournelles, where they rested until the Grand Tournament began the following Monday 13 November 1514.

Now Charles Brandon, more at home in the tiltyard than in the city or the corridors of power, came into his own. Wary of foreigners and their ways, he was beginning to dislike Paris as a 'stinking prison'. Weighing up his opponents, the French knights, he concluded that they wore their armour awkwardly. His confidence grew.

Originally, the tournament was to have been a series of friendly jousts between the English and French knights, held at Abbeville immediately after the wedding; but the Dauphin's ambitions had taken wing. The event would now take place in Paris, having grown from relatively modest beginnings into the kind of vast glittering Renaissance spectacular that Francis delighted in masterminding. He was determined to outdo any spectacle Henry VIII might put on, and also to humiliate the English nobles and steal their crown as Europe's premier jousters, by a dazzling display of personal prowess. Excitement was rife. Patriotic pride was at stake.

A huge stage had been erected in the Parc for the spectators, including the whole court. The Dauphin and his aides rode into the meadow to salute the King and Queen. Louis, once more crippled by gout, received their greeting reclining upon a couch. Mary, radiant with excitement, rose to acknowledge the cheers of the adoring multitude.

Among the most popular of the usual stunt riders and warm-up acts was Anthony Bownarme, who took the field dressed as a porcupine, with spears in his hand, under his arm and sticking out of his stirrups. To rapturous applause, he rode before the Queen and shattered ten spears into the ground.

The English had carefully selected their champions from among the country's best lances, led by Thomas Grey, Marquis of Dorset, and Charles Brandon. The combat would be ferocious. The peace was only six months old. Although the tournament was officially a sporting event, old animosities still smouldered.

Francis, spokesman for the French competitors, pledged to meet all 'answerers' both afoot and on horseback. Each contestant would run five courses over three days. The jousts proper comprised hand-to-hand combat on horseback with spears, and afoot with swords and lances, followed by the general tournament, or mêlée, at barriers, where groups of knights engaged simultaneously. In all, 305 men took part – some of whom, one chronicler commented, were slain and not spoken of. From the outset, public interest centred on the stars, the Dauphin Francis, his brother-in-law the Duc d'Alençon and the mighty English champions, Dorset and Brandon.

The knights were ceremoniously introduced individually, each galloping twice round the arena, pausing on the second lap to bow low before the royal stand, their plumes sweeping the saddle bow. On the first day the honours went to Brandon. He nearly killed one opponent, beat another to the ground and broke his sword on a third with such force that the man's horse was too terrified to approach him. Brandon knew his friend the King would have applauded his efforts. He wrote to Henry that he wished he had been there to witness his triumph to the honour of his country.

The Dauphin sported different armour and colours each day, first silver and gold, then crimson and yellow velvet, and on the third day, as a compliment to the Queen, the Tudor green and white. The English knights wore the red cross of St George. The sartorial glory of the French was spectacular; however, their sportsmanship fulfilled Brandon's low expectations. Overshadowed by the daring of the English, their praise was grudging. Francis, reluctant to court defeat, retired after injuring his little finger, substituting one of his seconds. Brandon, although injured, fought on, ignoring his wounds.

On the second day both Dorset and Brandon excelled, shivering many spears, but again Brandon overwhelmed all opponents, unhorsing his opponents in three successive rounds. Then the competition hotted up. Dorset later said the fighting was as furious as anything he had ever experienced. Horses and a French competitor were slain. Francis, nursing his finger and his dented pride, sent in Dorset and Brandon, who had agreed to act as his aides, to fight alone against all comers. His secret agenda was to discredit Brandon, already enjoying the Queen's delighted approval and the approval of more open-minded members of the French court, who realised that the English were being unfairly treated. Francis, resolved to salvage the remains of French prestige, replaced one of the French contestants with a massive unknown German mercenary in disguise, under orders to dispatch the English champion.

Brandon, suddenly finding himself facing a furious onslaught from a towering hooded figure, paused briefly, then rallied and counter-attacked, eventually, after the exchange of many savage blows, grabbing the giant by the neck: he 'pommeled [him] so about the head that the blood issued out of his nose'.[23] The defeated Goliath, blood streaming, was quickly removed on the Dauphin's orders. His identity was never revealed.

It was an English triumph. There were few injuries on the English side, and no deaths. Brandon made light of his own injuries. His account of his exploits was modest and matter-of-fact. He wrote to Wolsey on 18 November: 'The jousts are done and, blessed be God, all our Englishmen sped well as I am sure ye shall hear by others.'[24]

Dorset noted:

The Queen continues her goodness and wisdom and increases in the favour of her husband and the Privy Council. She has said to my Lord of

Suffolk and me that the King of France her husband said to her that my Lord of Suffolk and I did shame all France, and that we should carry the prize into England.[25]

Brandon and Dorset had also been charged with a secret diplomatic mission, so confidential that it was never recorded anywhere, lest the dispatches might be intercepted and the project become known in Spain and Italy: arranging a meeting between Henry and Louis. Henry wanted friendship with France, and French support in his projected war with Spain, both for his claim to Castile by right of his Queen, Katherine, daughter of Isabella, and military aid in order to drive Ferdinand out of Navarre as punishment for reneging on promises to both France and England.

The proposed meeting between the sovereigns had been much discussed, but there had been no agreement about its location, chiefly because Louis, set on his proposed Italian expedition, wanted to travel eastward towards Lyons. A tentative agreement was reached for a meeting in early April, somewhere between Boulogne and Calais. Louis tentatively agreed to support an invasion of Spain, demanding in exchange a loan of 200,000 crowns and Henry's assistance in enforcing French claims on Milan. There was a rumour in Venice that Brandon himself would join the Italian campaign at the head of 6,000 English troops.

Threats of war, like promises of marriage, featured widely in European diplomacy. There was no formal treaty; the two monarchs would discuss details when they met. Neither could know that this would never happen: by spring 1515 Louis would be dead and his successor, Francis, unwilling to honour his predecessor's commitments.

Brandon was no skilled diplomat, having little interest in the intellectual challenge of international political intrigue, and disliking subterfuge. But with his straightforward, soldierly personality and considerable charm, and the immediate entrée of his ducal rank, he made useful contacts among Francis's circle. Louis's councillors attempted to exploit Brandon's inexperience, but, at the bold suggestion that John Stewart, Duke of Albany, the possible claimant to the Scottish throne who had long resided at the French court, might be given safe passage to Scotland to negotiate, Brandon dug his heels in. Louis, impressed with Brandon's open, agreeable character, appreciated his loyalty to Henry, traits sadly lacking in his own son-in-law. 'That big lad will ruin everything,' he had recently remarked, remembering all he himself had sought to achieve for France and how little Francis seemed to care. By the end of their time together, Louis was promising to conduct all negotiations with Henry through Brandon and Wolsey. He assured Henry that no monarch had such a servant for both peace and war.

Brandon sent Henry gifts in token of friendship and reported to him directly on French matters. But, away from court, he had to rely on the goodwill of Wolsey to keep him informed about the King's intentions and reactions. He was reluctant to undertake diplomatic initiatives without direction from Wolsey. For the moment, Henry was delighted with Brandon, and Wolsey was happy to co-operate with him. But all that could change in an instant: Wolsey never let Brandon forget it.

Mary contributed to the success of the negotiations with grace and skill, ensuring that her husband was good-humoured and in a receptive mood. She displayed a talent for tact and diplomacy far beyond her years and experience by seeking the advice of de Longueville and other leading French courtiers. Brandon reported to Wolsey that she asked them 'how she might best order herself to content the King, whereof she was most desirous ... because she knew well they were the men whom the King loved and trusted, and knew best his mind'. The King and his Council were enchanted; Louise of Savoy and her circle remained aloof and sceptical.

The beautiful teenage Mary, surrounded by chattering courtiers whose daily topic of conversation was romance, must have compared the vigorous and dashing Brandon with her frail husband, recumbent on his couch. At the tournament held in her honour, Brandon was her champion, fighting for the glory of the Tudors and of England. Yet Mary's conduct remained impeccable, unlike that of the Dauphin. To the general embarrassment, Francis had fallen for his glamorous stepmother. His infatuation was public knowledge, hurtful and demeaning to Claude and infuriating for the Dauphin's clever and ambitious mother, Louise of Savoy. Patient Claude suffered in silence, but Louise furiously reprimanded her son, commanding him to control his desires, and warning him that he was putting his throne at risk.

The last act of the coronation festivities, and Mary's last ceremonial appearance as Queen of France, was a banquet held in her honour at the Hôtel de Ville by the University of Paris. People flocked to glimpse her, causing such a throng around the main door that the official party had to enter through the porter's lodge, filing up a narrow staircase to the vestibule where the dignitaries awaited them. After more effusive oratory and toasts in praise of the union between England and France, Mary was congratulated for marrying a monarch whose throne was secure. The insinuation was that England was prone to revolutions, unlike the more stable European powers.

The future Cardinal Jerome Alexander reported that he had never seen such a *'repas pantagruélique'* (feast of gargantuan proportions) or so many splendidly attired and distinguished personages at any one time. The Queen charmed everyone when, after enjoying a dessert especially prepared for her, she kindly ordered that a portion should be sent to the royal nursery at Vincennes for her 4-year-old stepdaughter, Renée.

The banquet brought the court season to a close. Their mission concluded, the English lords returned home for Christmas. Brandon alone lingered to complete his confidential assignment, although he itched to leave, weary of diplomacy for which he had little natural bent, and of penning endless reports and dispatches. On 27 November 1514, the King and Queen travelled to St Germain en Laye to spend three weeks at the King's country palace. Perhaps Louis hoped to go hunting, although it was becoming increasingly apparent that such strenuous activities were now beyond him.

In December the royal couple returned to Paris, where Louis took to his sickbed. Mary sat by his bedside, chatting with Francis, who, displaying little concern for Louis, made no secret of his obsession with her. Courtiers began to speculate whether the young Queen would soon share the honours of the Dauphin's bed with his official mistress, Madame de Châteaubriant. Francis, a year older than Mary, was considered charming and handsome, witty and affable. Already known at court as a womaniser, he spiced his conversation with insinuations which Mary, she confided to Dorset and Brandon, found distasteful. Mary was determined to play the devoted wife so long as Louis lived. But she could not afford to alienate the heir to the throne, upon whom she would be dependent if Louis died. She recalled the fate of her friend Katherine of Aragon, widowed, left without means in a strange land. Mary suspected her brother would probably be as little help to her in such a situation as Ferdinand had been to his daughter.

Because of the difference in their years and physical health, Mary and Louis had already been the subject of lewd gossip, speculation and sniggering. Mary was accused of being dizzy and flirtatious – one author claimed she could be giddy in six languages – and deliberately irresponsible. Francis's old chum Fleuranges, now Marshal of France, wrote vividly of the ailing monarch valiantly struggling to satisfy his young bride:

The King left the palace and took lodgings at Tournelles in Paris because it had the best climate and also he did not feel very strong because he had desired to be a pleasing companion with his wife; but he deceived himself, as he was not the man for it … he lived on a very strict diet which he broke when he was with his wife; and the doctors told him that if he continued he would die from his pleasure.[26]

Parisian gossipmongers ascribed Louis's decline to English trickery; they had sent him a 'young filly' to hasten his demise, darkly recalling the proverb 'an old man in love hugs death'.

The round of dinners and parties was resumed. Louis, abandoning his diet and early nights, plunged into pursuits suited to younger, fitter men – dancing, hunting, riding, indulging in copious amounts of food and drink. Louise of Savoy watched and waited; in her diary she recorded that these 'nights of love' hastened the King's end.

The King, having recovered his zest for life, continued in good spirits. Mellowed by age and illness, and the late flowering of happiness with his adored young wife, he lavished gifts on Mary and his daughter Claude. When Marco Dandolo asked him on 22 December when exactly he planned to set out on his Italian campaign, he told him not to hassle him, as he was keener than anybody and the expedition was imminent. 'This gout rather troubles me,' he admitted, adding stoutly, 'By Candlemas I shall be at Lyons, send troops into Italy and have with me my guard of 8,000 foot and 1,000 men at arms.'[27]

Brave words. Louis would not see another Candlemas.

Although ill, the King wrote on 28 December to his 'good brother the English King', expressing his continued delight in his Queen, and commending the service of Brandon, whose 'virtues, manners, politeness and good condition' deserved that the King should hold him in even greater honour.

Brandon would later have good use for this royal reference.

This was the last letter Louis wrote. Three days later, on New Year's Day 1515, he was dead.

When they broke the news to Mary, she fainted.

La Reine Blanche

At 19, after eighty-two days of marriage, Mary was a widow, Queen Dowager of France. Before the news of Louis's death reached London, fate had dealt Henry another blow. Katherine had been delivered of yet another premature child. The Tudor succession was still not secure. Now the future of the French monarchy, too, hung in the balance. Despite Mary's devoted vigil at his bedside, Louis had drawn his last tortured breath, not in the arms of his adored wife but of his successor, the Dauphin Francis.

Immediately after death, Louis's corpse was disembowelled, embalmed and laid in state in the great hall at Les Tournelles, with crown, robes and sceptre befitting a worthy prince. Monks were paid to keep vigil as the public shuffled respectfully past for a last glimpse of their late monarch. The next day, at the Church of Saint-Denis, Louis had his wish. He was buried with Anne of Brittany, whom he had loved so well and mourned so intensely, if so briefly.

The lying-in-state and the funeral lacked nothing in ceremony, but the unseemly haste with which they were executed betrayed the Dauphin's impatience to mount the throne. Mourning cost money: Francis cut short the wake. On the eleventh day the household ministers' staves were struck. The old reign was over. The Dauphin's mother, Louise of Savoy, had consulted the stars, desperate to read the future. For nineteen years her life had centred on the hope of seeing her son on the French throne. She heard the tolling bells with joy. Like Louis, Louise had long suffered from an agonising arthritic condition; now, in her hour of triumph, she defied her disability, riding the 100 miles to Paris within 48 hours, in time to witness her son's coronation.

Despite the impatience of Francis and Louise, Francis could not be formally crowned until it was certain that Mary was not pregnant with a male heir by Louis. According to ancient custom, Mary had to don the hideous white robes which earned a childless queen dowager of France the title of *la reine blanche* (the white queen), and retire to the palace known as the Hôtel de Cluny, a former Benedictine Abbey on the left bank of the Seine, to wait. The term of isolation imposed on the Queen Dowager was an old safeguard in France dating back to the death of Philip the Fair in 1314, whose three successors had all died before their heirs expectant were born. This calamity had led to the Salic law and the vexed question of female succession.

Mary found her sojourn profoundly depressing. Her chamber, although handsomely appointed, was a cheerless, sunless cavern, virtually soundproof, airless and unheated, hung about with black cloth, its long windows heavily curtained. Flickering tapers cast weird shadows on the dark walls. Here, day after day, the vivacious Tudor princess, so recently the petted and adored Queen, lay on her bed fretting, with no friend or confidante. Francis's controlling female relatives, Louise of Savoy and her daughter Marguerite, the self-appointed 'curators of the womb', still suspicious of Mary, had seen to that. Her few French attendants had been handpicked and commanded to monitor Mary's movements. Small wonder that Mary, lonely, highly-strung and now in a state of emotional fragility, grew irritable and frightened. She complained to her brother that she felt desolate and bewildered. To make matters worse, she had toothache. She begged Henry to allow his chief surgeon John Verye to attend her, which he did.

Usually, the heir presumptive delayed his coronation until all doubt had been removed. But Francis, impatient to plan his coronation, had already extracted assurances from Mary that she was sure she was not pregnant. But his mother was more sceptical. Devious herself, Louise imputed similar duplicity to Mary. There had been whispers at the French court that Mary was with child before Louis's death. For those first three weeks of January, Louise lived on edge. Fearing lest her ambitions for her son might yet be foiled, she resented Mary, as she had secretly hated Anne of Brittany, while maintaining a superficial relationship of cordiality. When Anne had given birth to a son, Louise suffered a frenzy of frustration. His death was a huge relief; in her journal she exulted that the child would not 'retard the exaltation of my Caesar, for he did not live'.[1]

At 21, Francis was a tall, broad-shouldered youth with an athletic figure already inclined to corpulence. His portraits show a superficially handsome oval face, with dark curling beard and narrow black eyes, their louche and saturnine expression both calculating and cynical. He considered himself an Adonis, but his long Valois nose was so disproportionately large that behind his back he was nicknamed 'Le Roi Grand Nez'. When Mary knew him he was liberal, cultured and suave, but the signs were already there of the sly despot and voluptuary he would become. Ironically, while a great womaniser, convinced he was irresistible to the opposite sex, he was at the same time so dominated by his powerful and doting mother and sister that the earlier years of his reign were called a petticoat government. Louise and Marguerite were the first beneficiaries of his new-found wealth and power. He bestowed upon Louise two counties, two duchies and a barony, and the title of duchess. To his sister he gave the county of Armagnac and a lucrative monopoly in the appointment of guild officials.

While Francis jousted, hunted and feasted, lavishing money freely on his princely lifestyle and apparently fulfilling the gloomy prophecies of those who had predicted that he would bankrupt the French treasury, his mother gathered the reins of power into her own capable hands, ruling in all but name. Francis indulged his artistic temperament, building châteaux, collecting art and playing at patronage, diplomacy and military campaigns. Brandon advised Henry to address official correspondence directly to Louise: 'Sir, [it is] she that rules all, and so may she well, [for I] never saw woman like to her.'

Depressed by her tiresome sequestration at Cluny, Mary was irritated to receive a letter from Wolsey, warning her to exercise caution, and 'if any motions of marriage be made unto you, in no wise give hearing unto them'. She thanked Wolsey for his wise counsel, promising not to do anything without the direction of 'the King my brother and his Council'. But in her few months as a King's consort and a fêted Queen, Mary had matured. She sharply reminded Wolsey that she was no longer a child. As she dictated the letter to a secretary, her indignation rose:

> I trust that the King my brother and you will not reckon in me such childhood. I trust I have so ordered myself, so since that I came hither, that I trust it hath been to the honour of the King my brother and me since I came hither and if here is anything that I may do [for] you, I would be glad for to do it. And no more to you at this time.
> Written at Paris the 10th day of January 1515.[2]

Francis's relationship with Mary has provoked much speculation, even claims that Mary, even before her husband's death, was so desperate to shore up her situation that she was willing to take a lover to give her a male child. Francis was notoriously infatuated. According to the French historian Brantôme, Mary made a play for him, and they embarked upon an affair which became the scandal of the court. Louise and her circle, alarmed, ordered their spies to increase their vigilance. Francis was taken to task by Jean de Talleyrand:

> In the name of Heaven, what are you about? Can't you see that this woman, who is a cunning and subtle creature, is merely trying to attract you so that you can give her a child? And if she succeeds in getting one, then you are then only Count of Angoulême for the rest of your life and will never be King of France as you hoped. The King her husband is old and will never give her any children ... You are young and hot and so is she. Good Lord! She'll snare you, just like that; she'll have a child, and you're done for! After that, you may as well say: Goodbye to my kingdom of France.

Brantôme inventively presents Mary as a manipulative minx who hoped to ensnare Francis in order to keep her position as Queen of France. Francis realised the danger, but, 'tempted time and again by the clever tricks and caresses of this fair Englishwoman, he rushed more than ever into it. For such is the ardour of love!' The scandal-mongering chronicler later claimed that Mary, during her seclusion at Cluny, paraded about padded with *'linges et drapeaux'* (sheets and linen) in a feigned pregnancy, until dramatically unmasked by a furious Louise. This is almost certainly a fantasy. Mary had already frequently complained to her brother and to Wolsey about the unwelcome importunities of Francis. She was inexperienced in the game of courtly love as practised at the French court, and did not dare protest too much in case she appeared ignorant. The French court was larger, livelier and more cosmopolitan than she was used to. Francis had gathered about him a group of celebrities from the worlds of letters and diplomacy, garnished with young beauties. As Francis himself said, 'A Court without ladies is like a year without springtime, or a spring without roses.' Whereas in England the King set the tone at court, in France the example was often set by the Queen. Allegedly, in the days of Anne of Brittany, who was lame, fashionable ladies affected a limp. While Mary was Queen, they had begun to adopt what they thought of as cool English reserve. While Louis lived, Francis had restrained his passion for Mary, hoping through her to reach the ear of her brother, the King of England. He had always feigned approval of her marriage to Louis, even though he had secretly schemed to prevent it because it was a threat to his own ambitions.

Henry ordered an impressive memorial service to be held at St Paul's for the French King, his brother-in-law, creating work for many craftsmen on the royal payroll, chandlers, haberdashers, the court painter, and bell-ringers. Knowing Francis's reputation with women, Henry was concerned for his sister when he heard rumours that the new King was considering divorcing his pregnant wife, Claude, and marrying Mary instead.

Mary herself believed Francis's designs were dishonourable. Some historians have dismissed this as unlikely, in view of the fact that he scribbled a disobliging comment on a drawing of her in the *Album d'Aix* (Bibliothèque Méjanès) some years later. However, it is possible that Francis, a notorious philanderer, genuinely hoped to seduce Mary; his blatant flirting with her while she was his father-in-law's wife had incurred rebukes from his own mother. Now Mary was no longer the wife of the King, he could importune her with impunity, as he could not have done while Louis lived without jeopardising his own future aspirations. Moreover, scrawling the words 'more dirty than queenly' (*plus sale que royne*) on a portrait smacks of lust spurned and sour grapes ... or possibly it was a reference to what Francis regarded as Mary's 'theft' of the Mirror of Naples.

Whatever Francis's intentions, Mary's brother now took a fateful step. He appointed as his ambassador, charged with bringing the widowed queen home to England, together with what could be recovered of her dowry, none other than his trusty servant, Charles Brandon, Duke of Suffolk.

Meanwhile, on 28 January, Francis, having dispensed with prolonged mourning, went ahead with his coronation at the ancient cathedral of Rheims, where holy oil was said to have been miraculously brought down from heaven by a white dove on Christmas Day 496. Legend held that French kings anointed from this sacred phial were thrice blessed. Francis was duly anointed, ceremoniously recognised, prayed for, enthroned and offered homage. By the authority of St Marcoule, he was now so thoroughly God's anointed that he could 'touch for the King's evil'.

The coronation had taken place so swiftly that the English ambassadors arrived too late to attend; luckily, they were in time for the celebratory jousts. Besides offering their condolences on the death of Louis and congratulations to Francis on his accession, they were to take possession of Mary's jewels and plate, and make an inventory of all her English valuables in order to obtain compensation and restitution for the costs of her transport to France, and arrange for her return. Francis demanded the restoration of Tournai, conquered by Henry the previous year. This was to form the basis of the negotiations. Wolsey had set his heart on the bishopric of the town. Throughout the negotiations between Henry and Louis XII, this had been promised to him, despite the Pope's disagreement. There were other matters, too: the French debt of a million gold crowns outstanding from the previous reign; the asylum offered to Richard de la Pole, the 'White Rose'; the movements of the Duke of Albany.

Despite his reluctance to undertake foreign assignments not of a military nature, embassies being both onerous and expensive, and offering opportunities during his absence for his enemies at court to stab him in the back, the chief burden of mediation fell on Brandon. Although the least experienced of Henry's three ambassadors, Brandon spearheaded the embassy by virtue of his rank and his closeness to the King. He knew Francis, and had been personally recommended by Louis. Now he hoped to ingratiate himself and Wolsey with the new King, although he knew it would not be easy. Francis was as distrustful as his mother, manipulative and venal. He had no intention of making any concessions, even though his predecessor's councillors had only months previously signed documents confirming that, in the event of Louis's death, Mary would be free to return to England with her 'servants, jewels and effects'. Part of her dowry had been offset against the French debt of one million crowns. There was also the question of whether the spectacular jewellery bestowed upon her so liberally by Louis now belonged to her or to the French crown. Henry expected his envoys to drive a hard bargain. Transporting Mary with all her retinue and baggage in September had cost an eye-popping sum, settled on 28 January at Greenwich. Compensation had also been paid out to the survivors of her ship the *Great Elizabeth*, wrecked off Sandwich in the storm during the crossing.

Henry was aware both that his sister loved Brandon and that the couple had no understanding; Mary was inhibited by her upbringing and delicacy, and Brandon by their difference in status. A letter, 'revealing a most extraordinary fact in the history of Suffolk's love for the Princess Mary, of which historians have been quite at fault', was sold in 1840. No trace of this vital document remains at the time of writing.[3] Brandon's attractiveness to women and his affairs of the heart were well known in the English court. Henry guessed that Mary, homesick and depressed, might fling herself at Brandon. In early January 1515, at Eltham, the King extracted a promise from Brandon not to propose to her. Letters written by Wolsey later imply that Henry would have been willing to keep his waterside promise, made as Mary was about to embark for France, allowing her to marry Brandon, but he wanted to keep his options open, retaining Mary as a bargaining chip on the European marriage market as long as possible. He also wanted to preserve the French alliance, especially in view of the new catastrophic turn of events in Scotland.

Brandon was charged with making sure Francis did not renege on Louis's promise to restrain the Duke of Albany and prevent him from rallying to the aid of the renegades.

Mary, still in seclusion in Cluny, had finally put her foot down and dismissed her unsympathetic French atttendants. She had been permitted to have some of her English ladies to keep her company; but she was still confined to the *chambre de la reine blanche* (the bedroom of the white queen), draped in the unbecoming nun-like white robes, when on 4 February Henry's other ambassadors, Nicolas West and Sir Richard Wingfield, visited her, accompanied by Brandon. The rules of Mary's seclusion had been somewhat relaxed; she was permitted to receive the English ambassadors and accept their condolences. Their arrival cheered her immensely. Brandon passed Mary's thanks on to Henry for sending 'in her heaviness my Lord of Suffolk and others as well to comfort her as for obtaining her dower'.

But Brandon found Mary in a highly nervous state. Immediately after Louis's death, Friar Bonaventura Langley and another friar had been sent to Cluny from the English court, presumably by Henry, or possibly by Katherine, who had previously used Langley's services, sending him to offer condolences to her sister-in-law Queen Margaret of Scotland after the Battle of Flodden. It has also been claimed that Langley was serving the Duke of Norfolk. Langley, appointed Mary's confessor, tried to extract from her a confession of her feelings for Brandon, and instructed to warn her against marrying Brandon by persuading her that Wolsey and Brandon were plotting to control Henry's mind through diabolical means. Brandon, according to Langley, was evil personified and in league with the devil: the Friar quoted the sinister affair known as 'Compton's leg'. Sir William Compton, like Brandon, had grown up at court as a companion of Henry. One day, it was said, a jealous Brandon had inflicted an ailment of the leg upon his rival by invoking satanic powers.

The friars also appalled Mary by warning her that her brother had no intention of honouring his waterside promise, hinting that Henry only wanted her home so he could marry her off to Prince Charles of Castile.

Brandon himself suspected that his enemy Norfolk and his supporters on the Council were plotting to bring down himself and Wolsey and to destroy the Anglo-French alliance. He had already confided his suspicions to Wolsey months before, after the summary dismissal of Lady Guildford. Handwritten drafts of Mary's own letters, in the Cotton Manuscript, show Mary's desperate state of mind. The drafts are unevenly scrawled, filled with crossings-out and repetitions.

The friars were recalled to England and reprimanded by Wolsey.

The wolf pack was already eagerly eyeing the Dowager Queen of France, young, beautiful and rich. All over Europe, prospective suitors were gathering. The English ambassadors advised Henry to bring her home as quickly as possible, for her own protection and to foil any plotting by Francis. Mary was no fool. She was well aware that neither Henry nor Francis was motivated so much by a concern for her welfare as by mercenary considerations. Francis entertained notions of marrying her off, his top contenders being Anthony the Good, Duke of Lorraine, or Charles III, Duke of Savoy, his 28-year-old uncle, who was at least the right age. Henry, however, thought Mary's hand could more advantageously be bestowed elsewhere, another reason for bringing her home, together with whatever could be clawed back of her dowry.

Emmanuel the Fortunate of Portugal made a bid for his son John. Germany put forward William, Duke of Bavaria, and Charles of Castile, after all his dithering, had the nerve to renew his suit. Even old Emperor Maximilian was stirred by rumours of Mary's looks. He asked his daughter the Archduchess Margaret to procure a portrait of Mary for his inspection. He was so captivated, his secretary informed the Archduchess, that he stared at the portrait for a full thirty minutes. Reassured that it was a good likeness, he wrote off to Henry 'to get the lady into his own hands', warning Henry that if she were married in France and died without heirs his kingdom would be in jeopardy. As usual, Maximilian shilly-shallied until it was too late.

Brandon, in his late 20s, at the height of his physical powers, had known Mary for years. His charm, daring and skill in the tiltyard, as well as his close friendship with the King, were legendary. But there had been no hint of a romance. As a royal princess, no flirtatious behaviour had ever sullied her name. A secret liaison would have been the riskiest of indiscretions for both. Their names had never been linked, not even by the prurient gossipmongers of Henry's court. But Brandon suspected how Mary felt, because he wrote to Henry how pleased he was to see how she controlled her feelings when he first met her again in France after her marriage to Louis. Her restraint 'rejoiced me not a little,' he wrote, adding, 'your Grace knows why.'

Before Francis left for his coronation at Rheims, Mary confessed to him her love for Brandon. On 3 February, after the English envoys brought Henry's official congratulations to the new sovereign, Francis summoned Brandon to a private audience in his bedchamber, at first feigning lofty indignation, declaring that he knew Brandon had come to France with the treacherous intention of wedding 'the Queen, his master's sister'. Brandon stoutly denied the allegations, sensibly pointing out that he could hardly marry the Queen Dowager of France without the permission of the present ruler of France or of his own King. But Brandon was deeply embarrassed when Francis revealed how much he knew, including a secret 'ware word' or endearment which he had thought nobody knew.

'I knew no man alive could tell them but she,' he later confided to Wolsey. Seeing Brandon aghast by this revelation, Francis now changed his tactics. He became chummy and reassuring. 'Be not disturbed,' he said. Brandon had found in him 'a kind friend and a loving, who would help them both as keenly as if it were for himself'. Later, Mary would reveal to Brandon that on 15 February she had written to Henry, confessing that she had told Francis of 'the good mind I bear towards my Lord of Suffolk'. She had, she said, been forced to do this to stop Francis pestering her.

Seeing how the thought of Henry's fury paralysed Brandon, Francis promised that he and Mary would both write to Henry 'in the best manner that can be devised'. Brandon, honourable and straightforward himself, ingenuously believed Francis to be sincere, rather than craftily acting in the best interests of France. Mary had refused the suitors proposed by Francis. If she married an English subject, bringing no political advantage to England, this would deprive Henry of a potentially valuable foreign alliance.

After this meeting, Brandon wrote at once to Wolsey, who congratulated him on his discretion and at this stage raised no objection to a marriage at some future date. Wolsey advised Brandon to urge Francis to write to Henry in support of his suit. Moreover, Brandon was informed that the King had bestowed on him the whole of the de la Pole estates and the lordship of Claxton, worth 1,000 marks in cash.

The next day was occupied with Francis's triumphant entry into Paris.

By 20 February there was open talk of a marriage between Mary and Brandon. On 3 March the couple were married in secret. As soon as the secret marriage had been consummated, Mary was sure she had conceived. Brandon, panicked at their recklessness, and correctly anticipating Henry's outrage, wrote to Wolsey 'with as heavy a heart as any man living', hoping the brilliant Archbishop of York would handle the King and solicit his forgiveness on Brandon's behalf. 'The Queen would never let me rest till I had granted her to be married,' he explained, 'and so, to be plain with you, I have married her heartily, and l have lain with her insomuch I fear me lest she be with child.'[4]

Wolsey was aghast. In rushing into a marriage without the King's consent the couple had been foolhardy beyond belief. He felt obliged to show Brandon's letter to the King, stating that 'he had secretly married the King's sister, and they have lived together as man and wife'.[5] Hitherto, Wolsey had been a benign fatherly figure on Mary's horizon. Now was the time for severe talking. There followed an exchange of letters of greater formality. Wolsey attempted to make the best of things, pointing out that Brandon's description of the secret wedding made it sound like a contract *'per verba de praesenti'*, which could still be annulled. There followed the suggestion that a full public marriage ceremony might follow, but this could not take place in Lent according to English custom, whereas it could according to French custom by episcopal dispensation.

Brandon also wrote to the King that Mary had been told by Friar Langley that she would never be allowed to marry Brandon if they returned to England first. They would send her to Flanders to Charles. '... she said she had rather to be torn in pieces than ever she should come there, and with that wept. Sir, I never saw woman so weep.'[6]

Brandon tried his best to assure her the friar was lying, but 'in none ways I could make her believe it'.[7] He had gently suggested that Mary should write to obtain her brother's goodwill, and then he would have had an easy conscience. He explained that he had given Henry his word not to marry her without Henry's consent. Mary was adamant. She had already confessed her feelings to Francis; if Brandon did not marry her forthwith he would never again have the chance.

Brandon, overwhelmed by her distress and entreaties, was persuaded against his better judgement into a precipitous action, risking his career and even his life. 'And so,' Brandon wrote to Henry naively 'she and I was married.'[8] Only ten witnesses were present at the Cluny Chapel in Paris. Neither Wingfield nor West attended. They had not been invited: Mary knew they would raise objections.

Brandon was right to be concerned. Henry, incandescent, flew into a fine Tudor rage, chiefly because their marrying without his consent broadcast to the world that the King's sister and his favourite had no qualms about flouting his authority. In truth, Henry was more upset about Brandon's betrayal than Mary's, for women were notoriously weak creatures, a prey to fantasies and ruled by their emotions. But oathbreaking was a grave offence against the very root of the chivalric code. Brandon, 'the man in all the world he loved and trusted best',[9] had promised not to wed Mary before they returned to England.

Wolsey had been present at Eltham when Brandon gave the King his word. Wolsey, like Henry, found it incredible that Brandon should so far forget himself. Wolsey knew he would have to pick up the pieces. But first he would say his piece: he told Brandon he would have thought that rather than break his oath Brandon would be 'torn with wild horses', and cursed the 'blind affection' that had brought him to such a pass. Despite Wolsey's intervention, the nobles, especially Norfolk and the Howards, smarting with jealousy over Brandon's meteoric rise to power and resentful of his influence over the King, fanned the flames of the King's wrath. The Privy Council, led by the Howards, were baying for blood. They urged the King to have Brandon imprisoned or executed for treason. Marriage to a blood relation of the monarch without royal permission was a capital offence. Moreover, Brandon was vaguely understood to be betrothed to his 13-year-old ward, Lady Elizabeth Lisle.

From Montreuil, on his way back to Calais, in April, Brandon wrote pleading for his life, gambling on the King's affection for him, and throwing the blame on his enemies.

> Most gracious sovereign Lord, so it is that I am informed divers ways that all your whole council, my lord of York [Wolsey] excepted, with many other, are clearly determined to tempt your Grace that I may either be put to death or be put in prison, and so to be destroyed. Alas, Sir, I may say that I have a hard fortune, seeing that was never one of them in trouble but I was glad to help them to my power, and that Your Grace knows best. And now that I am in this none little trouble and sorrow, now they are ready to help to destroy me.[10]

He cast himself on Henry's mercy, humbly acknowledging his offence and calling himself a most sorrowful wretch.

Mary supported his plea for clemency, assuming all the blame: Brandon had not actively courted her. She had persuaded him to break his promise. She spelled out their bargain to her brother:

> whereas for the good of peace and for the furtherance of your affairs, ye moved me to marry with my lord and late husband King Louis of France, whose soul God pardon, though I understood that he was very aged and sickly, yet for the advancement of the said peace and for the furtherance of your causes I was contented to conform myself to your said motion, so that if I should fortune to survive the said late King, I might with good will marry myself at my liberty without your displeasure.

She reminded Henry that he had agreed to this,

> as ye will know, promising unto me that in such case ye would never provoke or move me but as mine own heart and mind should be best

pleased, and that whosesoever I should dispose myself ye would be wholly contented with the same ...

Free again, she had remembered

the great virtues which I have seen and perceived heretofore in my Lord of Suffolk, to whom I have always been of good mind, as ye well know, I have affixed and clearly determined myself to marry with him, and the same I assure hath proceeded only of mine own mind, without any request or labour of my Lord of Suffolk or any other person.[11]

Wolsey advised them that Brandon's diplomatic mission to secure the friendship of Francis needed to succeed, and also, as Mary and Brandon knew, they would have to make some financial sacrifice to appease the King. When Mary received Wolsey's letter informing her of her brother's rage, she smuggled out as a peace offering the greatest treasure she possessed, the stupendous Mirror of Naples, which Louis had given her and which was the hereditary property of the Queens of France. Brandon alerted Wolsey to the imminent delivery of 'a diamond with a great pearl' to the King. Mary could not write herself, he explained, because her toothache had flared up again. Optimistically, he added, 'My Lord, she and I remit these matters wholly to your discretion.'[12]

In March, Francis demanded the return of the Mirror of Naples. Henry's refusal, even when Francis offered to pay 30,000 crowns for it, triggered a diplomatic row. Venetian sources suggest Henry flaunted his ill-gotten gains, wearing the 'Mirror' in public, even during his historic encounter with Francis at the Field of the Cloth of Gold, sporting it on his cap as a gesture of defiance.

Mary knew Henry would fulminate and threaten, but in the end he would accept the situation, especially if it were sweetened by financial gain. She also knew that Wolsey needed Brandon's help against Norfolk and his enemies on the Council, and would support them. She clung to Henry's promise that she would be free to choose her second husband, having complied with his wishes in marrying her first.

Paris was in uproar. Everyone knew that Mary and Brandon had technically put their lives in danger by marrying without Henry's permission. Francis, gloating secretly over Henry's discomfiture, wrote to Henry. Mary wrote, threatening, unless she heard 'comfortable words' from her brother, to enter a nunnery; even kindly Queen Claude, whose affection for Mary had survived her own husband's indiscreet attentions to her, wrote.

On Saturday 31 March, during Lent, the second, public, marriage took place. This ceremony advertised their union and proved the legitimacy of their offspring. It was impossible to conceal their relationship. Mary insisted on having Brandon with her the whole time, at dinner and in her rooms. Louise of Savoy noted: 'On Saturday the last day of March the Duke of Suffolk, *homme de bonne condition*, whom Henry VIII hath sent as ambassador to the King, married Mary, sister of the aforesaid Henry, widow of Louis XII.'[13] Sixteen days later she wrote with satisfaction that the Mary Tudor chapter was over so far as France was concerned. 'Marie d'Angleterre, widow of Louis XII, left Paris with her husband, the Duke of Suffolk, to return to England.'

During her last days in Paris, Mary's loss of political status was made subtly clear. A handsome gift from the Signory of Venice, a black silk hat in a jewelled black velvet box, with a pendant balas ruby and pear-shaped pearl attached to the band, had been intended as a wedding gift to mark her marriage to Louis but its delivery was delayed by the illness of the envoy. It was valued at £225. When Mary received the ambassadors, they extended their condolences on Louis's death, but refused to take her hint that they might have a gift for her. Instead, they kept it, for presentation with other gifts, to Henry VIII and the English nobles.

Poignantly, Mary's last use of her official seal as Queen of France was to transfer everything she possessed to her brother. She was now penniless and completely dependent on her husband. She retained the courtesy title 'Queen of France' for the rest of her life, but she was now Duchess of Suffolk. The French seal was brought back with her and archived as a souvenir of her past glory as wife of a reigning monarch. She and Brandon left Paris for Calais, there to await Henry's permission to cross the Channel and return to England. Francis escorted them as far as Saint-Denis. As a last gesture of goodwill he presented her with four rings.

Ambassador West noted that they were 'of no great value'.

The little town of Calais, within Henry's jurisdiction, entertained Mary and Brandon honourably; when word came from Henry, they were soon able to embark for England. Mary had been away from home exactly seven months.

They reached Dover on 2 May. Henry's fury with the two people he loved most on earth had been violent but short-lived. Wolsey came to meet them the next day and escorted them to the King at Lord Bergavenny's house at Birling. Henry rode out at the head of a great cavalcade to greet his sister. He accepted her confession that she was entirely to blame for the secret marriage. On 9 March, Mary signed a document agreeing to give up her jewels and plate to Henry. It was also agreed that the Suffolks should pay him a huge fine of £24,000 in annual instalments of £2,000 by way of compensation. Brandon, despite his rank, was not a man of means. The debt to Henry was a strain on his finances, but that was nothing out of the ordinary for a sixteenth-century peer. Henry could be a ruthless creditor, but he was indulgent towards the Suffolks and allowed their indebtedness to increase year by year without foreclosure. Brandon would hand over to the King the lucrative wardship of Lady Elizabeth Lisle. Mary was also bound, against a penalty of £100,000, to surrender all her valuables. By 11 May, the financial arrangements had been completed.

Many members of the Council felt Henry had been unduly lenient. As the question of the succession became more acute, the threat posed by random marriages by princes and princesses of the blood intensified. After 1536, it was treason by Act of Parliament for royals to marry without the consent of the sovereign. Mary and Brandon's granddaughter, Katherine Grey, and her beloved husband the Earl of Hertford would feel the full weight of Queen Elizabeth's vengeance when they defied her.

But in 1515 there was no real threat to the throne, despite the mutterings of Brandon's enemies. At the King's insistence, the couple now underwent a third marriage ceremony on 13 May in the Church of the Observant Friars at Greenwich, in the presence of the entire court. Because of public disapproval, the celebrations were low-key. The guests included some who had pressed for Brandon's execution. Public feeling was expressed in one of several copies made of a wedding portrait of Mary and Brandon. It showed a court jester whispering to the Duke:

Cloth of gold do not despise
Though thou be matched with cloth of frieze;
Cloth of frieze be not too bold
Though thou be matched with cloth of gold.

Wolsey, by saving Brandon's life through his intervention, had made of Brandon a client seeking patronage. However, Brandon was now the King's brother-in-law: 'much honour and respect were paid him'. After Wolsey, he had the second seat on the King's Council, although he attended only when matters of importance were at stake, spending most of his time looking after the royal interests in East Anglia.

The Venetian envoys, noting the general disapproval and lack of public celebration, waited two months before congratulating Brandon on his marriage. Encountering him with the King at a public audience, they addressed him in Latin. He answered 'very lovingly' in English. The chronicler Edward Hall recorded that many men 'grudged against the marriage', and said it was a great loss to the realm that Mary had not married Prince Charles of Castile, but wiser men were content, because another foreign marriage would have involved expenditure. As matters stood, Mary brought 9,000 or 10,000 marks into the realm. And 'whatsoever the rude people said, the Duke behaved himself so that he hath both the favour of the King and of the people. His wit and demeanour was such.'

The handsome Suffolks rode out the storm with their customary charm and dignity.

Duchess of Suffolk

At 20, Mary, brimming with zest for life, detested prolonged periods away from court. However, her presence there depended upon her brother's whims and upon her own precarious financial situation. She and Brandon spent the remainder of 1514 re-establishing their relationship with Henry. Other court favourites were shrewder than Brandon, possessed a readier wit, shone with greater intellectual brilliance. Yet Brandon was soon reinstated as the King's favourite: brave, loyal and honest, his was a refreshing presence in a court teeming with sycophants and intriguants. Henry had had his tantrum, punished the lovers, and quickly forgiven them. Within the year, Mary and Brandon were back in favour. Mary had benefited from her brief experience as Queen of France. English fashions had always lagged behind the Continent. Mary now became the arbiter of taste, introducing new fashions in dress and manners to the court ladies, keeping herself up to date with trends by studying long accounts of banquets and balls at continental courts.

In 1515 Brandon's life changed dramatically. Not only had he obtained the de la Pole estates, but his marriage to Mary meant that any children had a legitimate claim on the throne of England. This would prove a curse rather than a blessing for the young Brandons and their descendants, at times heartbreaking, at others fatal. The royal connection and royal godparents would be a privilege, but Brandon's marriage to Mary was problematic. The jointure designated for her by Act of Parliament included all the de la Pole manors as well as eighteen others. Her frail health distracted Brandon from other important enterprises. Mary's financial links with France were a constant political liability, while Brandon's friendship with Francis engendered suspicion. It was rumoured that the Brandons' household harboured French spies. The gossip may not have been without foundation: in 1517, the French Government paid

Mary's treasurer, George Hampton, 300 crowns for an undisclosed secret mission. Hampton made numerous trips to France – he was arrested there in 1522 – while other agents of Brandon were in Bordeaux purchasing wine. William Fellowe, Brandon's future pursuivant, was involved in an attempt to sell off some of the more than 200 judicial offices at Mary's disposal, the most valuable of which would fetch £800.

Brandon constantly urged a meeting between the French and English sovereigns. Tournaments would play a major role and Brandon would be largely responsible for organising the jousts for the Field of the Cloth of Gold. He felt indebted to Francis, whom he admired, and seemed so in thrall to the French that he was virtually an additional ambassador for France at the court of England. He severed his ties with the Low Countries, requesting the Archduchess Margaret to send home his daughter from her court.

Shortly after their marriage Brandon settled the customary property jointure on Mary, designed to give her financial independence in the event of his death. Mary owned no land except for her 'great properties in France', guaranteed to her by Francis before she returned home. The annual income from this, some £6,000–7,000, was dependent on the goodwill of Francis. If war broke out between France and England, and this source of funds was cut off, Mary would be penniless. Brandon was cash-strapped but land-rich, at least in theory. He settled on Mary forty-seven manors, to revert to the Crown on her death; however, these formed part of the de la Pole lands in which he had only a reversionary interest. Neither he nor Mary lived long enough to acquire them.

Brandon had to establish a power base on his newly granted estates. Henry had been dispensing de la Pole possessions up to 1 February 1515 when he granted the lands to Brandon. Later that month, Margaret, Countess of Suffolk, widow of the executed Edmund de la Pole, died, freeing her jointure for Brandon, but some of the manors had reverted to her feoffees in 1513. Brandon's officers Oliver Pole and Humphrey Wingfield had to buy them back for £1,000. Consolidating his East Anglian properties meant repurchasing them from the Earl of Surrey at extortionate interest rates. His own income and Mary's fluctuating French pension provided an uncertain financial basis for their lifestyle; Mary did not really have a country seat worthy of her status until 1527, when Brandon built Westhorpe.

When Brandon was granted the de la Pole properties, he was still having to borrow money to finance his stay in France, which was never reimbursed, so his acquisition of the estates was delayed. He never managed to secure the whole estate. The Brandons would fall deeper and deeper in debt as they struggled to repay Mary's huge debt to the King. Worried about the cost of keeping up appearances at court, Mary remained on their East Anglian estates while Brandon was in attendance on the King. This economy reduced her dressmaker's and other bills, and the number of paid attendants she required when she needed to live up to her status as the 'French Queen'.

Brandon, needing officers he could trust, followed the example of other peers by employing his own relatives in key positions. Many of them had helped him during his troubled stay in France: Sir Richard Wingfield, his cousin, had written to Wolsey on his behalf, calling him 'the said unhappy Duke', and another cousin, Sir William Sidney, was dispatched to Paris to persuade Francis to conceal the Parisian marriage, because it was potentially damaging to Brandon and the House of Tudor. Another of Brandon's relatives, Humphrey Wingfield, a gifted lawyer, once had to plead Brandon's cause while riding alongside the Cardinal, advancing his arguments as their horses stepped over puddles.

Replacing the de la Poles as a major landowner in East Anglia required Brandon's presence. In the summer of 1515, he seized the opportunity to accomplish this while accompanying the King, who was hunting in the area. The Suffolks went on a progress round Norfolk and Suffolk: Mary, as Dowager Queen of France, outranking every woman at court, except for Queen Katherine, stole the limelight. Brandon was content that it should be so, especially as the progress proved successful. They were both showered with gifts and regally entertained. Brandon's efforts in East Anglia suited both the King and Wolsey, both keen to see a strong, reliable magnate in the south east to replace the de la Poles. The menace of the exiled but scheming Richard de la Pole was ever present. He and the French, who unscrupulously flaunted him as a threat to England, bragged that they could raise support among the remaining Yorkists. In 1523 Richard, primed with funds from his supporters, contemplated an invasion. East Anglia was the obvious target, being accessible by sea and the site of the majority of the de la Pole lands.

Brandon strove to replace the de la Poles, altering his seal to include the Brandon lion rampant, *queue fourchée*, reminiscent of an earlier seal of the de la Poles. He employed members of families who had been prominent in the de la Pole administration, thus ensuring continuity and defusing potentially treacherous activities. Building Westhorpe in 1527, Brandon now had a residence close to his East Anglian heartland. Outside East Anglia, too, Brandon's sphere of power and influence continued to increase. Sir Edward Guildford handed over to him the stewardship of Sir Edward Burgh's estates in the south east in October 1515.

The same month, Brandon and Mary attended the launching of another of the King's new ships, the *Virgin Mary* (*la Pucelle Marie*), which would later become known as the *Princess Mary*. The vessel was huge, 600–800 tons, with 120 oars, 207 guns and the capacity to carry 1,000 men. Henry, wearing a sailor's suit of cloth of gold, piloted the ship down the Thames himself, to the great delight of his Queen and his sister. Round his neck on a golden chain he sported a whistle, which, according to Wolsey, he blew 'as loud as trumpet'.

The *Princess Mary*, with the *Peter Pomegranate*, the *John the Baptist* and the *Katherine Pleasaunce*, would form the nucleus of Henry's navy, destined to become the most powerful maritime fleet in Europe. Other monarchs grew uneasy as they observed the massive amounts Henry spent on his ships. Wolsey did his best to assure the French envoy that the great vessels had been built 'solely to give pleasure and pastime' to the two queens, but the French recognised the potential threat. There was some truth in Wolsey's assertion: the dedication ceremony for the *Princess Mary*, 'the greatest cheer and triumph that could be devised', was chiefly designed to delight the King's sister, now fully restored to favour.

The Suffolks lacked the means to stay at court for long periods without financial assistance from Henry. At first this was not forthcoming, and they retired to Tattershall, one of their largest Lincolnshire manors, returning to court in the autumn for the ceremony on 15 November 1515 when the papal prothonotary entered London bearing the Cardinal's hat for Wolsey. Suffolk and Norfolk greeted the Cardinal at the door of Westminster Abbey the following Sunday after the ceremony and escorted him to York Place at Charing Cross, where a banquet awaited them. As French Queen Dowager, Mary sat at the top table with Henry and Katherine. Both Mary and Katherine were pregnant.

At Christmas 1515, the King and Brandon amused themselves by running at the ring, Henry sporting a wreath of green satin embroidered with the Queen's pomegranate badge. He had kitted out the competitors at his own expense at a cost of £142; at the end of the day each man was told he could keep whatever he was wearing. Brandon was also given the horse, armour and saddle he had been using. The courtiers watched the event from elaborate pavilions with chivalric names: White Hart, Harp, Greyhound, Flower-delice, Leopard's Head, Ostrich Feather.

Mary remained in the country awaiting the birth of her child. Brandon wrote to Wolsey from Butley about their debts, and the couple agreed that he should send some of Mary's jewels to Wolsey as an earnest of their intent to pay. Brandon also sought to consolidate Henry's favour with the gift of a prized goshawk. He announced his intention of bringing Mary up to London for her confinement in March, adding plaintively that he had heard the King was planning 'some pastime' in May, but that he himself was hard up and ill-equipped to cut a dashing figure. They both assured the King that they desired nothing so much as the pleasure of the King's company.

Mary was finally summoned in February for a joyous occasion: Queen Katherine had at long last succeeded in bearing Henry a viable child. Her labour had been an ordeal throughout which the Queen clasped the holy girdle of her patron saint St Catherine. At 31, poor Queen Katherine, described uncharitably by one contemporary observer as 'rather ugly than otherwise', had already buried four children. The King was only 25 and in full vigour. He had hoped for a son, but the longed-for child was a girl. However, the King was delighted to have a healthy child. 'The Queen and I are both young, and if it is a girl this time, boys will follow,' he told Giustinian, the Venetian ambassador.[1]

The little princess, the future 'Bloody Mary', was a tiny Tudor redhead who never cried. She was named for her beautiful aunt, and baptised at Greenwich in the little Franciscan chapel of the Friars Observant, where her parents had married seven years before and where Henry himself had been christened. The ceremony followed the solemn time-honoured ritual established by Lady Margaret Beaufort in the Household Ordinances. The silver font had again been transported from Canterbury, the processional route was spread with rich carpets, the church was hung with tapestries. The baby, three days old, was divested of her robes and ermine-trimmed train of cloth of gold in a specially constructed cabinet containing a brazier and towels, and then immersed naked in the font, set on a raised dais in view of the congregation. She was then anointed with holy oil and the white chrisom cloth was wrapped about her tiny head. Her little fist was closed around a lighted taper and she was borne to the high altar, where she was confirmed by Archbishop Warham.

Mary, far advanced in pregnancy, did not attend. It was an ice winter. From her windows she watched children sledging on the frozen Thames, and carts crossing the great river on a highway of ice. Brandon represented the family, presenting the infant with a New Year's gift of a golden pomander. This practical piece of jewellery was worn on the girdle by women of all ages. It contained perfume, usually based on ambergris, musk or civet or aromatic spices, to be delicately sniffed at when confronted by 'foule, stinkying aire'. Wolsey stood godfather, and the baby's great-aunt, Lady Katherine Courtney, Countess of Devonshire and daughter of Edward IV, and the Duchess of Norfolk were the godmothers.

On Tuesday 11 March, late at night, at Bath Place near Temple Bar, Mary gave birth to her first child, a son. In an impressive ceremony the baby was given his uncle's name, Henry. The King and Wolsey were god-fathers, Lady Katherine was godmother to this child, too, highlighting Mary's links with the royal house of York. The font in the Hall at Suffolk Place was filled with lukewarm water for the baby's comfort. Fires blazed on the hearths in the corners, the light of 24 torches flickered on the wall hangings and bench cushions, embroidered with red Tudor roses and white Yorkist roses. It was a state occasion attended by everyone of importance except Mary herself. She waited in the nursery to receive her son and his baptismal gifts.

The walk from the nursery to the door of the hall had been newly spread with gravel and rushes, enclosed by an ornamental rail and lit by flaring torches. Outside the hall a substantial timber porch had been erected, covered and lined with cloth of gold. The christening procession passed along this artificial aisle. After the ceremony, spices and wine were served by the peers, headed by Norfolk. The christening gifts were presented one by one. Lady Katherine Courtney gave two pots of silver and gilt, the King a salt cellar and cup of solid gold.

Those who resented Brandon's influence and despised his humble origins observed with ill-concealed envy the auspicious launching of this royal child, who might one day become King. Obsessed with dynastic succession, people reflected that, if the ageing Queen continued to fail to produce a male heir, baby Henry Brandon might eventually inherit the throne.

The birth of a healthy princess had brought out the sunny side of the King's volatile nature. He was equally delighted with his small name-sake, Mary and Brandon's son. The whole month of May was devoted to revels and enjoyment, in celebration of the births and also the visit of Henry and Mary's older sister, Margaret. The costly christening had drained Brandon's coffers, but the Suffolks remained at Southwark for several weeks in anticipation of a reunion with the widowed Queen of Scots, and the attendant festivities.

Margaret, Queen of Scotland for ten years and Regent for two, widow of James IV and mother of 3-year-old James V, was in trouble. Determined to retain the power in Scotland for herself and her son, her position as Regent was threatened when John Stewart, Duke of Albany, cousin and potential successor to her son, arrived in Scotland. Although usually courageous and resourceful, Margaret now destroyed her own powerbase with one act of romantic folly. The handsome young Earl of Angus, Archibald Douglas, had been introduced into her court by his grandfather, Lord Drummond, the Chief Justiciary of Scotland and the father of the murdered Lady Margaret Drummond, Margaret's husband's mistress.

On 14 August 1514, aged 24, Margaret married Douglas in a secret ceremony at Kinnoul Church. This disastrous action alienated many clans who nurtured a deep hatred of the Douglases. The Scottish lords foregathered and solemnly voted to depose the Queen from the Regency. Sir William Comyn, Lyon Herald, who the previous year had had to face Henry VIII with James IV's declaration of war, now confronted another unpleasant task. He had to inform Margaret of the lords' decision. Ushered into Margaret's Presence Chamber, he addressed her by her new title decreed by the Council: she was no longer 'the Queen's Grace' but 'My Lady the King's mother'. Enraged, old Lord Drummond rose from his chair, squared up to Lyon Herald and slapped him across the face with his glove.

The Duke of Albany was chosen as Regent by the Scottish Parliament. He immediately seized custody of young James. Scotland was on the brink of civil war.

By August 1515, Margaret realised she had lost both her Regency and her children. She fled from virtual captivity in Edinburgh, to live quietly in northern England. At Harbottle Castle in Northumberland on 8 October, after a difficult labour in which she nearly died, Margaret bore her seventh child and third daughter, Margaret, the future Countess of Lennox.

On 3 May 1516, Margaret rode out to Tottenham Cross to meet her brother. She was destitute and suffering from sciatica. Neither of her siblings had seen her since 1503 when she left London to become the bride of James IV, but they had followed her turbulent career with amazement and alarm. Queen Katherine had sent a white palfrey upon which Margaret rode in triumph into London followed by a large procession of courtiers and dignitaries. Later that year Wolsey would arrange for her to occupy Scotland Yard, once the ancient London residence of the Kings of Scotland, but now incorporated into York Place. For the time being, she was to be accommodated in Baynard's Castle. Arriving there with her escort at 6 in the evening, Margaret must have remembered how she and Henry, two carefree children, had danced there, fifteen years previously, at their brother Arthur's wedding feast.

Margaret was formally received by the King and Queen at Greenwich and reunited with her sister Mary. She was overawed by the magnificence of her brother's court and overwhelmed by the gifts lavished on her. Margaret had inherited the Tudor taste for pomp and pageantry and luxurious living. It was reported to Henry that the gifts and gowns he had sent her in Northumberland after the birth of Margaret Douglas had done her more good than all the pysicians in the world. After a state banquet at Lambeth in Margaret's honour, there followed a series of celebrations and jousts at Westminster or Greenwich. The climax was the Grand Tournament on 19 and 20 May, where the King, with Essex, Suffolk and young Nicholas Carew, were the challengers. The three Queens, Mary, Margaret and Katherine, surveyed the spectacular parade of gorgeously apparelled contestants, tricked out courtesy of the Great Wardrobe in black velvet overlaid with a tracery of honeysuckle in 'fine flat gold' so that the leaves and branches appeared to move and shimmer in the May sun.[2]

Brandon was Henry's first aide. The King, Brandon, Essex and Carew all dressed alike, but only the King's and Brandon's retainers wore yellow damask. The King's other attendants were clad in blue velvet fringed with gold. On the first day Henry won many accolades for his performance. Next day, Brandon outshone him in a series of thrilling contests in which all his opponents broke at least four lances on him in their eight runs. Henry and his attendants were resplendent in purple velvet embroidered with golden roses and foliage, the noblemen's mottoes picked out in gold on the borders of their trappings. The officers of the tiltyard wore yellow satin edged with cloth of gold. Their opponents wore white and gold.

But the King felt the quality of his opponents did him little honour. He announced that in future he would 'never joust again except it be with as good a man as himself'.[3] Thereafter he usually chose outstanding competitors, principally Brandon. At the end of the official programme, Henry and Brandon delighted the spectators by running 'volant at all comers' with a dazzling exhibition of freestyle jousting.

Shortly after the tournament, Mary and Brandon retired to the country. Mary's sister Margaret remained in England for just over a year. There was much speculation about her separation from her husband, and the possibility of a marriage with the Emperor. One of the many people who reported back to Louise of Savoy swore he had heard Wolsey say he would willingly renounce his cardinal's hat or 'lose a finger of his right hand' if he could bring about such a marriage.[4]

Margaret had no intention of being married off to an elderly infirm monarch as her sister had been. She still loved Angus. Moreover, had the marriage been declared void, little Lady Margaret Douglas, for whom her uncle the King of England had conceived a great liking, would have been rendered illegitimate. In June, Queen Katherine's favourite Lady-in-waiting, Maria de Salinas, left the royal service to marry William, Lord Willoughby d'Eresby, Master of the Royal Hart Hounds. The Queen provided Maria with a handsome dowry and frequently invited her to court after her marriage. She was probably a godmother to Maria's daughter Catherine, born in 1517 and named in her honour.

Catherine Willoughby would one day become Brandon's wife and Duchess of Suffolk.

Wolsey, now in full command of the Council, was directing foreign policy. Brandon appeared to be temporarily out of favour. He spent the rest of the year in the country, unwilling to return to court unless the King sent for him. Mary wrote a sad little letter to her brother from Letheringham, Suffolk, in September, saying she hoped soon to be with him again. She longed to be recalled to court. But Brandon was even more heavily in debt to the King than usual. By the end of 1516, he owed £1,200.

Margaret, Dowager Queen of Scots, was in even worse financial straits. By Christmas 1516, she had to beg Wolsey for funds to enable her to make the traditional New Year's Day gifts to her servants and attendants, both for her brother's honour and her own. It would be a disgrace were she unable to honour her obligations. Wolsey delayed replying, so Margaret wrote him a note in her own hand, entreating him to advance her £200, against her expectations of receiving her promised income from Scotland. By the spring of 1519, Margaret would be reduced to pawning her jewellery and dismissing her household servants. The Scottish lords had given her 'nothing but fair words'.[5] She declared she would rather be dead than live among them. While she was in England her husband Angus seized her Scottish estates and rekindled his affair with his old flame, Lady Jane Stewart of Traquair. The couple were boldly cohabiting in Margaret's home and at Margaret's expense. Margaret's passion now turned to black hatred.

Nonetheless, Christmas 1516 was celebrated with the usual immoderate sumptuousness at Greenwich, graced by the presence of the three Queens. There was moderate optimism: Wolsey had saved Margaret's face by lending her £200 to pay for her gifts; Brandon was back in favour, having been chosen to command Henry's army in the event of the outbreak of war with France. Their reconciliation included a new financial arrangement by which Mary's annual repayment could be made in kind – jewellery – rather than cash. Brandon was also granted an extension of the loan, to be paid off by instalments. Brandon managed to stall his other creditors, including the Earl of Shrewsbury, indefinitely.

In the spring of 1517 Brandon's financial difficulties were partially relieved by being granted the wardship of the two young sons of Sir Thomas Knyvet, bringing in lucrative resources from their estates in Norfolk and Wiltshire. Brandon tended to take a relaxed view of finances, and refused to allow his indebtedness to depress him. Nor did he curtail his lavish lifestyle. Confident of the King's leniency, he imported expensive tapestries from the Continent and spent vast sums on his houses, building a fine brick residence in London on his ancestral estate by the Thames, Suffolk Place, in what is now known as Southwark High Street, and carrying out renovation and improvements on his country seat, Westhorpe Hall in Suffolk. Here Mary spent most of her time, attended by a staff of fifty, while Brandon was at court. He also maintained five other properties in East Anglia, Berkshire and Oxfordshire.

It was now almost a year since the birth of the Princess Mary, and there was still no sign of the longed-for son and heir. Katherine undertook another pilgrimage to the renowned shrine of Our Lady of Walsingham at the Austin Priory. The Suffolks travelled to meet her at Pickenham Wade in Norfolk and accompanied her to the priory. On the return journey, they entertained her 'with such poor cheer as we could make her Grace', Brandon recorded modestly, but so graciously that the Queen felt obliged to return their hospitality the next month.

The Suffolks spent much of the rest of the year in the country, a money-saving exercise. Brandon would have cash-flow problems and remain in debt for most of his life. But the Suffolks much preferred the luxurious and exciting life at court. Mary, loved by both the King and the Queen, was with her beauty and magnetism an acknowledged ornament, while Brandon was once more the King's favourite companion, in constant demand for jousts, pageants and other royal pastimes. Henry and Brandon often rode out of the lists together, their contests ending symbolically in renewed eternal brotherhood. Seventeenth-century surveys of the Tower of London found complementary sets of arms and armour, one belonging to the King, the other to Brandon. Often, two equally splendid jousting suits were made for them. They invariably opened the tournament, running the first eight courses, always brilliantly.

In late April 1517 the Suffolks visited Richmond, where Henry and Katherine were spending Easter. Henry always fled at the slightest hint of an epidemic, and an outbreak of the plague was once again ravaging London. There was also growing social unrest. Foreign merchants, French and Genoese, had begun to dominate trade through unfair practices, driving up prices and disregarding the rules of commerce laid down by the mayor and aldermen. Eventually the English workforce revolted. On Easter Tuesday, they were inflamed by a sermon preached at St Paul's Cross by Dr Beal[e], a canon of St Mary's Hospital, who assured his audience that under God's law any man had the right to fight for his country against foreigners. England was for the English: 'As birds would defend their nest, so ought Englishmen to cherish and defend themselves and to hurt and grieve aliens for the common weal.'⁶ Violence erupted. Artisans and apprentices rioted. During the night of 30 April, a furious mob sacked the houses of foreign craftsmen.

On 1 May 1517, always thereafter remembered as 'Evil May Day', hundreds of Londoners thronged the streets seeking out foreigners to attack. Wolsey and the Earl of Surrey rode to the gates of London only to find that the apprentices had locked the city gates. Surrey forced an entry and his father, the Duke of Norfolk, brought up reinforcements. The troops quickly suppressed the rising and rounded up the ringleaders. Forty rioters were hanged, drawn and quartered, hundreds more imprisoned. Gibbets were erected at the city gates where the grim remains of the victims of rough justice were displayed. On 22 May, in a choreographed piece of theatre, more than 400 miscreants, including 11 women and many young boys, were brought to trial before Wolsey and the King in a packed Westminster Hall, hung with banners and arras of cloth of gold. The accused were paraded before the dignitaries, cutting wretched figures, in shirtsleeves, barefoot, with ropes about their necks.

In a long address, Wolsey, as Lord Chancellor of England, reprimanded the culprits and the city authorities who had failed to keep the peace. With tears in his eyes, he urged future loyalty. Then first Wolsey and then Queen Katherine, weeping, begged the King to show mercy. The prisoners fell to their knees, taking up the cry: 'Mercy! Mercy!' The mighty Cardinal fell to his knees also, pleading for mercy. The King ordered them to be released. The prisoners leapt and shouted for joy and threw their halters in the air. There were tears of relief all round. 'Then were all the gallows within the city taken down and many a good prayer said for the King.'⁷

Both Mary and Katherine were pregnant again. On 18 May, Margaret had set out to return to Scotland, to attempt a reunion with her wayward husband. Henry had worked out her itinerary and rode north with her for the first four days. He had entertained her for over a year at a cost of more than £2,000 and she left England laden with his gifts of gold, valuable textiles and equipment and trappings for her horses. His generosity was based on the understanding that Margaret would promise to take no further part in government and administration. But by September she was plotting to take control. She failed. On 30 October, Wolsey learned that she was 'badly treated and no promise kept to her'.

But Henry was too preoccupied with his own affairs of the heart; he sent neither money nor troops to help Margaret. His Queen was expecting her fourth child, but Henry was deeply involved in his romance with young Bessie Blount, now one of the Queen's maids of honour. Bessie had first attracted the King's attention when he had partnered her in a Christmas pageant at Greenwich back in 1514. Bessie seems to have been a popular and lively young lady: in October 1514, Brandon, still single and already in France, had added as a postscript to a letter to Henry, asking him to remind 'Mistress Blount and Mistress Carew' to reply to him when he wrote to them or sent them love tokens, the implication being that both the King and Brandon were on familiar terms with both ladies and possibly shared their favours.

Margaret now wrote to her brother, pleading to be allowed to return to England and live separately from her husband, although she did not mention the word 'divorce', nor did she mention Wolsey's notion of marrying her to the Emperor. She did, however, meekly promise that she would never marry again unless Henry selected her bridegroom.

Henry's response demonstrated the double standard of Tudor morality: at Margaret's suggestion of leaving her husband, Henry was outraged and sent Friar Bonaventure Chadworth to Scotland to lecture Margaret on moral values and wifely duty. Despite her pleas to be allowed to return to England, both Henry and Wolsey found it more expedient, as well as cheaper, to keep her where she was. Over the next few years Mary heard from her sister occasionally, but neither she nor Henry ever saw Margaret again.

Queen Katherine's son was born in February. The child did not live long and its name was never recorded. Bessie Blount would eventually bear Henry a healthy son, Henry Fitzroy, Duke of Richmond. Henry was overjoyed by this living proof of his ability to beget male heirs.

Married Life

At the first sign of infectious disease, the court rushed to their country houses, seeking purer air and less congestion. The dreaded sweating sickness had first appeared in England in 1485, causing some to view it as divine retribution visited upon the Tudors for usurping the throne. Europeans called it 'the English sweat', because it appeared to have originated in England and raged with great virulence there. Victims usually died within twenty-four hours, often succumbing within four or five hours. In summer 1517, when the sickness again broke out in London, Brandon and Mary left town. They needed a spell away from the expenses of court life, their finances being more precarious than ever. Brandon, so dependent on the King's favour that he dare do nothing to jeopardise their relationship, had added his signature to a treaty of friendship with Spain, although reluctantly, well aware that, if he alienated Francis, Mary's French income, which fluctuated at the best of times, could be terminated at any moment.

Notwithstanding, in July the Suffolks happily returned to court in July to participate in the lavish reception of the envoys sent by Charles and Maximilian. From playing the military commander, Henry had now recast himself in the role of international peacemaker, intent on maintaining the balance of power between Francis and Maximilian. He modestly informed the Venetian envoy Giustinian that he was content with what he had, and wished only to govern his own subjects.

The diplomatic mission arrived with an imposing retinue of 100 horses and a twenty-four-waggon baggage train. Henry responded by sending out 400 nobles to meet the ambassadors and escort them to Greenwich, where they were received in audience with great magnificence. Queen Katherine and Mary, Duchess of Suffolk, resplendent in cloth of gold, displayed their priceless jewellery; but the King outdid them, wearing a splendid garment 'in the Hungarian fashion' with a heavy collar of 'inestimable value' about his neck.[1] The Venetian minister recorded that 'everything glittered with gold'. The foreign delegates were dumbfounded by English opulence and culture. They were lavishly wined and dined, and entertained with concerts, pageants, jousts and exhibitions. In these events the King always starred, demonstrating his talents at tilting or music.

On St Peter's Day, after mass, the terms of the accord were discussed. The event culminated in a joust held before 50,000 spectators. A special walled tiltyard had been built, which the awed Venetians declared to be three times larger than the Piazza di San Pietro at Mantua. There were grandstands for guests, tented pavilions of cloth of gold for the contestants. Henry had at first declared his intention of challenging all comers single-handed, but he was persuaded, on time considerations, to content himself with a single opponent, Brandon. The pair 'bore themselves so bravely that the spectators fancied themselves witnessing a joust between Hector and Achilles,' recorded Sagudino, secretary to the Venetian ambassador. In a four-hour contest, the champions tilted eight courses, shivering their lances, 'to the great applause of the spectators'.[2] The King, mounted on a succession of splendid destriers, executed breathtaking caprioles.

A defensive league comprising the Papacy, the Empire, Spain and England was proclaimed. The ambassadors left with a loan of more than £13,000, to be repaid in instalments, and laden with gifts worth £3,000. The papal nuncio Francesco Chieregato was impressed with the English and their King, their wealth, elegant manners, decorum and politeness, blessed with a worthy and eminent sovereign. Chieregato would find Wolsey's demeanour less decorous: the great Cardinal's usual affability concealed ruthlessness. On a later occasion, he cursed and struck the papal nuncio, and threatened to have him put to the rack.

Wolsey supervised Brandon's finances. None of the total debt for which Brandon had contracted in 1515 had been paid. In May 1517, Wolsey moved the goalposts. The payments remained at 1,000 marks a year, but Brandon was now to pay 500 marks a year towards his own debts, even when no dower was forthcoming from France for Mary. Instead of falling due within forty days, Wolsey tightened the timescale to fourteen days. In the event of Mary's death, all her personal jewels and valuables would revert to the Crown. She had to promise not to resign her dower to Francis. Jewels to the value of 2,000 marks were handed over, and the total debt was increased by more arrears on the Welsh lordships of which Brandon was the Receiver; additionally, in an unprecedented sideswipe, the Suffolks were charged £600 for their lodging at court.

In the end, the debt remained merely a threat, just so long as Brandon retained the King's favour. The Suffolks remained the King's greatest debtors, after Francis himself.

After the departure of the Burgundian envoys, the court dispersed. Mary set off for Walsingham Priory, but when her labour started she was forced to accept the hospitality of her old acquaintance Nicholas West, Bishop of Ely. Hatfield, 17 miles north of London, had been the seat of the bishops of Ely since the Middle Ages, but the palace had been leased to the King's farriers and was Crown property. In this idyllic and secluded mansion set amid orchards, early on 16 July, St Francis's Day, Mary gave birth to her first daughter. The baby was christened two days later at the local parish church before a congregation of seventy-five people. She was given the name Frances, ostensibly after the saint but perhaps also in honour of the King of France. The ceremony was illuminated by eighty torchbearers. The godfather was the Abbot of St Albans. The godmothers, Queen Katherine and the infant Princess Mary, were represented by Elizabeth Grey and Lady Boleyn, probably Lady Anne Boleyn, the wife of Edward Boleyn and a favourite of the Queen's. Katherine had little idea that Lady Anne's niece and namesake would one day cause her such grief.

This christening was less formal than that of Mary's first-born, Henry, since the King was not present. Besides, Frances's birth was less dynastically important. The King already had a healthy legitimate daughter and a thriving illegitimate son, his child by Bessie Blount. No one could have foreseen that baby Frances Brandon's own daughter, Lady Jane Grey, would pay a terrible price for her royal Tudor descent.

The epidemic continued to sweep through England's cities, keeping many of the nobility away from London for the rest of the year. The Suffolks remained mostly at Westhorpe Hall, in the green heart of rural west Suffolk with its windmills and dovecotes. Westhorpe was a comfortable manor house nestling within its moat, boasting a cloistered court and a private chapel, the latter beautifully lit by high stained-glass windows. Under Mary's influence, the gardens were laid out in the French fashion. The fourteenth-century parish church was within walking distance. It still contains the royal pew, once occupied by Mary and Brandon on Sundays. Only 75 miles from London as the crow flies, the journey along meandering country roads usually took four or five days. The Brandons started out at dawn at a leisurely pace, their little cavalcade of carts and horses passing up the Great North Road – the Old Watling Street of Roman times – to St Albans, where they would spend the first night. Mary and the children travelled in a small carriage with the nurse, the others on horseback; servants took care of the packhorses and baggage train. Brandon had much to occupy and interest him in the country. His parks were well stocked with red deer, and he enjoyed hunting and took pride in his herds of valuable horses and mules.

The Suffolks spent that winter quietly with friends and family. Both of Brandon's daughters by his wife Anne Browne were present, and possibly also Magdalen Rochester, the girl whose life he had saved in France, now aged 13. His older daughter, Anne, a good-looking 16-year-old, returned from the court of the Archduchess Margaret, kept Mary company during Brandon's frequent absences. Her sister Mary was only 8.

The sweating sickness continued its ravages in the cities. The court was closed to all but those whose official business required their presence. Wolsey stoically remained at his post, fighting off four attacks. The King, terrified by any threat of disease, fled from one residence to another before the spreading infection. Even Mary and Brandon were not often permitted to join him, except when he sent for them out of boredom or anxiety. The Suffolks had yet again narrowly avoided financial ruin, and were once more enjoying the King's favour. This was confirmed in March 1518, when to their delight they were invited to spend Easter with the King and Queen, who were currently staying in Abingdon. Henry wanted to celebrate Easter with his sister as he had done in 1516.

When the Brandons arrived on 1 April, the atmosphere was tense; there were rumours of plots to overthrow the King. Henry had intended to return to London, but had once again lost his nerve upon learning that the capital was still infested with disease. He decided he was better off in Abingdon, where there was less danger and where people did not depress him by coming to him every day bringing news of yet more deaths. Buckingham and other members of the Council were dismissed, but the Suffolks stayed on, accompanying the King and Queen to the royal manor of Woodstock at the end of the month. Mary was loath to leave, and Henry found it difficult to deny his adored younger sister anything. She was an ornament to the court. Besides, she was ill.

That Easter brought the added strain of political concerns. Wolsey was in London negotiating a rapprochement with France. He frustrated Brandon by keeping the King, Sir Henry Marney and Sir Thomas Lovell informed of his progress, but excluding Brandon. Brandon's enemies claimed he had promised the French the restoration of Tournai, thus destroying Wolsey's main bargaining point. Brandon, eager to vindicate himself, bombarded Wolsey with assurances of good faith for two months. At the end of July he hurried from the Bury St Edmund's Abbey of Elmswell, where he was staying, to Enfield to confront Wolsey. He found Wolsey more relaxed than expected: the treaty was just about signed and sealed. Brandon sensed that the temporary coolness between them had evaporated. The King came to stay at Wanstead, where Brandon was still Keeper, and enjoyed Brandon's entertainment.

At the end of July, Brandon attended Wolsey in Council at Westminster, having been commanded by Henry to be present. But Mary, laid low with repeated attacks of fever, remained longer at Woodstock than intended. Brandon apologised to Wolsey for the delay. 'The French Queen was unable to depart the court so soon as was appointed, for, Sir, it hath pleased God to visit her with an ague, the which has taken her Grace every third day four times very sharp, but by the grace of God she shall shortly recover.' He added that she was attended daily by the King's physicians, who were able to assuage much of her suffering.

By late September, Mary was sufficiently recovered to visit London for the reception of the French envoys, headed by Admiral Bonnivet, her old admirer. The French had three objectives: to negotiate the return of Tournai, to sign a peace contract between England and France, and to celebrate the betrothal of Princess Mary to the Dauphin, the infant son of Francis and Claude, still a babe in arms. Princess Mary, aged 2½, was brought in for their inspection. On catching sight of Friar Dionysio Memmo, the court chaplain, a skilled musician born in Venice, the little princess captivated the company by squealing 'Priest! Priest!', begging him to play for her. The King jovially swept his daughter up in his arms, and the musician obliged, to the general delight.

On 3 October a general peace, the Treaty of London, was proclaimed between England and France at St Paul's. The French regained Tournai, paying Henry compensation. The remaining 323,000 crowns outstanding on Mary's dower was to be settled and proper arrangements were to be made for her income as Queen Dowager to be sent to her. Bonnivet wrote to Francis that the King of England processed to mass accompanied by a 'great train of gentlemen, richly dressed', and by the Cardinal, and the ambassadors from Spain and Venice. The Mass was celebrated by all the bishops and abbots of the kingdom. In an atmosphere of 'solemnity too magnificent for description', Henry swore to observe the peace.[3]

After the solemn proceedings, the King and his company dined at the house of the Bishop of London. In the evening it was Wolsey's turn to feast the dignitaries. He threw a banquet at York Place, which overwhelmed the Venetian Giustinian by its opulence. 'We sat down to a most sumptuous supper, the like of which, I fancy, was never given either by Cleopatra or Caligula: the whole banqueting hall being so decorated with huge vases of gold and silver that I fancied myself in the tower of Croesus.'⁴ After supper there was mummery, starring the talented Suffolks, then twelve masked gentlemen and as many gorgeously dressed masked ladies took the floor. At the end of the dance, they removed their masks, revealing that the two principals were Henry and Mary. The dancers were plied with 'countless dishes of confections and delicacies';⁵ great bowls were placed on the tables containing ducats and dice, for guests wishing to gamble.

In the excitement of the constant diversions – masses, banquets, pageants and dancing – Henry even forgot his dread of illness and threw himself into the swing of things with his old zest, his favourite companions, Brandon and Mary, ever at his side. Mary and the Queen were the centre of attention. Mary was in her element, delighted with everything. She smiled at the amazement of the Londoners when they saw the French capering about the streets mounted on mules, and at the gallant efforts of the French courtiers, who had been urged by Bonnivet to 'warm up these cold ladies of England'. The French brought the hottest fashion news from Paris. Modish gentlemen were now affecting the 'shemew', a gown 'cut in the middle', or worn loose and open. This was soon to gain popularity in England. Henry would wear one, the gift of the French King, at the Field of the Cloth of Gold.

Two days later the court embarked for the barge trip along the Thames to Greenwich for the espousals of the two babies, Princess Mary and the French infant prince. In the Queen's Great Chamber, the French Admiral stood proxy for the Dauphin. The princess, a tiny figure in cloth of gold, and a little black velvet hat studded with jewels, stood in front of her mother Katherine, who was once again heavily pregnant. After an eloquent Latin oration in praise of marriage, the little princess was lifted up so that Wolsey could slip onto her finger a ring with a huge diamond. As the Admiral pressed it into place, to everyone's amusement, the child looked up at the Admiral and demanded sagaciously: 'Are you the Dauphin of France? If you are, I want to kiss you!'⁶

In the royal chapel, to which the company now proceeded, the scene was spectacular, the rich clothing of the courtiers being set off by the whole choir, draped in cloth of gold. Brandon, the Dukes of Buckingham and Norfolk, served the King when he washed his hands before the feast. The Queen retired early, but the splendid festivities continued until 2 a.m. A grand joust on 7 October was followed by another banquet and a pageant in honour of the peace and the betrothal. That evening, Henry wore a long robe of stiff gold brocade lined with ermine. When Admiral Bonnivet admired it, Henry, in one of those fits of impulsive generosity for which he was renowned, threw it off and presented it to him.

He then invited the company to Richmond to hunt, and proposed that Wolsey should now entertain them all at Hampton Court, which he had been embellishing since 1514. While Henry and Bonnivet set off for Richmond, Wolsey's staff were thrown into a frenzy of activity, preparing the banquet. Wolsey's gentleman usher George Cavendish recorded that they were commanded 'to spare neither expense nor labour, to make the French such triumphant cheer that they might not only wonder at it here, but make a glorious report in their country to the King's honour and that of this realm'.[7]

Wolsey was a brilliant host. Costly delicacies were brought in by the cartload, the cooks toiled night and day to devise subtle dishes to surprise the eye and delight the palate. The rooms where the French envoys were to spend the night had beds of silk and walls hung with rich tapestries. When they were shown to their rooms they found roaring fires in the grates and fine wines to refresh them. At supper time they were escorted to banqueting halls draped with rich hangings. The first dining chamber was imaginatively illuminated by placing candelabra on polished silver salvers, reflecting the light on all sides. The tables were spread with snowy damask, the sideboards groaned under an array of precious plate. In the Presence Chamber, where the most important guests would be seated, the tablecloths had been perfumed; the gold plate on display was so precious that it was barricaded off. The plate was for show only. The great Cardinal, in the course of his career as the star of European diplomacy and Henry's chief minister, had acquired so much plate that there was an abundance of gold and silver salvers and dishes left to serve the banquet.

A fanfare of trumpets greeted the guests, followed by music that entranced the French envoys. But they still glanced around for their host, who had not arrived. As they admired the second course, a triumph of the pastry-cook's art, a model of St Paul's Cathedral, complete with steeple, dishes in the shape of birds and animals, edible models of English soldiers fighting with swords and cross bows, and a chessboard made of spiced sweetmeats, Wolsey rushed in, booted and spurred as though fresh from travelling, bade everyone welcome and dropped into his seat still in his riding clothes, 'laughing and being as merry as ever I saw him in my life,' Cavendish reported. Wolsey offered the edible chessboard to one of the French guests, who declared it was too beautiful to eat. A special case was made in which it could be carried back to France as a memento of the occasion.

The highlight of the evening was the loyal toast to the two Kings, proposed by Wolsey, lifting a golden bowl filled with spiced wine. The company joined in enthusiastically. A document was signed promising that the two Kings would meet face to face before 31 July 1519.

But the Queen, approaching the birth of the child that was to be her last, had much to ponder. For the first time she found herself at odds with the Brandons, usually her close and supportive friends. Katherine's kinship with Spain and the Netherlands meant she secretly deplored the French alliance, and had been quietly working behind the scenes to further the cause of her nephew, Charles of Castile. As the proposed summit meeting approached, she felt it should not have been with Francis I but with the Holy Roman Emperor. With this preying on her mind, and desperate to produce the son and heir her husband and the whole country yearned for, in November 1518 she bore her sixth child. The baby girl died before she could be christened.

Two months later, in January 1519, the Emperor Maximilian died. This required the election of a new Holy Roman Emperor, even though Maximilian's grandson, Charles of Castile, nephew of Queen Katherine and the former betrothed of Mary Rose, was the obvious candidate. Undeterred, Henry VIII put his own name forward, and awaited with impatience the outcome of the election, which took place on 28 June 1519. He was playing tennis with the French hostages at the Duke of Buckingham's residence, Penshurst Place, when he was informed that his candidature had been unsuccessful. Henry took his disappointment very well: when he learned how much bribing the electors had cost Charles, Henry snorted that he was glad he had not bothered.

After the Queen's disastrous confinement, Mary retired to the country, spending the winter and most of the summer of 1519 at Westhorpe; sometimes she and Brandon stayed at Letheringham Hall, where they were occasionally visited by Wolsey, or at Butley Priory, near Westhorpe, which, with its annual income of £400, was well able to cater for distinguished guests. The Brandons were received into the Augustinian Order in 1518. If the canons of Butley hoped for financial patronage, they were disappointed – the Brandons enjoyed their hospitality but made no major donations. They were given an apartment within the main building where they could have privacy, although during the summer they took their meals with the canons on the sacrists' garden. They went fox hunting in Staverton Park or Scuttegrove Wood until late afternoon, staying out for a picnic supper afterwards. On their last recorded visit, in 1530, they stayed for two months, hunting, riding and gaming. On excursions to Yarmouth or Norwich, they always enjoyed royal receptions. During these months they were also frequently at court in the royal household, dining at the top table. When in London the King often dined with them and spent the evening at Suffolk Place. Brandon was granted various fees and annuities in Wales, and Henry made him the gift of a 'big bald black horse bought at the Hague'.

Brandon's relationship with Wolsey had also improved. Brandon wrote to tell Wolsey that Henry was dissatisfied with the French hostages left by the French delegation as earnest of their master's good intentions regarding fulfilment of the peace treaty. Henry did not think the hostages were of sufficiently elevated status nor held in high esteem by their own sovereign. Besides, they so often beat the King at gambling on dice and cards that he was reputed to be losing 6–8,000 ducats a day. These losses hardly endeared them to him.

Concentrating on the imperial election, Henry had postponed his meeting with Francis I until the following year. By 1520, Queen Claude was pregnant and, as both kings were insistent that their spouses should attend the occasion, the date for their encounter could not be safely set much later than early June. The two kings joked that such was their eagerness for this personal encounter that neither would shave his beard before it took place. The King's beard grew golden, but Katherine so objected to it that she nagged him constantly to shave, and before long he gave in, breaking his promise. Francis's clever mother, Louise of Savoy, managed to avert an international incident by declaring that the love the two kings bore one another 'was not in the beards but in the hearts'.[8]

The Brandons now had three children, Henry, born in 1516, Frances, 1517, and Eleanor, born in 1518. After Eleanor's birth, Mary's poor health kept her away from court, but by 1520 she was recovered and in excellent spirits. The court was buzzing with the forthcoming summit meeting between the two monarchs. In March 1520, the enormous preparations began for the historic encounter, which would be immortalised as the Field of the Cloth of Gold. Six thousand workmen were dispatched to start work on the English quarters. At this momentous event, Mary, her charm and beauty outshining all others, would again prove an inestimable political and diplomatic asset to her brother the King.

Field of the Cloth of Gold

In spring 1520, the arrangements for the Field of the Cloth of Gold, the legendary summit meeting between Francis I and Henry VIII, which would go down in history as the Eighth Wonder of the World, snowballed rapidly. Wolsey, his power approaching its zenith, personally selected those who would accompany the King and Queen of England. But Mary was the Dowager Queen of France. There was no precedent for determining the number of a former queen's attendants. In March 1520, Wolsey contacted Brandon. Brandon replied that Mary had again fallen ill. He apologised for his absence from recent Council sessions, explaining that Mary had sent for him from her sickbed. 'The said French Queen hath had, and yet hath, divers physicians with her for her old disease in her side, and as yet cannot be perfectly restored to her health.'

But at the prospect of another glorious occasion, Mary rallied. As Dowager Queen of France, she was Henry's trump card. During the spring she and her sister-in-law Katherine threw themselves whole-heartedly into the preparations for their visit to France. Henry, resolved to dazzle the French, gave the two queens carte blanche to order sensational finery. The meeting with Francis I would cost Henry £15,000; it would take the French ten years to pay their share of the expenses. Bishop Fisher, scandalised by the extravagance, wrote: 'Never was seen in England such excess of apparelment before.'[1] Courtiers in both countries spent vast sums, bringing their families to the brink of ruin.

The historic meeting was to take place 6 miles from Calais at the Val d'Or, the Golden Valley, on a great plain near the English-held town of Guisnes, where Henry would stay, and the French town of Ardres, where Francis would be based. Five thousand people would be transported across the Channel. Calais, England's last remaining continental possession, would be the storehouse and centre of operations. The English ambassador to Paris, Thomas Boleyn, would conduct the diplomatic negotiations. Both monarchs had entrusted the formidable logistics of the operation to the capable hands of Wolsey, who also had to rule on matters of precedence and etiquette, and resolve the numerous arguments that arose. A lesser man would have quailed before the challenge.

Henry, determined to present a show of breathtaking magnificence, unprecedented and unforgettable, dismissed Guisnes castle as inadequate; a temporary palace, the 'palace of illusions', was to be constructed from wood and canvas, designed like a banqueting house or one of the elaborate stage sets which featured in court entertainments, 328ft square, with an inner courtyard, gatehouse and battlements. Completed in less than three months, this triumph of Tudor ingenuity amazed the French with its brick foundations and real glass windows; the diamond panes were described by Fleuranges as the clearest and finest he had ever seen. An Italian observer remarked that even Leonardo da Vinci, who had died the previous year, could have created nothing finer.[2] The pièce de résistance was a banqueting hall with a ceiling of green silk studded with golden roses and carpeted with patterned taffeta. There was a King's side, a Queen's side and a suite for Wolsey, who conducted the whole operation from it, and another suite for Mary, each with spacious chambers furnished with costly tapestries, Turkey carpets, beds of estate, sideboards laden with precious plate. The whole edifice was a triumph of *trompe-l'oeil*. The pitched roof was of canvas painted to resemble slate. Pennants featuring the royal arms fluttered from flagstaffs carved with Welsh dragons, English lions, the white harts of the Angevin monarchs and the legendary Beaufort yales, deer whose antlers allegedly swivelled round on their heads.

On the lawn before the palace, beside a gilded pillar bearing a statue of Bacchus, God of Wine, a fountain 'of ancient Roman work' flowed with wine of three types, white, Malmsey and claret. An invitation in Old French was carved in the stonework, welcoming all comers to partake of this munificence: '*Faicte bonne chere quy voudra*' ('Let he who wyshes make good cheere!'). Silver drinking cups were chained to the fountain. The French were amazed that nobody attempted to steal them. Both princes kept open house throughout the proceedings. Grand marquees were erected for entertainments and banquets. A 9ft-high rampart encircled the whole camp. Leading courtiers were to be accommodated in the Castle of Guisnes, others in the 2,800 brightly coloured pavilions set up at nearby Balingham, but there was not enough accommodation. Some nobles paid local farmers to put them up on a bed-and-breakfast basis; some even had to sleep in hayricks.

The food bill came to £8,839 (£440 was spent on spices alone): 2,200 sheep, 800 calves, 1,300 chickens, 340 beeves, 26 dozen heron, 13 swans, 17 bucks, 9,000 plaice, 7,000 whiting, 700 conger eels, 4 bushels of mustard, mountains of sugar for the refined pastries that were to astound the French, gallons of cream for the King's cakes. The bill for wine and beer was £7,400.

The King's retinue would comprise 4,000 persons, including 100 peers and princes of the Church, dukes, chaplains, the entire staff of the Chapel Royal, heralds, poursuivants, 200 guards, 70 Grooms of the Chamber and 266 household officers, each attended by his own household servants.

Queen Katherine's suite numbered almost 1,200; her attendants included the disreputable Mary Boleyn, who had served Mary Rose in France in 1514, staying on at the French court in the service of Queen Claude after Mary returned to England in 1515. Francis ungallantly referred to Mary as 'my English mare'.[3] Even twenty years later, he would refer to her as 'a great whore, the most infamous of all'. Mary Boleyn had later become the mistress of Henry VIII, supplanting Bessie Blount, the mother of his son. Both parties conducted the affair with unaccustomed discretion. But in 1528 when Henry asked the Pope for dispensation to marry Anne Boleyn, he admitted that he had placed himself within the forbidden degrees of affinity by having sex with her sister. The secret was out. That Mary Boleyn had recently managed, despite her notoriety, to secure a husband in William Carey was probably thanks to King Henry's interest in her. Now Mary, a respectable married woman at last, would witness the meeting between her two old flames.

Besides personnel and provisions, there was a huge cargo to be shipped: tapestries, furnishings, equipment required for the tournaments, planned for 11–22 June, under the direction of Brandon and Admiral Bonnivet: 1,500 spears from the Tower arsenal, 1,000 Milanese swords, many valuable horses, which could only be transported in favourable weather conditions. The armourers' steel mill was brought from Greenwich for the repair of weaponry.

The French eyed all this English bustle and expense askance. There would be no prefabricated palace for Francis: the French court would occupy a town of 400 glittering tents. The French also constructed a spectacular tiltyard. Lest either King should lose face, it was agreed that neither would joust against the other. The terrain was levelled out to ensure neither side had the advantage.

The area was soon crowded with sightseers, lured by the promise of thrilling spectacles and free drink. When the tournament finally got underway, so liberally did the wine flow that Francis issued a royal proclamation forbidding access to unauthorised persons, on pain of hanging. His officers turned away 10,000 people, but not before the streets were littered with drunken ploughmen, labourers and vagabonds lying in heaps. Still the crowds poured in; the Provost Marshal of the Field appeared powerless to stop the flow.

Henry, leaving England in the hands of Norfolk and Bishop Foxe, set off, arriving at Canterbury on 25 May 1520, with Brandon, Buckingham, ten earls, five bishops, the great Cardinal, the Archbishop of Canterbury, Queen Katherine, Mary Rose, their ladies, and 3,000 horses.

But before he met Francis, Henry planned another summit meeting. The death of the Emperor Maximilian had radically altered the political balance of power in Europe: three dynamic young monarchs, power-hungry, ambitious and wily, now directed the course of history. Both Francis I, at 25, and Henry VIII, almost 28, courted the favour of Mary Rose's former betrothed, the hatchet-faced 19-year-old Habsburg Charles, the new Holy Roman Emperor. While Francis and Henry were assuring one another of mutual support and affection, behind the scenes each was manoeuvring to ingratiate himself with Charles. Henry, dismissing the fact that his daughter was already betrothed to the Dauphin, and that Charles himself was pledged to the Dauphin's sister, offered Charles the hand of the Princess Mary.

Wolsey had arranged this hasty meeting between Charles and Henry to enhance Henry's firepower in his subsequent discussions with Francis. Henry, hoping to meet Charles on English territory in France, had suggested Calais. But Charles announced that he would land at Sandwich in mid-May, on his journey from Spain to his northern dominions for his coronation at Aachen. Charles was keen to meet Henry before the latter had a chance to sign any binding contracts with Francis. But his ship was delayed by contrary winds, so he only just made it to England by 26 May, the date Henry had set as the deadline for his own departure to France. The Emperor's ships put in at Dover to a thunderous salute from the English flotilla lying in the straits of Dover. Charles strode ashore beneath a canopy of cloth of gold emblazoned with his device, the black eagle. Wolsey welcomed him and escorted him to Dover Castle, where he spent the night.

The moment he learned of the Emperor's arrival, Henry galloped off to the castle to greet him. One account claims that Henry arrived after Charles had retired for the night, and had at Henry's insistence to be roused from his bed. Another version reports that Henry reached the castle just after dawn, and the two men bumped into each other on the stairs as they hurried to greet one another. The departure of Henry's fleet was now delayed for a further five days. Henry escorted the Emperor to Canterbury, where the citizens welcomed him rapturously, having loathed the French since time immemorial.

After high mass in Canterbury Cathedral, King and Emperor knelt in prayer at the shrine of St Thomas à Becket and were shown the martyred saint's hair shirt, his battered skull and the sword that had inflicted the fatal blow, all of which sacred relics they devoutly kissed. Afterwards, on the marble staircase of Greenwich Palace, the Emperor met his aunt, Queen Katherine. Elegant in ermine-lined cloth of gold, exquisite ropes of pearls looped about her neck, Katherine, overjoyed to be united at last with her nephew, burst into tears.

To enhance the glorious spectacle with which he proposed to astonish the French, Henry had encouraged the royal ladies to devise sumptuous new wardrobes. As they processed to Canterbury Cathedral for mass, Mary Rose, walking with Katherine immediately behind the Emperor, was resplendent in cloth of silver trimmed with gold cord and studded with pearls. When Charles beheld the matchless beauty of the princess to whom he had been betrothed for six years as a boy, it was said he shed bitter tears in contemplation of the prize he had rejected.

Charles brought with him in his train another famous beauty, Queen Katherine's stepmother, Germaine de Foix, Dowager Queen of Spain. King Ferdinand had married the young widow after Isabella's death. Germaine endured the same salacious rumour-mongering as Mary Rose: people whispered that her charms had hastened the demise of an ageing husband, debilitated by his efforts to beget an heir of her. When Ferdinand died in 1516, Germaine had married the Margrave of Brandenburg. At the three-hour state banquet all three queens graced the royal table, and enjoyed 'much revelry' till daybreak. The fun was fast and furious. According to the Venetian ambassador, one young visiting gallant 'made love so heartily that he had a fainting fit' and had to be carried bodily from the chamber.[4] Mary was in great form, dancing with her brother the King and her husband Brandon, but the Emperor ungraciously refused to take the floor, although his new little proposed bride, Princess Mary, was present, in her party dress. One romantic interpretation ascribed Charles's moroseness to his being mesmerised by Mary Rose's beauty and tormented by his repudiation of her. However, marriage or romance were probably the last thing on the Emperor's mind. He was desperate for an alliance with England that would guarantee him the military assistance he knew he would soon need.

The two monarchs parted on excellent terms. Henry rode five miles with Charles, satisfied with the outcome of their talks, and now looking forward with greater confidence to his meeting with Francis. Wolsey escorted Charles to Sandwich, while Henry proceeded to Dover, embarking on 31 May with twenty-seven ships, after five vessels had swept the Channel to make sure no threats lurked anywhere. Arriving a few days later at Guisnes, they found a monument to Renaissance splendour and ingenuity, a worthy backdrop for the intended display of late medieval pageantry. The gateway of the English headquarters was guarded by four huge golden lions, above which hovered a naked winged cupid, symbolising the celebration of love and amity between the two nations. The English encampment, twenty-eight brilliantly coloured tents, gleamed in the June sun; on the Ardres side the French tented town flashed in gold and silver around the huge royal marquee, lined in blue to represent the heavens, set with gold foil stars. Here, Francis entertained Henry and Wolsey, beneath the golden statue of St Michael the Archangel, until the gales of the Picardy plain blew the tent away, occasioning much mocking laughter from the English workmen, and scathing comments about French workmanship. After this humiliating disaster Francis moved his headquarters to Ardres, borrowing money to provide new halls and pavilions and a Roman theatre.

On 7 June, to the thunder of cannon, the two monarchs, accompanied by a host of courtiers, rode out from their respective headquarters to their historic meeting on the plain. Despite the protestations of friendship, their two nations had so recently been sworn enemies that fear of an ambush lingered, and both sides came in battle array. Henry VIII, attended by the Yeomen of the Guard, glittered in cloth of gold and silver, heavily bejewelled, with a feathered black bonnet and his golden Garter collar. He had grown his beard again, and it glinted reddish gold in the scorching Picardy sun. As his great bay horse trotted out the gold bells on its harness jingled. The sun gleamed also on the apparel of Francis I, also in bejewelled cloth of gold. He sported white boots and a black cap, and was attended by his Swiss Guards.

The two young kings paused dramatically on the perimeter of the Val d'Or, and then, to a fanfare of trumpets and sackbuts, galloped alone towards each other, doffed their bonnets and embraced as brothers-in-arms, still mounted on their destriers. After dismounting, they linked arms in a physical parade of amity, and entered Francis's gold damask pavilion. Here they chatted cheerfully until evening, sipping hippocras, a spiced wine popular in Roman times.

Aware of the hostility and continuing suspicion, the young kings took care to display no hint of rivalry. Henry diplomatically insisted that their shields should be placed side by side on the tree of honour, so that neither should appear dominant. During the tournament they ran an equal number of courses, breaking an equal number of spears.

On 10 June they rode out to visit each other's queens. Henry, accompanied by Mary Rose, rode over to Ardres to pay his respects to the heavily pregnant Queen Claude. Francis, meanwhile, arrived at the English headquarters at Guisnes riding a mule. During the banquet held in his honour he was entertained by the choir of the Chapel Royal. Francis was in gallant mode. When 130 English ladies were presented to him, he insisted on kissing each one – with the exception of four or five who were 'old and not fair'.[5] Competition between the ladies was as fierce as the jousting between their lords. The English ambassador Sir Richard Wingfield, having learned that Francis's staff had been ordered to scour the country for the 'the fairest ladies and demoiselles', urged that the English ladies should be hand-picked for their looks. The French leading ladies were Francis's mother Louise, said to have invested in a 'whole emporium of cloth of gold', his sister Marguerite and his current mistress Françoise de Châteaubriant. Queen Claude was no beauty. She was, however, a pious and dutiful wife. Madame de Châteaubriant was a noted belle, but she, like everyone else, was eclipsed by Mary, who led the procession of lords and ladies to the French camp, 'scintillating in her saddle',[6] wearing a Genoese costume of white satin with a headdress and flowing veil.

Italian observers admired the wealth of gold chains worn by the English, but found the French more elegant. The Mantuan ambassador thought the English ladies badly dressed and overfond of alcohol. The English tut-tutted at the revealing gowns worn by the French ladies. Mary, however, had acquired cosmopolitan tastes during her brief time on the Continent, and wore French fashions herself to splendid effect. She invariably stole the show; always described as 'superbly arrayed',[7] she was an invaluable asset to Henry and he knew it, not only because as Dowager Queen of France she was assured of an ecstatic welcome, and knew personally all the major players in both camps, but because her extraordinary beauty illuminated every occasion. Following Mary's example, the English ladies soon threw caution to the winds and embraced the daring French fashions, by which 'what they lost in modesty they gained in comeliness'.[8]

On 11 June, the Dowager Queen of France was borne to the tiltyard in a litter of cloth of gold embroidered with fleur de lis and the late King's porcupine emblem, as well as monograms of the initials L and M interwined. The French spectators went wild, seeing their own Reine Blanche, Louis XII's bride, so exquisite, widowed so heartbreakingly young and lost to France. The three carriages that followed Mary's, draped with cloth of gold, crimson and azure, carried beautiful women, splendidly dressed. Queen Claude, wearing cloth of silver, followed, with Louise of Savoy, the King's mother, stylish in black velvet, accompanied by a large number of ladies in crimson velvet, their sleeves lined with cloth of gold. Even Queen Katherine attracted attention when she wore a Spanish headdress with her still luscious auburn hair, her remaining beauty, hanging loose over one shoulder. But for sheer crowd-pleasing charisma, Mary was without rival.

One morning she and Henry led a party of masquers into the French camp, Mary and her ladies mounted on palfreys caparisoned in white and yellow velvet. Francis went to dine with Katherine, attended by nineteen gentlemen in elaborate disguise. Outside the English head-quarters the fountain continued to gush forth fine wines: one day claret, another malmsey. During the two weeks of entertainments, feasting, jousts, dancing and 'midsummer games', the two courts vied for supremacy. Superficially, all was amicable, but tensions remained between old enemies. Francis half-jokingly misquoted Virgil's *Aeneid* to Henry, remarking 'I fear the English, even when they bring gifts'.[9]

Shrewd Venetian observers noted, 'These sovereigns are not at peace. They hate each other cordially.'[10]

Between 11 and 22 June 300 contestants competed in the tournaments organised by Brandon and Bonnivet in the great tiltyard. Only blunted swords and lances were allowed. Henry and Francis meticulously continued their charade of courtesy. When an English herald began to read out a proclamation in the old style used by English kings since they laid claim to the Kingdom of France in the fourteenth century, 'I, Henry, by the Grace of God King of England and France ...' Henry interrupted, saying, 'That I cannot be, for you are here!'[11] For the rest of the visit he would be styled 'Henry, King of England' only.

But the old rivalry between the young monarchs soon resurfaced. On 13 June, after watching a wrestling match between the Yeomen of the Guard and Francis's Bretons, Henry challenged Francis to a similar contest. He was ignominiously thrown on his back. He should have asked for a return match according to the rules of chivalry, but Francis was persuaded to refuse, by the queens and by his own courtiers, who perceived that the incident could disrupt the harmonious atmosphere. Fortunately, Henry soon regained face by scoring victory in an archery contest. Francis was determined to show Henry that no offence had been intended, so, ignoring the counsel of his lords, on 17 June, accompanied by only two gentlemen, he rode over to Guisnes at dawn, and crept into Henry's bedchamber. Henry awoke to find the King of France standing over him, offering to act as his valet, helping him on with his shirt. Henry, always delighted by diversions, was charmed by this original token of respect. 'Brother,' he exclaimed, 'you have played me the best trick ever played, and shown me the trust I should have given you. From now on, I am your prisoner.'[12] He gave Francis a priceless collar of rubies. Francis returned the honour with the gift of an even more valuable bracelet.

The last public event took place on Saturday 23 June. The sun still glared down, it was 'hotter than in St Peter's in Rome'.[13] The tiltyard had been converted into a chapel and here, at noon, Wolsey, assisted by five other cardinals and twenty bishops, celebrated a solemn mass for both courts. The choir of the Chapel Royal sang, alternating with its French equivalent, La Chapelle de la Musique du Roi, and Richard Pace gave a Latin oration on peace. During the service, a firework in the shape of a salamander, Francis's personal emblem, was accidentally set off, causing great alarm. There was another delay, the situation approaching the comical, when each king tried to allow the other to be the first to kiss the Holy Gospel. Queen Claude and Queen Katherine were not backward in showing similar tact: when the Cardinal of Bourbon offered them the Pax to kiss, they kissed each other instead.

The two kings had agreed to found and maintain a chapel to Our Lady of Peace on the site of their meeting, and after mass Wolsey laid its foundation. The solemn proceedings were concluded by a jovial banquet alfresco, a final joust and the official fireworks display. The next day the kings again visited each other's queens, and after one last feast, where the entertainment included mummers and dancing, Queen Katherine presented the prizes to the champions of the jousts. The jousts had not been an unqualified success: Brandon, who had injured his hand, felt he had underperformed, Francis had sustained a black eye, Henry had managed to kill his own horse, and one of the French contestants had lost his life.

On 25 June, after lingering and effusive farewells and the exchange of many precious gifts, including jewels, horses and a litter, the French court departed for Abbeville, while the English contingent moved to Calais, where Henry intended another diplomatic rendezvous with the Emperor Charles. Their route was lined with the comatose bodies of drunken stragglers. Henry thanked his lords for their support and, realising that many had beggared themselves to do him honour at the Field of the Cloth of Gold, gave them permission to dismiss half their suites, and bade them live 'carefully' for the rest of the summer. Most had enjoyed the occasion; few harboured regrets over the massive expenditure.

Politically, the concrete achievement of the Field of the Cloth of Gold was negligible. Despite the superficial display of friendship and cordiality, the old undercurrents of mutual suspicion and jealousy persisted. The chapel to Our Lady of Peace remained unbuilt, the splendid temporary structures were demolished, the marriage between Princess Mary and the Dauphin never took place. Within three years hostilities had once more broken out between England and France. To all intents and purposes, the event had been a costly masquerade. But Henry chose to regard it as a triumph. Many years later, around 1545, he would commission – probably for Whitehall Palace – two large commemorative paintings from artists, probably Flemish. In one painting, the King is depicted as a tiny figure embarking on the *Katherine Pleasaunce*. The other work presents a composite view of events, including Henry's arrival from Guisnes with Calais in the distance, the meeting of the two kings, feasting in a pavilion, with a tournament in the background. Above, the sky is illuminated by the firework salamander.

However, all had not been futile. The two kings had gained insights into each other's intentions and capabilities. Henry, by his show of magnificence, had enhanced his international prestige. Moreover, Henry's meeting with Francis had paved the way for his meeting with Emperor Charles, a low-key event which was, nonetheless, of much greater political significance. On 10 July, Henry and Katherine, with their reduced retinue, left Calais for Gravelines in Flanders to meet Charles V and his indomitable aunt, the Archduchess Margaret, now Regent of Austria. Mary now met face-to-face her '*chère tante*', to whom she had written when a young girl, as betrothed Princess of Castile. There had been rumours of a match between Margaret and Mary's husband, Brandon. Moreover, had the high-spirited Margaret not flatly refused to marry the ageing King Henry VII of England, she might once have become Mary's stepmother.

Returning to Calais with Charles and Margaret, Henry had intended to entertain them in a temporary banqueting hall painted with heavenly bodies, constructed 'upon the masts of a ship, like a theatre'.[14] But it was the turn of the English craftsmen to fall foul of the French gales. The pavilion was blown down, and Henry and his courtiers, in their gorgeous masquing gear, were forced to attend upon the Emperor in his lodgings instead.

Charles was a political animal, not a prancing peacock like Francis. He neither desired nor encouraged great demonstrations of sociability, and baulked at any indication that he was being manipulated. Under the expert guidance of Wolsey, who understood the Emperor's temperament, matters passed off satisfactorily. Henry was enthusiastic, the ladies were charming, Charles was agreeable. A contract of friendship was signed,

promising support in the event of war with France. The betrothal of
Princess Mary to the Dauphin was annulled, and her hand offered to her
cousin Charles, subject to the necessary papal dispensation. Charles had
broken off his engagement to numerous ladies, starting with Mary Rose.
He now showed no compunction in breaking off his betrothal to Princess
Charlotte of France.

Friendly relations with the Empire progressed, as cracks appeared in
the Anglo-French alliance. The Emperor, desperate for an ally, enticed
Henry with promises of a joint invasion of France, the partition of
conquests and the recognition of Henry as King of France. The new
Anglo-imperial union was to be sealed by the betrothal of 22-year-old
Charles to 6-year-old Mary Tudor. On 2 March 1522 Henry held more
jousts, riding a horse caparisoned in silver and the motto '*elle mon
Coeur a navera*' (she has wounded my heart). This mysterious message
may well have been dedicated to Mary Boleyn, but according to the rules
of the game of courtly love, it could have been anyone.

Two days later, the imperial envoys were guests at Wolsey's palace,
York Place, where a grand pageant was staged, featuring a green castle
occupied by ladies in white satin gowns, with their pageant names
embroidered in gold on their jewelled head gear. Mary, as Beauty, led the
dancers. Mary Boleyn was Kindness, Jane Parker, Lord Morley's daughter (later to marry George Boleyn and die on the scaffold), portrayed
Constancy, while Mary Rose's former attendant, Anne Boleyn, about
to launch her brief stellar career, represented Perseverance. Anne had
recently been recalled from the French court because of the political
situation. She had remained in France after Mary returned to England,
serving as maid-of-honour to Queen Claude. Mary had never warmed
to Anne Boleyn. She soon had greater reason than ever to distrust and
dislike her.

Mary and Brandon played a leading role in honouring the Emperor
Charles, Mary's former fiancé, entertaining him to dinner at Suffolk
Place, followed by a hunt in the park.

Mary and Emperor Charles would never meet again.

Doubts and Divorce

After 1523, although her husband's career was at its peak, Mary herself spent less time at court. When in London, the Brandons lodged and dined on the Queen's side of the Royal household. When Mary was in the country and he was alone, Brandon stayed at the 'King's house', where meals were served daily between 10 and 11 a.m, and 4 to 6 p.m. Like other members of the household, they benefited from the usual allowances for the 'King's honourable house', the weekly 'bouche' of court providing materials for heating and lighting and extra food and drink for their private consumption. The size of the allowance varied according to rank: dukes and duchesses were regarded either as having greater need of food and heating than other people, or as needing to entertain more extravagantly. In addition to their regular meals, they received two coarse grey cheat loaves of wheaten bread and three manchets (fine white bread), three gallons of ale and one pitcher of wine a day. The King could withdraw his bounty at any moment.

After the outbreak of war between Henry and Francis I in June 1543, Mary's French income ceased. Francis seized her 60,250 livres revenue and this meant further renegotiation of the Suffolks' debt to Henry VIII. Technically, Brandon was supposed to pay the King 2,000 marks a year, but by February 1521 only a small part of the total owing, £25,234 6s 9d, had been settled. In 1522, Brandon had courted the Emperor's favour and patronage during his visit to Canterbury, gaining imperial pensions for himself and his followers, but these were not sufficient to make up for the loss of Mary's French revenues.

However, lack of funds had never dampened the Brandons' spirits. They entertained the Emperor lavishly at Suffolk Place, and probably named their second daughter, Eleanor, for his sister. When the war with France broke out, Brandon took the field in command of one of the most impressive armies Henry VIII ever sent to war under a lieutenant. Great deeds were expected of Brandon. He had not seen action since 1513. This promised to be his greatest opportunity for military glory, and his greatest test. Henry first ordered him to besiege Boulogne, but his orders were changed. Instead, he was to lead a bold march over the Somme into the heart of France towards Paris, and link up with a rebel French leader, the Duke of Bourbon. But Bourbon's revolt crumbled.

Charles V had pledged that the Archduchess Margaret would support Brandon with troops and supplies. Her difficulties in meeting these commitments meant that Brandon's departure from Calais was delayed long enough for many of his troops to succumb to disease. Brandon commanded competently, but was forced to retreat because of lack of support. A freak spell of frost transformed his already disease-ridden army into a mutinous rabble. The Welsh warrior Elis Gruffydd, who would later make a career in the Calais garrison, described the calamity in his vivid *Chronicle* of November 1523:

> Some said it was too much for them to be lying there on the earth under hedges and bushes dying of cold, another said that he wanted to be home in bed with his wife ... and yet they had no reason to complain except of their own sluggishness and slovenliness. For there was no lack of food, or drink, or wood for fire or making huts, and plenty of straw to roof them and to lie on, if they only fetched it ...
>
> At last on Wednesday night there rose a noise and shouting amongst the host and especially around the tents of the duke, and some of the soldiers said they would stay there no longer, and that they would go home willy nilly the next day ... against this some of their comrades said ... that ... was no less than treason ... to this these obstinate senseless men answered that it was no worse being hanged in England than dying of cold in France. My master, Sir Robert Wingfield, heard all this noise and talking, and made me get out of my bed, where I was as snug as a small pig, to listen to the talk, and to take note of those men who were making this noise ...[1]

Next morning, the mutinous feeling had spread throughout the host; men began shouting 'Home! Home!'[2] Brandon and his captains conferred about the best course of action. The men set off to march against the freezing wind all day – one of the worst days the oldest man in the army had ever seen, though many of them were more than 60 years old.

This day ... many men on horse and on foot died from sheer cold. Others said that some had lost the use of their limbs from the force of the frost wind. And others said that they had lost the use of their water-pipes, and could not pass any water that way until they had got fire and warm water to thaw them ...[3]

In December, Brandon, defying the King's order to stay put, brought his wretched demoralised army home. Henry demanded furiously how the Anglo-Flemish alliance of two great armies, which had sworn to win him the crown of France, had dissolved into a pathetic stream of sickly scarecrows drifting back into Channel ports, but, learning of the misfortunes they had suffered, he realised that Brandon had followed his orders as best he could. The catastrophe did not diminish either his affection for Brandon or his faith in him. The campaign brought Brandon little material benefit, but his martial reputation remained undimmed.

A few months later, Brandon almost caused his monarch's death. As the chargers of the country's greatest jousters, Brandon and the King, thundered towards one another, the spectators' breathless anticipation turned into a gasp of horror. People screamed 'Hold! Hold!'[4] The King, desperate to try out his latest invention, a new harness he had designed himself, had forgotten to lower his visor. Brandon's lance was pointed at the King's exposed face. But Brandon, behind his own heavy helmet, could neither see nor hear. As he crashed into Henry, his lance struck the King on the brow under the guard of the headpiece and shattered, filling the King's headpiece with splinters. Brandon, tearing off his armour, rushed to the King, swearing that he would never run against him again.

Henry sought to calm the general consternation and Brandon's distress, assuring everyone that it was his own fault. To prove he was unhurt, he ran six more courses, to huge acclamation. The severe headaches from which the King suffered in later life may have been a direct result of this blow to the forehead.

The incident caused a panic. The King had almost been killed, leaving no son to succeed him, thus raising the spectre of a potential civil war over the succession. Many people would never accept the rule of a woman. A handful of potential claimants descended from the Plantagenets were still around. It was five years since Katherine's last pregnancy. At 38, her child-bearing years were ending. Since 1522, prompted by doubts raised by his confessor John Longland, Bishop of Wilson, the King had been pondering the validity of his marriage. Now Henry asked himself in earnest why Katherine's sons had been stillborn or died in infancy. Seeking his answer in the scriptures, he stumbled upon the passage in

Leviticus which condemned a marriage between in-laws as impure, and the penalty as childlessness. Although Pope Julius II had granted a dispensation for his marriage to Katherine, the King began to see his lack of sons as God's judgement. But the Queen was popular, and he was fond of her. Moreover, she was the Emperor's aunt. Henry knew that to put her aside would jeopardise the imperial alliance.

Christmas 1524 saw another grand tournament, originally intended as part of a great pageant, for which a massive Castle of Loyalty was built to the King's design in the tiltyard at Greenwich. The Queen was seated in the model castle when two 'ancient knights' appeared before her, begging leave to 'break spears'.[5] When Katherine praised their courage in performing feats of chivalry at their age, they threw off their masks to reveal the 33-year-old King and Brandon.

This would be Henry's last major tournament.

In February 1525, the Emperor inflicted a resounding defeat on the French at the Battle of Pavia, taking Francis prisoner. When he heard the news, Henry leapt from his bed, threw on his shirt and enquired after Richard de la Pole, the troublesome last Yorkist pretender, who had been among Francis's officers.

'The White Rose is dead in battle,' the herald replied.

'God have mercy on his soul,' Henry said piously, adding, 'All the enemies of England are gone.'[6] He told the messenger he was as welcome as the Archangel Gabriel had been to the Virgin Mary, and called for him to be plied with wine. He ordered bonfires to be lit in the streets of London and free wine to be dispensed to the citizens.

Henry's old dream of replicating the glory of Henry V and reclaiming England's lost possessions flared alive again briefly. His ambition had seen the country taxed hard to pay for futile wars. The attempt to levy an 'Amicable Grant' to enable him to lead an invasion of France in person met with a refusal, and provoked a revolt in Suffolk, which the two East Anglian Dukes, Norfolk and Suffolk, united forces to suppress. Howard and Brandon were both concerned that Wolsey and the King did not seem to appreciate the depth of feeling against the projected campaign, and together demanded a council meeting so they could make their views known to the King. The Amicable Grant was abandoned and Wolsey made peace with France. Charles V had no intention of allowing England to regain Normandy, Picardy and Brittany, and the Treaty of More, signed at Wolsey's house on 30 August 1525, made more modest arrangements.

It also made provision for both of Henry's sisters. The arrears of Mary's dower rents, some £2,000 a year, were paid for the three years when they had been interrupted by the war. Wolsey also negotiated a deal that left the Suffolks some 22,000 livres a year better off. Brandon maintained a prominent ceremonial role at court; after 1526, the strengthening of the French alliance placed him once more at the centre of foreign diplomatic affairs. In late 1525 the French ambassadors travelled to Reading to thank Mary for her part in bringing about the new rapprochement, and her husband replied on her behalf that she would do her utmost to maintain it.[7]

Mary's feelings for Francis were equivocal. He had importuned her with his attentions in her youth, but Brandon admired him. On 9 May 1526 he and Mary wrote a joint letter to Francis congratulating him on his release from captivity after the defeat at Pavia. Mary assured him that the ladies of England had been praying for his release, both those ladies who had met him and those who had only heard tell of his God-given grace and virtue. Brandon offered Francis all that a gentleman had in his power, namely, to die at his feet in his service.

Though Henry had gloated over the capture of the French King, he and his court were still in awe of French Renaissance culture, which Henry was bent on emulating. Mary Rose, still widely known as the French Queen, remained the court authority on French style, following Paris fashions, and an important patroness of French cultural innovations. In 1530, she presented her brother the King with a French *Book of Hours* illustrated with classical architecture and playful putti. She was the leader of an inner circle of younger nobility and distinguished foreigners, one of whom was probably Anne Boleyn recently returned to England. At one of Wolsey's revels in 1522, Mary Rose, Anne and six other ladies were rewarded for their part in the entertainment by the gift of the gowns they wore, of richly decorated yellow satin.

Long before her notorious relationship with the King, Anne had incautiously become romantically involved with a member of Wolsey's household, Lord Henry Percy, heir to the Earl of Northumberland. Percy would frequently 'resort for his pastime unto the Queen's chamber, and here would fall in dalliance among the Queen's maidens'. Percy was already engaged to Lady Mary Talbot, daughter of the Earl of Shrewsbury, a better match than a Boleyn. He had the effrontery to ask Wolsey if his betrothal could be broken off, earning a stern rebuke. The Cardinal, aware that the King had been Anne's sister's lover and had certainly noticed Anne, sent for Percy's father. Northumberland told his wayward son he was a 'proud, presumptuous, disdainful and very unthrift waster', dragged him back to the north and married him off to Mary Talbot forthwith.[8]

The age gap between the King and Queen was becoming increasingly obvious. Katherine had lost her youthful bloom with the years of disappointment and repeated pregnancies, while Henry was still on fire with energy and zest for life. Mary Rose's affection for the ageing Queen deepened. She helped her friend Katherine entertain Charles V's sister, the Queen of Denmark, on a royal visit in 1523; the German ambassador noted with surprise that 'La Reine Blanche' was given precedence over the Danish Queen at the dinner table.

Two years later, on 18 June 1525, Mary and Brandon were excited to be in London again when a peerage was conferred upon their second son, Henry, aged 2 (their first son, also Henry, had died at the age of 6): '... the lorde Henry Brandon, sonne to the duke of Suffolke and the Frenche Quene the kynges sister, a childe of twoo yere old, was greated Erle of Lincolne ...';[9] '...The King's nephew, Henry [...] was so young that Sir John Vere was appointed to carry him ...'[10] Several other young boys were honoured at the investiture at the new Bridewell Palace on 18 June. But the event was overshadowed by the elevation to the Earldom of Nottingham and the Dukedom of Richmond and Somerset of Henry Fitzroy, the King's 6-year-old natural son by the enchanting Bessie Blount, now safely married off to Gilbert Tailboys, the son of Lord Kyme, 'an lunatic'[11] kept in the custody of the Duke of Norfolk. In a hot, stifling room packed with courtiers, Henry Fitzroy entered to a fanfare, knelt before his father and was robed in the mantle of crimson and blue, sword, cap of estate and coronet of a duke, as the patent of creation was read out. He then took his place on the dais beside his father the King, taking precedence over every other peer in the room.

Katherine concealed her fury, but she was bitterly offended by the insult to her own daughter and the threat to Princess Mary's position. England had no Salic law. Henry had shown no qualms about leaving Katherine as Regent when he marched off to fight the French. Katherine had exhorted the troops as her mother, the heroic Queen Isabella, had done, rejoicing in her title of 'King' of Castile. She distrusted Wolsey, blaming him for the advancement of Henry Fitzroy. In June 1525, his spies in the Queen's household informed Wolsey that three of Katherine's Spanish ladies were encouraging her to protest. The Cardinal had them dismissed, and when Katherine urged Henry to rescind the order, he refused. It was becoming apparent to Katherine that she no longer held much sway with her husband. She felt increasingly isolated. The Emperor had also jilted her daughter, deciding that the beautiful Isabella of Portugal with her million-pound dowry was a better bet. Katherine's dreams of a Spanish marriage for Mary seemed unlikely to be fulfilled. Mary Rose sympathised, but both she and Brandon kept their feelings to themselves. Their own son, now Earl of Lincoln, remained a potential heir to the throne.

In 1526, Mary was principal guest at the spectacular banquet at Greenwich in honour of the French and Italian ambassadors. The Queen, meanwhile, was comforted by the presence of her favourite lady-in-waiting, Maria de Salinas, Lady Willoughby de Eresby, who had returned to Katherine's service after the death of her husband in October. Lord Willoughby's death meant that an eminently suitable heiress became available, the ideal match for young Henry, Earl of Lincoln. Brandon had known the now-widowed baroness since at least 1511, when she stood godmother to his daughter Mary. He had had further dealings with her over the years, and now, supported by Wolsey, quickly put in a bid in November 1527 for the wardship of her daughter Catherine. That Christmas and every following Christmas for eight years he was to pay 500 marks until he had paid off the debt of 4,000 marks. The price was high, but it would prove a worthwhile investment for the future.

In 1527, Mary stayed for more than a month in the peaceful surroundings of Butley Priory, visiting friends, and distributing largesse to the monks. Brandon joined her briefly, but could spare little time to hunt and picnic with Mary: his responsibilities in the counties had grown, and now, when in the country, he was very much on business, rushing from one appointment to the next, meeting his chief supporters, attending sessions, then speeding back to London for official receptions.[12] In the late 1520s, after the death of Richard de la Pole at Pavia, and the removal of the Yorkist threat, Brandon's chief role in the south east was to quell popular unrest, in co-operation with the Duke of Norfolk.

In 1527, Mary was in London attending the celebrations of yet another betrothal for the King's only legitimate child. Having been rejected by the Emperor Charles, Princess Mary was now being wooed by that notorious womaniser Francis I. Widowed for less than a year, Francis was exploring every available matrimonial avenue, although he was most interested in an alliance with the Empire. Reports stated that he was so keen to cement his relationship with Charles V that he was willing to propose to any woman even if she were aged 100, even to Caesar's mule. Charles's sister Eleanor, Dowager Queen of Portugal, was available. Her brother ordered her to 'cast off her widow's weeds'. Eleanor obeyed, and even began somewhat prematurely calling herself the Queen of France, although Francis made no secret that he found her unattractive. Francis swore as a monarch and a gentleman to keep the troth, and at the same time swore to the English that he was free of all ties and longed for nothing more earnestly than to wed the young Princess Mary, being aware of her 'manifold virtues and other gay qualities'.

Wolsey, aware of these double negotiations, pointed out that Madame Eleanor, at 30, was too old for Francis, and lacked the malleable good nature and humility possessed by 'my lady Princess'. The monarch, Wolsey cajoled, deserved a lady of more tender years and nature, of better education, beauty and other virtues. If she was not to be the King's bride, perhaps Mary would suit his second son, the Duke of Orléans. At the end of February 1527 an embassy arrived from Paris to discuss a Treaty of Eternal Peace, to be sealed by the marriage of the Princess Mary to Orléans. If Henry continued to lack a male heir, Orléans would one day rule England as Mary's consort. Not ideal, but a provisional solution. After much feasting and revelry, the treaty of betrothal was signed at the end of April 1527. Francis offered a bride price of an annual tribute of salt, 2 million crowns and a personal pension to Henry of 50,000 gold crowns.

The only fly in the ointment was a throwaway remark made at Bridewell, questioning the validity of the King's marriage and therefore the legitimacy of the Princess Mary.

At the time, Henry dismissed it, but he would remember it later, when he had decided to discard Mary's mother in favour of his new love, with whom he had become obsessed, the Lady Anne Boleyn.

At the same time as conducting negotiations with France, Henry was eagerly planning yet another war, this time against the Low Countries. Brandon, Wolsey, Francis I and Henry discussed strategy. Brandon was commanded to buy armour. He was the French King's choice for the task of attacking the Netherlands with 10,000 English troops in 1528, if the Emperor refused to return the French princes held hostage for their father's humiliating treaty of 1526. Brandon's importance increased as he and Wolsey prepared for war. Troops were mustered in London, word was sent to prepare Guisnes, and the co-operation between Wolsey and Brandon was closer than ever. However, in June 1528 economic concerns – disruptions to the cloth trade and the fishing industry – forced a truce with the Low Countries; Brandon's captains disbanded their troops.

Mary Rose and Queen Katherine sat side by side watching on 5 May after mass when the French envoys were welcomed to the King's new banqueting house at Greenwich; in this splendid new construction, the hand of Holbein was evident in much of the sumptuous decoration. Next day there was a tournament, a recital, a banquet and masques. In one of these the King and his daughter participated. As they danced, the proud father could not resist pulling off her netted caul and letting her 'profusion of silver tresses' tumble cascading about her shoulders for the admiration of the French envoys. After the masque the dancing continued till dawn. Henry, who had injured his foot playing tennis, was wearing black velvet slippers, and every courtier did the same, so that he would not be made to feel conspicuous on the dance floor.

The revels were rudely interrupted by terrible news. Mercenaries in the Emperor's armies, exasperated by lack of pay, had run amok and sacked Rome. The Pope had barely escaped with his life, and was now a prisoner. The French envoys departed quietly.

That summer, the whisper that the King's marriage was unlawful began in the taverns of London. When Henry got wind of it he summoned the Mayor of London, Sir Thomas Seymour, and 'charged him to see people should cease this rumour upon pain of the king's high displeasure'.[13] Henry had confided his doubts about his marriage to Katherine to Wolsey. As a preliminary to divorce, Wolsey and Archbishop Warham had convened a secret ecclesiastical court at Westminster on 17 May 1527, at which Henry was cited for living in sin with his brother's widow. This would allow the original papal dispensation of 1503 to be further examined by experts in canon law. This was the first step. Henry was furious that news of it had leaked out to the court.

He had been toying with idea of making his son Henry Fitzroy King of Ireland, to make him a more acceptable match for Charles V's niece, Maria of Portugal. Katherine protested, fearing this might be a move towards Henry's naming the boy his heir.

Worse was to follow: on 22 June, the King marched into Katherine's chamber and announced that after 18 years their marriage was over. He had asked the Pope for an annulment. He himself would receive absolution for committing adultery through ignorance, Katherine could spend her remaining years in a nunnery, leaving Henry free to marry Anne Boleyn and sire a male heir.

Katherine, distraught, threw herself on the advice of Mendoza, the Spanish ambassador, and the aid of her nephew, the Emperor Charles.

Henry and Wolsey realised that the Pope, currently the Emperor's prisoner, would be unlikely to antagonise his captor by annulling the marriage of his aunt. In July, therefore, Wolsey left for France with great pomp. When his men were seen loading huge chests at Dover, reputedly containing £240,000 of the King's money, intended as bribes, people's suspicions were aroused. Officially, Wolsey was on Church business, bound to attend a convention of cardinals at Avignon, and to solicit Francis's support for the restoration of Pope Clement. But he also intended to conduct private discussions with Francis about a possible marriage between Henry and the French King's sister-in-law, Madame Renée. Meanwhile, the plan to have Henry's sister Margaret's son, James V of Scotland, declared his heir was dropped; Mary Rose's son, Henry, Earl of Lincoln, would be second in line to the throne – after the son Henry hoped to beget with Anne.

There was sufficient genuine doubt about the validity of Henry's marriage to Katherine for the theological debate to occupy the minds of European scholars. The Pope issued a bull in 1527 granting the King a dispensation to remarry when he was free to do so. Anne Boleyn's relationship with Percy had to be clarified. There was also paperwork, left incomplete when Brandon married Mary Rose, to be cleared up. Pope Clement VII, who had fled for his life from the rioting imperial troops, first took refuge in the Castel Sant'Angelo and later in Orvieto. Here on 12 May 1528 he signed the bull which recognised the legitimacy of the Brandons' three children, the Earl of Lincoln and the Ladies Frances and Eleanor Brandon.

One of the mysteries in the story of Mary Rose and Charles Brandon is why either Brandon or his lawyers never addressed the matter of Brandon's messy matrimonial status in 1516. In 1507, Brandon had obtained a dispensation to allow him to marry Margaret Mortimer, thus invalidating his previous contract with Anne Browne, and bastardising his elder daughter. At the time of his marriage to Mary Rose, Brandon required another dispensation to repudiate Dame Margaret. A lawsuit brought by Margaret's daughter by another marriage, attempting to gain possession of her mother's properties, brought the oversight to Brandon's notice. Margaret, bewildered by the lawyers' jargon, appealed to Brandon for help, thus alerting everyone to the fact that he was bigamously married to Mary Rose, and that in spite of the splendid wedding ceremony Henry had arranged for the couple at Greenwich, their children, designated heirs to the throne, were illegitimate. Perhaps, in the haste and emotion of his secret marriage to Mary, Brandon simply forgot to sort things out, or possibly he felt overwhelmed by the intricacies of canon law and felt unable to proceed until he had the King's support. Now Henry, perceiving parallels between his own case and Brandon's, supported him, encouraged by the fact that the Pope had granted a divorce to his sister Queen Margaret of Scotland on even flimsier grounds.

Wolsey fixed things for Brandon with his usual efficiency. He promptly sought a bull confirming that the dispensation to marry Margaret Mortimer had been founded on error. Lady Margaret had since died, so the issue was concluded as far as the Church was concerned. The Orvieto bull found that the dispensation to marry Dame Margaret had not been viable. This legalised Brandon's subsequent marriage to Anne Browne, who thus became his only previous legal spouse. Anne Browne was safely dead before Brandon married Mary. The bull was perfect: decisive in threatening with ecclesiastical sanctions anyone who challenged it, and at the same time suitably vague about two dubious points, the consanguinity which invalidated the Mortimer marriage, and the dates of birth of Brandon's two daughters by Anne Browne. It set the record straight in more ways than one: it confirmed the legitimacy of Anne Brandon, his elder daughter by Anne Browne; by March 1525, Anne had become the bride of Lord Powis. The marriage had been planned long before, and Brandon had contributed the £1,000 dowry. With a few strokes of the papal pen, all four of Brandon's children were rendered legitimate. The most important effect of this was to confirm his son Henry, Earl of Lincoln, in the line of succession.

Brandon's second daughter by Anne Browne, Mary, married Thomas, son and heir of Edward Stanley, Lord Monteagle. In youth, Thomas had been raised in Wolsey's household, where he had acquired a taste for luxury. He was heir to a major fortune and his wardship had been purchased by Lord Darcy and Sir John Hussey, on the understanding that he would marry Hussey's daughter. But before the summer of 1527 Brandon managed to secure the young man's wardship and within a year he married Mary Brandon. If Brandon congratulated himself on a dazzling match and the birth of a grandchild which followed, he would have cause to regret the match. Monteagle was thrilled to come into his inheritance in summer 1528, but he was soon running up vast debts which his father-in-law would eventually have to settle. His creditors included the royal goldsmith and the royal shoemaker.

In May 1528 the successful conclusion of the Suffolks' case encouraged the King to look for success in his own, but it also increased his sense of frustration that matters were not progressing faster. Wolsey, facing the greatest test of his career, was exerting all his powers of diplomacy and his skill in ecclesiastical law and politics to secure a papal annulment of the King's marriage to Katherine, but progress was slow. Frustrated, Henry now began to doubt Wolsey's commitment.

Throughout that summer while the sweating sickness once more ravaged the country, the court sought refuge in less dangerous areas. Henry and Katherine went on progress to several religious houses but the tension between them made their sojourn less cheerful than the Brandons' pleasant holiday at Butley Priory. They were relaxing, enjoying the autumn sunshine under the oaks of Sholgrove Wood after an excellent morning's hunting, when suddenly their idyll was shattered. A messenger burst in upon the happy scene, summoning Brandon to court to welcome the papal legate.

Mary's mood changed from one of happiness to deep foreboding. Throughout the difficult summer Mary, who had known and loved Katherine since childhood, had listened sympathetically to the Queen's increasingly despairing confidences. She was appalled by the thought of a royal divorce, and broke out into bitter lamentations. Katherine had stayed with the Brandons after making a pilgrimage to Walsingham after the birth of the Princess Mary. Mary Rose had commiserated with her sister-in-law's difficult births and her bitter disappointments. She was godmother to Princess Mary, she understood and sympathised with Katherine's anger over the elevation of Henry Fitzroy in 1525.

From now on, precedence over Katherine of Aragon, Queen of England, and Mary Rose, Dowager Queen of France, would go to Anne Boleyn. When Wolsey returned on 17 September from his Embassy to France, he realised with a horrible shock that he had lost ground. His monopoly on power had been gradually eroded.

That Christmas, the Brandons played their usual leading role in the revels and celebrations. Katherine went to Richmond at the beginning of December, and when she returned, after the season of misrule, she found Anne Boleyn comfortably installed in a suite of rooms in the royal palace. Katherine struggled for composure, but she was grim-faced, 'made no joy of nothing, her mind was so troubled'.[14] Katherine's private life would become common property, to be picked over salaciously and lewdly gossiped about. The King was hell-bent on marrying Anne Boleyn.

Brandon kept quiet and did as his King bade him. But he would find many of the duties he would be called upon to perform over the coming months distasteful. The Imperial Minister, Chapuys, had no doubt where the Suffolks' sympathies lay.

'Suffolk and his wife, if they dared, would offer all possible resistance to the marriage,' he wrote to the Emperor.[15]

The Great Whore

During the early months of 1529, the legates prepared for the hearing of the King's nullity suit. The Great Matter polarised opinion among the elite, leading to a vicious power struggle. By 1528, three distinct factions had emerged: those who supported Wolsey and the King; the aristocratic conservatives, who discreetly supported the Queen and hoped to break Wolsey's iron grip on power; and the Boleyns' supporters. Through Anne Boleyn's influence, Wolsey's power was declining. Wolsey had left no stone unturned in his efforts to ensure that the King's case was watertight. When the legatine court opened on 31 May in the Great Hall of the Priory of Blackfriars, he was confident of a happy outcome.

After the Christmas celebrations at Greenwich, Mary Rose had slipped quietly back to her peaceful country estate, and the company of her own children and her stepdaughter Mary Brandon, soon to wed. Until Henry had begotten a living legitimate male heir, little Henry Brandon, Earl of Lincoln, remained high in the line of succession. Mary Rose had two daughters of her own and one stepdaughter to be matched and married, a large household to run, charitable enterprises to be fostered. Westhorpe had been enhanced with a grand new wing, surmounted by battlements and decorated with terracotta figures, costing £12,000, a sum mainly derived from Mary's French incomes. In East Anglia, Mary was still revered as the French Queen. At the summer fair at Butley Abbey she held state in a cloth of gold pavilion. At court, she had taken precedence over every lady but the Queen. Although Mary loved court life and the exhilaration of London, she welcomed the opportunity to retreat from a debate she found repugnant. In the country, she did not have to suffer the indignity of finding herself outranked by the woman now generally nicknamed 'the Concubine' or 'the Great Whore'.

Brandon was dispatched on an embassy to France to canvas Francis I's support for Henry's planned marriage to Anne Boleyn. Although an unattractive mission, the trip provided a welcome escape: it meant that, even though he had been among Prince Arthur's attendants who witnessed hearing the young bridegroom's boasts the morning after his wedding, Brandon would be spared having to testify against Katherine in June.

The case aroused huge public interest. No royal couple had ever been summoned to appear before a court, or to subject their private lives to public scrutiny. Eyes were popping when the Queen swept into the chamber, scorning the chair designated for her. She fell on her knees before the King, proclaiming loudly that she had been a true wife to him and had come to him as a virgin. She rose, curtseyed deeply and left the court as swiftly as she had appeared, disregarding the shouts urging her to return.

There followed days of depositions and heated and unsavoury debate. Much of the evidence focused on whether Prince Arthur had effectively consummated his marriage with Katherine. Several noblemen boasted that they themselves had been fully capable of performing the sex act at Arthur's age. The King maintained that Katherine's unsuccessful pregnancies were God's punishment for their incestuous marriage. Katherine repeated that Arthur had never 'carnally known her'. Doña Elvira had spoken true when she insisted that her princess had emerged from her bridal chamber each morning still a virgin.

But the courtiers had watched the young couple go off to bed each night, with the usual lewd nudges, and the squires of the bedchamber, now middle-aged men but then lusty young blades in their prime, had sniggered knowingly when they heard young Prince Arthur's bragging in the morning.

The Pope's representative, Cardinal Lorenzo Campeggio, listened impassively. Finally, on 23 July, he announced that he was referring the whole matter to Rome, as he had been secretly instructed to do by the Pope. A horrified silence greeted his announcement. As the King strode out in a fury, Brandon, purple with rage, thumped his fist on the table and yelled, 'By the Mass, now I see that the old saw is true, that never cardinal or legate did good in England!'

Wolsey, aghast, conscious that he faced ruin, replied with great dignity: 'Of all the men in this realm, ye have least cause to dispraise or be offended with cardinals. For if I, a simple cardinal, had not been, ye should have at this present no head upon your shoulders!'

This was a sharp reminder that he had saved the Suffolks over their secret marriage in Paris. He advised Brandon to behave himself and hold his peace, 'for ye know best what friendship ye have received at my hands, the which yet I never revealed, to no person alive before now, neither to my glory, nor to your dishonour'.[1]

Henry had already stormed from the room. Brandon followed in silence.

Brandon's outburst against Wolsey may well have been provoked by two characteristically high-handed actions of the Cardinal's: the first was the 'Amicable Grant', the forced loan of 1525 levied on property and goods to enable Henry to finance yet another military campaign. Brandon had resented having to impose the levy and then endure obloquy for an unpopular policy not of his devising. Open resistance had obliged the use of force and soured relationships.

Second, Brandon's circle had suffered for Wolsey's determination to leave a legacy of educational memorials. His desire to found a college at Oxford and a preparatory school for it in his native Ipswich had entailed the seizure of land in the area, including three valuable properties belonging to the Brandons: Snape Priory in Suffolk and the manors of Sayes Court and Bickling in Kent. The Brandons, now realising that Wolsey's assistance in securing Mary's French revenues had not been free of self-interest, had reminded him that, without Brandon's efforts and his cordial relationship with Francis, negotiations with France would be much more precarious.

Throughout August and September, no one moved against Wolsey; there remained a faint hope that he would by some miracle succeed in outmanoeuvring the alliance of Pope, Emperor and Queen of England.

After his return from France, Brandon's usually robust health suffered a setback. Enforced rest allowed him to spend part of the summer in East Anglia with Mary and their family. Now that their daughters were of marriageable age, they took care to have Brandon's own divorce papers notarially attested before witnesses. The bull, signed the previous year at Orvieto by Pope Clement VII, was presented to the Bishop of Norwich on 20 August. Now unquestionably legitimate, Mary's daughters, Frances and Eleanor, were extremely desirable brides on the aristocratic marriage market. In 1530, a marriage was discussed between Frances and the Norfolks' eldest son, Henry Howard, Earl of Surrey. It seemed the ideal arrangement, in view of the proximity of their estates. At this point the rivalry between the two dukes was in abeyance and their co-operation in council was relatively amicable. But although 13-year-old Frances was the King's niece, in Norfolk's eyes her royal birth was insufficient to compensate for her meagre dowry.

Brandon returned to court in the autumn to find Wolsey's enemies in full cry. Anti-clerical feeling was running high. Against his own inclinations, Brandon found himself drawn into the increasing circle of Boleyn supporters. Wolsey's fall was sudden and dramatic. On 6 October he chaired the Council meeting. On 9 October, he was charged in the court of the King's Bench with the offence of praemunire: in allowing the legatine court to be set up he had broken the law of England by introducing an illegal foreign body into the land.[2] Wolsey knew his enemies had triumphed. He made no attempt to refute the charges. On 19 October, Norfolk and Suffolk called on him formally to remove the seals of office. Du Bellay wrote:

> Wolsey has been put out of his house and all his goods taken into the King's hands. Beside the robberies of which they charge him between Christian Princes, they accuse him of so many other things that he is quite undone. The Duke of Norfolk is made chief of the council, Suffolk acting in his absence, and at the head of all, Mademoiselle Anne.[3]

The great Cardinal was sent to a modest dwelling in Esher, and later in the autumn retired to his see of York. The moment he left York Place, Henry and Anne Boleyn, aware that Wolsey had ordered his officers to conduct an inventory of his goods, hurried over to check out the spoils they had won. The word on the street was that Wolsey would be sent to the Tower. Agog, the good citizens of London clustered at the riverside to witness the great man's arrest. A thousand craft were said to be scouring the river, but Wolsey foiled pursuit by embarking on his barge from his own private steps, surrounded by his own attendants. He sailed to Putney, where he had arranged to be met with horses to transport him to Surrey.

Wolsey was banished. Anne's star had risen; Henry was lavishing priceless gifts in her. On 9 December 1529, at the banquet held to celebrate her father's elevation to an earldom, Anne, ablaze with jewels, occupied the seat of honour next to the King. She took precedence over Mary Rose, who, as Dowager Queen of France, had the right to be treated as a queen. Mary Rose forbore to comment but no doubt she was infuriated by the interloper's presumption, both on her own account and on behalf of her friend Queen Katherine.

Suddenly, in November 1530, the Earl of Northumberland – the former Lord Henry Percy whose affair with Anne Boleyn had been curtailed by Wolsey's intervention – appeared at Cawood and arrested Wolsey for high treason in the King's name. Wolsey travelled south with his captors. He knew he faced the block. At Leicester Abbey, where the company were to spend the night, Wolsey collapsed and died. His recorded last words:

'If I had served God as diligently as I have done the King, He would not have given me over in my grey hairs.'[4]

When the news of Wolsey's death reached London, a troop of players funded by Anne Boleyn's father staged a distasteful comedy 'of the descent of the Cardinal into Hell'. Norfolk, Anne Boleyn's uncle, ordered the text to be published, treating it as a huge jest.

Privately, the King registered the magnitude of his loss, sighing: 'Every day I miss the Cardinal of York.' He had good reason for his regret. For the next two years, he found ruling England alone a heavier burden than he had imagined possible. Initially, he tried to blame Wolsey for leaving affairs in a mess. But it soon became clear just how many and how diverse were the tasks that had been shouldered by the Cardinal, and how brilliantly he had performed them.

Wolsey's fall was a political victory in which Brandon had played no significant part. He had never actively joined the conspiracy against a minister who had never really harmed him and who, in respect of the secret marriage to Mary Rose, had shown him vital support. But he shared in the spoils: Wolsey's prize mules came to his stables, Wolsey's kitchen clerk entered his service and the manor of Sayes Court in Deptford was returned to him. The office of President of the Council was revived for him and for Norfolk, with whom he shared it. Suffolk had also been Henry's first choice as Lord Chancellor of England, but a jealous Norfolk opposed the appointment, protesting that Brandon was already too powerful: he objected to the Seal being given into 'such high hands'. Brandon himself may not have wished for such a responsibility. He had a realistic view of his own abilities, and knew his skills and interests lay elsewhere. In consequence, the post went to an initially reluctant Thomas More, who recognised that his views regarding the Great Matter differed from the King's, and anticipated the inevitable clash.

Meanwhile the divorce trial proceeded seamlessly. Eager to curry favour with the King, most people fell into line and spouted prearranged testimony. Brandon, who had always shared Mary's respect and affection for the Queen, was outwardly courteous to Anne, suppressing his personal feelings out of loyalty to the King. It was for that unwavering loyalty that Henry so valued him. On the surface, their friendship remained unchanged. They continued to exchange gifts. Brandon gave the King greyhounds and a gold-bound book containing a clock. Henry visited Ewelme in 1531, 1532 and 1535, and the two men continued to play tennis and gamble together, and listen to Mary Rose's sackbut players. When members of the Privy Council urged the King to seek reconciliation with Charles V, Henry snarled at them all except for Brandon.

But their relationship was complicated. The disinheritance of Princess Mary, which would eventually be followed by that of the Princess Elizabeth, the daughter whom Anne Boleyn would bear the king, reinforced the claim to the throne of the Brandon children. Their friendship with Katherine of Aragon was also problematic. Chapuys reported that the Brandons secretly deplored the divorce. At least one contemporary attributed Mary Rose's early death to her grief over the treatment of her friend Katherine. Lady Willoughby, the Earl of Lincoln's prospective mother-in-law, Katherine's former lady-in-waiting Maria de Salinas, remained devoted, rushing to Katherine's side when she lay on her deathbed. Maria's own daughter, Catherine, was second mourner at the ex-Queen's funeral in February 1536. The first mourner was the Brandons' younger daughter, Eleanor.

Brandon deplored the repeated missions to humiliate Katherine; so impressed was he by her dignity in May 1531 that he attempted to persuade the King to change his behaviour. Norfolk, Suffolk and thirty councillors held a conference with the Queen at Greenwich. Katherine insisted that she was Henry's lawful wife and that the case must be heard in Rome. Norfolk told the King what he wanted to hear, but Brandon told Henry that, although the Queen was ready to obey him in all things, she recognised two higher authorities. Henry was about to explode; he demanded who these two authorities were, thinking them to be the Pope and the Emperor. Brandon said bluntly: God and her conscience. Chapuys, relating the incident to Charles V, said Henry did not respond. 'Suffolk and his wife,' the ambassador added, 'if they dared, would offer all possible resistance to his marriage.' Two days previously he had heard Brandon and the Treasurer saying, 'The time was come when all the world should strive to dismount the King from his folly.'[5]

As time passed, the antagonism between Norfolk and Suffolk increased. They clashed both in council and back on their own turf over local issues. Their henchmen began to form bands. In April 1532 matters came to a head. Anne was now dominant at court, sharp-tongued, flashing her black eyes and flaunting her jewels. Henry planned to take his beloved to France to meet Francis I, and had asked the Queen to hand over her jewels. Katherine indignantly declared that she would not give up what was rightfully hers to adorn 'a person who is a reproach to Christendom and is bringing scandal and disgrace upon the King'.[6] But Katherine was forced to submit. Most of the jewels, including four bracelets with rubies and diamonds, were confiscated and reset for Anne.

Relations between Brandon and the arrogant Boleyns were strained. Anne was bitterly hostile to Brandon. In July 1531, she went to the lengths of smearing his name with charges of incest with his own daughter.

In April 1532, at last, Mary Rose gave rein to her feelings.[7] Up in London on business concerning her dowry, she openly criticised Anne. The King's sister's insults were gleefully repeated, first at court and then bandied about in taverns by the followers of the two great dukes, throwing the court into an uproar, and resulting in murder. One of Norfolk's henchmen, with a band of twenty heavies, goaded a group of Suffolk's supporters until violence broke out in Westminster Abbey. Sir William Pennington, one of Suffolk's gentlemen, sought sanctuary in the traditional way by throwing himself before the high altar. He was pursued and brutally cut down by Norfolk's people in the aisle. Brandon, furious, rushed to the Abbey 'to remove the assailants by force'.[8] The King sent Thomas Cromwell after him, 'for the turmoil displeased him'. Cromwell, Wolsey's former servant, was a self-made man of humble origins who was to rank among the greatest statesmen and politicians of the Tudor age. The King was coming to rely upon him increasingly.

The Venetian ambassador Capello reported of the fatal brawl: 'It was owing to opprobrious language uttered against Madame Anne by his Majesty's sister, the Duchess of Suffolk, Queen Dowager of France. The affair of the divorce becomes daily more difficult.'[9]

The Brandons, disgusted, retired to their estates, but their retainers were still spoiling for a fight and the King and Thomas Cromwell had to intervene to prevent further outbreaks of violence. Shortly afterwards, Henry himself called on Brandon. It took all his powers of persuasion to convince Brandon to return to court. The murderers, Norfolk's retainers Richard Southwell and his brother, were pardoned after paying a £1,000 fine.

Anne continued to ride roughshod over everyone. Hell-bent on appropriating every privilege of queenship, she ordered her Chamberlain to seize the Queen's barge, repaint it in her colours of blue and purple, burn off its coat of arms and replace it with her own. For her visit to France, she ordered stacks of gowns, furs and nightgowns. Unfortunately, it appeared that no royal lady at the French court was willing to receive her. To Henry's disgust, it was suggested that Francis's current mistress, the Duchess of Vendôme, should do the honours. In the face of this unspeakable insult, Henry decided that Anne would remain in Calais while he travelled on to meet Francis.

There was a holiday air on 7 October when Henry and Anne left Greenwich with a 2,000-strong retinue, including the King's bastard Richmond, the Duke of Norfolk and an unenthusiastic Brandon. Mary Rose had flatly refused to participate in the charade. Even the deliberate snubbing by King Francis's sister, Marguerite d'Angoulême, and his second wife, Queen Eleanor, did not set a damper on the festive air of the excursion. More conservative members of court deplored the unedifying spectacle of the King of England setting off to France accompanied by his bastard and by the woman referred to by London commoners and Marguerite d'Angoulême alike as 'the King's Whore'.

There was speculation among the courtiers whether the King would follow Mary Rose's example sixteen years earlier and simply wed secretly in France, returning to England to present the world with a fait accompli and, if this happened, what the consequences of such a rash action would be for them all.

In April 1533, Brandon was given the bitter task of informing Katherine that she was no longer queen. In December he was commanded to dismiss some of her attendants and move her into an insalubrious residence at Somersham. Katherine locked herself in her room. Lady Willoughby later told Chapuys that Brandon had been to confession and communion before he could man himself up to embark on this distressing mission, and had wished some accident might befall him to relieve him of the odious duty. His motto *'Loyaulte me oblige'*, by which he had conducted his life, had never been so hard to live up to.

The Greys

In the early summer of 1533, Lady Frances Brandon, the slim, good-looking 16-year-old daughter of a glamorous couple, starred in one of the most sumptuous weddings London had ever seen. The wedding at Suffolk Place was attended by her uncle, the King of England; to everyone's relief, his new Queen, Anne Boleyn, conscious of the hostility of the bride's mother, did not impose her presence on the festivities. Brandon shrugged off his perpetual indebtedness and splashed out £1,666 on the celebrations. Mary Rose, despite her poor health and her anxiety about her sickly son, cast care aside and shared this last joyous occasion.

Three years earlier, Frances had been ignominiously rejected as a bride by the ambitious Norfolks, unimpressed by her meagre dowry – Brandon's finances having been depleted by the demands of Lord Monteagle, the feckless husband of Frances's stepsister Mary Brandon.

This new match delighted her parents. Her bridegroom, Henry 'Harry' Grey, Marquis of Dorset, whose father the 2nd Marquis had died in October 1530, was six months older than Frances, 'young, lusty, well-learned and a great wit'.[1] Brandon had successfully negotiated the marriage with Harry's mother, the Dowager Marchioness. Dorset's royal connections made him a suitable match for the King's niece: his grandfather the 1st Marquis was the son of Elizabeth Woodville, and therefore the half-brother of Henry VIII's grandmother, Elizabeth of York. The Brandons, who once basked in the King's favour, had felt less welcome at court since the King's marriage to Lady Anne. Mary Rose made no secret of her dislike of Anne, about whom she made disparaging remarks. Their loathing was mutual. Anne retaliated by spreading slanders about Brandon. Frances's marriage to Dorset opened up avenues promising a possible return to the royal favour.

Dorset's father, Thomas Grey, had, like Brandon, earned the King's approval in the lists. He served with Brandon in the French war of 1513, and led the English team in the Parisian tournament celebrating Mary Rose's marriage to King Louis. In 1529 he had borne witness for the King in his efforts to secure an annulment of his marriage to Queen Katherine. In gratitude, Henry VIII created Harry Grey a Knight of the Bath at Anne's coronation. Self-willed, ambitious and successful, Harry had exhibited a rebellious streak since boyhood. He had been previously betrothed to the Earl of Arundel's daughter but had jilted her, buying himself free of the engagement.

The Brandons' younger daughter, Eleanor, had just become betrothed to Henry, Lord Clifford, eldest son of the Earl of Cumberland. When Frances left for her new home, Bradgate in Leicestershire, Brandon, as Earl Marshal, was obliged to stay in London. Mary Rose, accompanied by Eleanor, set out on the slow journey home. She had mustered her last shreds of energy to grace Frances's glittering wedding. She would never see London again. Brandon managed a brief visit to her at Westhorpe mid-May, but had to return to London to finalise the arrangements for Anne's coronation, scheduled for 1 June. Brandon, appointed High Constable of England specifically for this occasion, stage-managed the great triumph of the King's 'goggle-eyed whore'. Resplendent in pearl-encrusted doublet and robes of crimson velvet, mounted on a destrier similarly bedecked, Brandon supervised the whole proceedings, from the new Queen's entry into the Tower, her procession through London and the banquet for 800 guests in Westminster Hall.

Despite the pomp, Anne's reception by the people of London infuriated her. Many regarded her as an adulterous interloper who had ousted the rightful Queen Katherine. Few doffed their caps or cried 'God save the Queen!' Anne's fool yelled at them 'I think you all have scurvy heads, and dare not uncover!'[2] Undeterred by Anne's grim expression, at the sight of the royal couple's entwined initials, some wits burst out laughing, shouting 'HA! HA!'

In the midst of the hullabaloo Brandon knew in his heart that his wife was dying. He managed a flying visit to her bedside after the coronation, bearing a conciliatory message from the King, healing the rift between brother and sister. On 25 June, Mary died. She was 37. Exhausted, Brandon hastened from court back to Westhorpe. It was not the custom for a husband to attend his wife's funeral, so, after paying his respects, Brandon returned to court.

Mary's body was embalmed and laid in a lead coffin. In the sixteenth century, the funerals of the great exuded pageantry and symbolism.

Tradition demanded that the splendour of the deceased's obsequies must reflect their earthly status. The 'Orders of Precedence' drawn up by Mary's grandmother, Lady Margaret Beaufort, in 150, dictated the protocol, detailing the correct dress for public mourning, even the length of train to be worn by ladies. Heralds, mourners and a pursuivant were sent from France by Francis I to assist the English heralds with the complicated ceremonial befitting a Dowager Queen of France.

The science of embalming was well advanced in northern Europe. Mary lay in state for three weeks at Westhorpe in the chapel, where daily masses were said. Beside her coffin, draped in blue velvet, her family and retainers kept vigil night and day by the light of flickering wax tapers. On 10 July the King ordered a requiem mass to be sung at Westminster Abbey. This official ceremony was a public gesture, conducted with all the ostentatious formality befitting royalty. (Three years later, when it was suggested that a service be held at St Paul's to commemorate Katherine of Aragon, the King refused. His sister Mary, he said, was a queen. There was no need to go to the expense of commemorating Katherine.)

Brandon and the King were struggling to establish Henry's unpopular new queen. Neither could spare the time to visit Suffolk. In East Anglia, Mary's family gathered for the service on 22 July. The lords, wearing black hoods and gowns, the ladies with black trains, were led by Frances, the young Marchioness of Dorset, and her brother, the 17-year-old Earl of Lincoln. Eleanor, their sister, and Lady Catherine Willoughby, Brandon's ward and his son's fiancée, followed, and after them Mary's stepdaughters, Lady Powis and Lady Monteagle. After early mass, the family breakfasted together in the house that had been Mary's home, once filled with her grace and laughter.

The procession formed in the courtyard. Six gentlemen bore the coffin, draped in a black pall of cloth of gold with a white cross, from the chapel, setting it upon a hearse draped with black velvet embroidered with Mary's emblems and drawn by six horses. On the coffin was placed Mary's effigy, representing her as Queen of France, wearing a golden crown and holding a sceptre brought specially from France. Above the hearse a canopy was supported by four knights. The cortège proceeded at snail's pace along the narrow roads to Bury St Edmunds, preceded by 100 poor countrymen in coarse black hooded garments, glad to earn a few pence by trudging through the leafy lanes bearing wax tapers to honour the French Queen, of whose status they had been proud and whose kindness and beauty they remembered. The chapel clergy followed, carrying the cross, then came Mary's household staff, heralds, officials, mounted knights and nobles, and the hearse itself, followed by another 100 taper-bearing yeomen. After them rode Frances, as chief mourner, her palfrey caparisoned in black velvet, flanked by her husband and Lord Clifford, her sister Eleanor's betrothed. In single file rode ten noble ladies who had served Mary, each attended by a running footman. Mary's gentlewomen rode in two carriages. Yeomen and servants followed on foot. Along the way more people joined in. On the way through the Suffolk villages, delegations met the cortège at various points to pay tribute to the dead Queen and to receive money and torches.

At Bury St Edmunds the procession was ceremoniously received by the local clergy, the abbot and monks, and the Bishop of London in his pontifical robes. A catafalque had been prepared before the high altar for the coffin, draped in black and embroidered in gold with Mary's arms and her modest motto *'La volonte de Dieu me suffit'* ('Sufficient for me is God's will'). Banners decorated with the symbols of Lancaster and York, the Tudor portcullis and the fleur-de-lis were hung from the monastery gate up to the high altar. The mourners, their positions strictly governed by rules of etiquette, clustered about the coffin as the Dirge was sung and the French herald chanted: 'Pray for the soul of the right high excellent Princess and right Christian Queen, Mary, late French Queen, and all Christian souls.'[3]

The company then moved to the refectory for supper. Free food was distributed to everyone who had followed the procession. Eight women, twelve men, thirty yeomen and several clerks and priests were appointed to keep the last overnight vigil beside the coffin.

Requiem mass was sung early next day, and offerings of palls of cloth of gold were made by the chief mourners – the four Brandon daughters, Anne, Mary, Frances and Eleanor, and Catherine Willoughby and her mother. The Abbot of St Bennet's delivered a lengthy funeral oration, leaving Mary's daughters too exhausted and emotionally drained to attend the final farewell at the graveside in the crypt. They were sent home to rest and so were spared the breaking of the household staves and the general outburst of lamentation that accompanied this dismal last ritual. One tradition suggests that Mary's biological daughters had good reason to be upset beyond the ordinary transports of grief: their stepsisters, Mary and Anne Brandon, barged their way to the front of the funeral cortège just as the coffin was being lowered into the crypt, horrifying Mary's own children.

After the final funeral dinner, meat and drink were freely distributed. Paupers received 4 pennies as 'largesse of the grave'. On 23 July the funeral party dispersed. The catafalque remained in the church awaiting instructions from Brandon.

ANNA BOLINA VXOR—　　HENRI· OCTA

1 Anne Boleyn (unknown artist). © *National Portrait Gallery, London*

2 Thomas Seymour, Baron Seymour (unknown artist). © *National Portrait Gallery, London*

3 Mary Tudor; Charles Brandon, 1st Duke of Suffolk (George Vertue). © *National Portrait Gallery, London*

4 Eleanor Clifford (née Brandon), Countess of Cumberland (unknown artist). © *National Portrait Gallery, London*

14 Queen Elizabeth
I (George Gower).
© *National Portrait
Gallery, London*

15 Charles Brandon
(Wenceslaus Hollar).
© *National Portrait
Gallery, London*

16 Francis I, King of France (Titan).
© *National Portrait Gallery, London*

17 Kings of France including Louis XI,
Charles VIII, Louis XII, Francis I,
Henry II and Francis II (unknown
artist. © *National Portrait Gallery, London*

The memory of Mary's beauty, grace and benevolence lingered long in the countryside even after the whirligig life of court had moved on. Some claimed the shock of learning that her brother had secretly married Anne, and that she was pregnant by him, hastened her death.

After spending lavishly on Mary's funeral, Brandon found himself even deeper in debt, with a young ward and two unmarried children to support.

Mary's death diminished the prestige of the Suffolk household and strained Brandon's finances, causing him to reconsider his agreement to support Frances's husband Dorset at court until his majority. Frances's mother-in-law, the dowager countess, bombarded the new major influence at court, Thomas Cromwell, with appeals. Underhand attacks by her lawyers forced Brandon to capitulate; he ended up supporting the Dorsets for almost five years. His finances received a boost when he was granted the revenues of the vacant see of Ely, more than 12,000 ducats, and a crown debt of £1,000 was remitted. Within three years he had obtained remittance of all Mary's crown debts and refinanced his own. He and the King probably shared the cost of Mary's ornate alabaster monument at Bury St Edmunds. Both tomb and records were destroyed during the Dissolution, but the coffin itself was saved and quietly removed to the monastic church of St Mary's, its present location.

It was expected that a widower, still in the prime of life, should marry again. Brandon, at 49, had mellowed from a handsome young athlete into a distinguished and still commanding figure; his muscles, honed in the field and in tournaments, had, like those of his friend the King, started to turn to fat. Brandon's ward, Lady Catherine Willoughby, an attractive, intelligent, strong-minded girl of impeccable antecedents and impressive fortune, had reached the marriageable age of 14. Catherine, the daughter and heir of Lord William Willoughby by his second wife, Maria de Salinas, the Spanish lady-in-waiting so beloved of her mistress, Queen Katherine, was a baroness in her own right with an annual income of 15,000 ducats. Brandon had purchased her wardship for £2,266 13s 4d five years earlier, intending to keep her fortune in the family by marrying her to his son Henry, as soon as the boy was old enough. Henry's frailty was a constant worry to his parents. His older brother had died in childhood.

It seemed to Brandon a shame to lose Catherine, when his son could so easily make another advantageous match. A few hours before the future Elizabeth I came into the world, on Sunday 7 September 1533, Charles Brandon and Catherine were married. Mary had not been in her grave seven weeks.

The hasty remarriage raised few eyebrows. Marriage among the great had less to do with romance than with power, politics and economics.

A man needed a wife with a dowry and sufficient youth and robustness to produce sons. But Chapuys, reporting on the union to Charles V, noted not only the age gap between bride and groom, but also the speed with which Brandon hastened 'from the bier of one spouse to the bed of the next'.[4]

Within six months of his father's remarriage, in March 1534, Henry Brandon died. Spanish chroniclers, fond of attributing death to sentiment, noted that the young earl, jilted by his betrothed in favour of his own father, 'was so sorry he died'. Anne Boleyn reputedly commented: 'My Lord of Suffolk kills one son to beget another.'[5]

Despite malicious whispers and age difference, Brandon's last marriage was a success.

To his credit, Brandon had succeeded in maintaining relations with the husbands of his wayward older daughters. In 1538, Mary's husband, Lord Monteagle, had complained in vain to Thomas Cromwell about his wife's bad behaviour. Monteagle was incompetent, and Brandon had to enlist Cromwell's intervention in his inept administration of his estate. Two years later, Brandon's older daughter, Anne, caused a scandal by living openly with her lover. Her husband, Baron Grey of Powis, petitioned Henry VIII's Privy Council to punish Anne for adultery and for conspiring with her lover to murder him. Nothing came of the allegations. One contemporary source remarks that though 'handsome women, they took to evil courses, and became common women, the father, however, taking no notice of it'.[6] In reality, Brandon asked Cromwell to mediate between Lord and Lady Powis, and to favour Anne only if her behaviour was honourable. Following the violent removal of her lover in a night raid on their lodgings by Lord Powis, Cromwell renegotiated a maintenance agreement preparatory to a legal separation. Lady Powis was soon back in court circles. Whenever she needed cash she had no compunction about borrowing, either from Cromwell or her father.

Catherine was just 15 when their first son, Henry, was born. Brandon proved a loving husband to her for the last twelve years of his life. When he died in 1545 he left her and their two sons, neither of whom would survive to adulthood, both material and landed wealth, and strong alliances within the ranks of the English aristocracy. To Frances and Eleanor, Mary Rose's daughters, he bequeathed £200 worth of plate bearing the ducal arms. He had helped their husbands, buying lands for Cumberland and guiding Dorset through his military apprenticeship in France. In time, Dorset assumed leadership of the family. In 1551, after the deaths of Catherine Willoughby's sons, he was created Duke of Suffolk.

Brandon would be remembered for his military leadership and superb horsemanship. Charles Wriothesley lamented the death of 'so valiant a captain in the kings warres'.[7] The grizzled, cynical old warrior Elis Gruffydd, who remembered Brandon from the 1523 campaign in France, claimed the King grieved for the Duke 'with reason, because of his courtesy and ability, for he was the flower of all the captains of the realm and had the necessary patience to control soldiers'.[8] Brandon was remembered as heartily beloved of both high and low, rich and poor. The most affable, least devious and ambitious, of men at the Henrican court, this was the secret of his success and political survival. Just after Brandon's death, the King stated in an open council meeting that Brandon had never betrayed a friend nor taken unfair advantage of an enemy. Doubtless aware that his rosy view was not shared by all his Council, Henry warned them to hold their tongues, for which of them could say as much?

As the King grew increasingly disillusioned, he frequently recalled the loss of his last true friend, and of his beloved younger sister, who had loved him and shared his most carefree moments. Young, beautiful, dancing, jousting, making music, dazzling with their gaiety and grace, they had seemed to bear charmed lives. Where had it all gone wrong?

Brandon was scarcely cold in his grave when Henry VIII took a step that would prove disastrous for Mary and Brandon's descendants. He sought to secure England's security by a peaceful and uncontested succession. One legitimate male heir – Prince Edward, son of Anne Boleyn's mousy successor, Jane Seymour – was not enough. The succession could not depend on one fragile boy and two unmarried daughters. The first in a series of Succession Acts came in 1534, a year after Mary's death. In 1546, the Royal Will bequeathed the crown to the descendants of Henry's two sisters, should his own three children die without issue. Henry broke with the tradition of primogeniture. Preference was given to the Suffolks over the Stuarts. Politically, Henry distrusted the Scots; besides, there was the common-law rule that foreigners could not inherit English land. John Styrpe, however, may have been closer to the truth when he wrote that Henry was influenced by personal feelings, because he loved Mary and Brandon better than the heirs of his older sister, Margaret. In the second and third Succession Acts of 1536 and 1543 the will received parliamentary sanction, and in the First Edwardian Treason Act of 1547 it was confirmed; to attempt to alter it was decreed to be treasonable.

This lent support to the Suffolk claim for another fifty years, blighting the lives of several of Mary's descendants, for whom their closeness to the throne and Henry's affection for Mary would spell grief, imprisonment and death.

At the end of May 1537, Frances, praying her second child would be male and that, unlike her first-born son, he would survive, took to her great bed of estate with its fine sheets and fur-trimmed counterpane in the traditional womblike seclusion of a darkened room. The late Queen, Anne Boleyn, had borne a daughter: Frances's husband Harry Dorset had carried the salt at little Princess Elizabeth's christening – a pinch of salt was placed on the baby's lips as a symbol of purity, to ward off evil. But this living royal child had been followed by several miscarriages. The Queen herself had been executed on 19 May 1536 on charges of adultery and treason. The King's second marriage had been annulled; both his daughters, the Princesses Mary and Elizabeth, had been declared illegitimate. This raised the importance of Mary Rose's children and grandchildren in the line of succession, although the King was still determined to sire a son of his own to succeed him.

Dorset wanted a son, too, like all noblemen. Frances was only 19; they were both young, and when Frances was delivered of a daughter they were grateful that she was healthy, confident that sons would follow. The christening was arranged immediately, although this meant Frances, still recovering for the next month, could not attend. Often, new mothers did not even sit up in bed for the first fortnight. Frances chose as the child's godmother the new Queen, for whom she was named. Frances's uncle King Henry VIII had announced his betrothal to the pallid Lady Jane Seymour, the greatest possible contrast to his last Queen, sharp-witted Anne of the flashing black eyes, the day after Anne's execution. Jane Seymour was with child: nobody knew whether her pregnancy would result in the longed-for heir to the throne, but the Dorsets had hitched their waggon to the Seymour star, and their confidence was to prove justified. The two families would remain linked for many years. Frances's pushy stepsister, Lady Monteagle, was a favoured lady-in-waiting to Queen Jane, who gave her jewellery, and had her sketched by the Flemish artist Hans Holbein the Younger.

On 11 October 1537 word came that Queen Jane was in labour. Dorset hurried to London; a procession of clergy and officials prayed for the Queen. At 2 in morning, on the eve of the feast of St Edward, Henry VIII's legitimate son was born. At 9 a.m. Dorset joined the throng crowding about the door of the medieval church of St Paul, singing the *Te Deum*. Triumphal cannon fire thundered from the Tower, hogsheads of wine were distributed. There was general rejoicing: at last the succession was secure.

Frances and Dorset were desperate to be invited to the christening. Frances's father was to stand godfather at the confirmation that followed immediately afterwards. However, to their frustration, they found themselves banned from Hampton Court. There had been an outbreak of plague in Croydon, where Dorset's mother lived. The King's paranoia about infection had intensified, now he had the precious prince's welfare to consider.

Days later, Queen Jane suffered a massive haemorrhage, possibly caused by partial retention of placenta. She died on 24 October. Frances had missed the christening, but she and Dorset played leading parts in Jane's state funeral in November. Dorset, Brandon and four other leading courtiers rode beside the carriage bearing Jane's coffin to Windsor. Frances rode in the foremost of the carriages bearing the chief ladies of the court.

Away from court, the Dorsets resided at their family seat, the magnificent Bradgate Manor, a palace of rose-red brick patterned in deep lilac diamonds, built by Dorset's father and grandfather on the site of an ancient ruined castle. The glory of the Bradgate estate was the great park, created through the destruction of a medieval village; here the children exercised their father's greyhounds and accompanied their mother and her friends, hunting deer with longbows. The west wing housed the family's private apartments, the chapel, servants' hall, bakery, brewery and the bustling main kitchens. The Dorsets entertained on a lavish scale. When Dorset was in residence the house was crowded with scores of attendants, visitors and members of the extended family. The household dined in state on a raised dais at one end of the 8oft-long Great Hall in the heart of house, heated by a huge fireplace, with a minstrels' gallery.

In these idyllic surroundings Frances and Harry brought up three daughters: Jane, fiercely intelligent, her father's favourite and the focus of his ambitions; Katherine, the beauty of the family, affectionate, golden-haired, reminding many of her grandmother, the famous beauty, Mary Rose; and Mary, the youngest, warm-hearted like Katherine and clever like Jane, but without their looks. (Mary was later uncharitably described as crook-backed and hideous.) The Dorsets were determined that their girls should develop practical and intellectual skills. Frances was an excellent needle-woman, sewing shirts and collars as New Year gifts for her uncle the King. Dorset had received a fine academic grounding, having been brought up in the household of the King's illegitimate son, the late Henry Fitzroy, Duke of Richmond. He had learned Latin from a pupil of Erasmus and French from the great scholar John Palsgrave, and insisted that a love of scholarship should be passed on to his daughters, especially the brilliant Jane. By the age of eight, both Jane and Katherine were learning Latin and Greek. The study of the classics was intended to ensure moral understanding, moulding pupils into good subjects of King and deity.

Since Jane's birth in 1537, new divisions had arisen between conservative ideologues like Bishop Gardner and those who favoured the King's reformation. In the 1550s the term 'Protestant' became current. The 'evangelicals' advocated a return to a closer reading of the gospels. The Dorsets were regarded as holding radical views. The stage was being set for an ideological struggle in which the Grey sisters would play a key role, as members of the first generation to be raised as evangelicals, and also of royal blood.

In 1546, Frances, serving the King's sixth wife, Catherine Parr, as Lady of the Privy Chamber, started taking her oldest daughter Jane with her to court to prepare her for a role as Maid of Honour in the Queen's service. The court was the hub of social, cultural and political life, a hothouse of gossip and intrigue. At 55, Henry VIII no longer represented the picture of masculine beauty. Wan and obese, lumbering awkwardly on legs permanently damaged by hunting and jousting injuries, he usually remained in his private apartments, emerging occasionally, wheeled on chairs covered with tawny velvet through the corridors of the palace. Queen Catherine, a charming and sensual woman in the prime of life, bathed in milk, scented her body with rosewater and her breath with cinnamon lozenges, and favoured gorgeous robes of scarlet silk.

Kindly, intelligent Catherine had been married off twice in her youth to old men, and had found in religion an outlet for her passion. As the leading evangelical at court, she made energetic attempts to spread the new teaching in universities. Every afternoon evangelical chaplains would preach to her circle, followed by theological discussions. Such activities were dangerous: religious conservatives on the Privy Council were plotting the downfall of their evangelical rivals. They concentrated their attack against Anne Askew, a 25-year-old gentlewoman. Anne, a witty poet and evangelical, had broken a taboo by quarrelling with her husband over religion. In July 1546 she was condemned to death for heresy. The rumour-mill gained momentum: Anne was reputed to have allies in the Queen's Privy Chamber; she had apparently even been introduced to the Queen and to the King's favourite nieces, Frances and Eleanor Brandon. This introduction, everyone thought, must have been contrived by Frances's stepmother and childhood companion, the Dowager Duchess of Suffolk. Catherine Suffolk, blonde, blue-eyed, charming and forthright, was a remarkable woman. Her caustic wit and rages were legendary. Although the daughter of Katherine of Aragon's Spanish lady-in-waiting, Catherine had abandoned her childhood religion; foreign ambassadors called her 'the greatest heretic in the kingdom'.[9] A favourite of Catherine Parr, she also knew Anne Askew. Askew was taken to the Tower where she was hideously tortured and interrogated persistently about any connection to the Brandons and the Greys, who waited anxiously, wondering what she would reveal.

Anne was torn apart 'until the strings of her arms and eyes were perished',[10] but she named no names. Her torture and condemnation sparked a public outcry. In an official attempt to restore calm, she was offered a pardon if she would recant. She refused. On 16 July 1546 she was brought to Smithfield to be burned. So broken that she could not stand or sit upright, she had to be tied to the stake in a chair. The Queen's cousin, Nicholas Throckmorton, and two of his brothers stood shouting support for her as the flames consumed her. Foxe, the sixteenth-century martyrologist, viewed this attempt to detect heresy in the Queen's Privy Chamber as the prelude to an attack on the Queen herself. However, Henry's temporary disillusionment with Catherine Parr had less to do with her reformist zeal than with the fact that his eye had fallen upon the alluring young Catherine Suffolk. Clever Catherine Parr managed to soothe her increasingly unpredictable lord, and was soon restored to his good books. He was not to live long thereafter, dying in January 1547. He was 56.

His successor, 9-year-old Prince Edward, described by the Catholic ambassadors as 'the prettiest child you ever saw', was an angelic-looking lad, with blonde locks and pink cheeks. Crowds cheered wildly as he processed from Whitehall to Westminster for his coronation. Thoughtful attendants had positioned two cushions to give him extra height. It was important that the new young King should seem commanding rather than a vulnerable child. His coronation departed from the norm: Thomas Cranmer, Archbishop of Canterbury, had rewritten the coronation oath. The ancient promise to uphold the liberties and privileges of the clergy was omitted. Instead of swearing to accept laws presented by his people, the people were obliged to accept Edward's laws – in reality, the laws of the Council, presented under the monarch's authority. Henry VIII had regarded as his greatest achievement 'royal supremacy' in religious matters, placing him above the laws of the Pope and the laws of England. In his sermon, Cranmer stressed that the boy King was to be a new Josiah, the destroyer of idols. England's Catholic past was to be obliterated from minds and memories.

At the conclusion of the ceremony, Dorset, with Frances's young half-brother, Henry, Duke of Suffolk, stepped forward to assist the King, helping him grasp his sceptre and the 'ball of gold with the cross',[11] and propping him up to present him to the congregation as their monarch.

Henry VIII's will had decreed that 16 executors should act as co-rulers until Edward came of age. These executors established themselves as the Privy Council on the day Henry's death was announced, three days after he had expired. They elected Edward's evangelical elder uncle, Edward Seymour, a successful soldier-politician, on whom Henry VIII had come to rely heavily towards the end of his reign, as Lord Protector of England. Seymour was also created Duke of Somerset. Somerset's elevation and arrogance annoyed Dorset. The 'good Duke', as Somerset delighted in being known, despised Dorset in return. However, Somerset's younger brother, the dashing Thomas Seymour, was already pondering a political alliance against his brother.

Thomas Seymour was charismatic, ambitious and allegedly the handsomest man in England. Somerset had sought to tame his brother by appointing him to the Privy Council, creating him Lord Admiral and giving him the title of Baron Sudeley. But these trappings did not satisfy Thomas's lust for power. What Thomas really hankered after was the post of Governor of the King's Person, which would have allowed him to share the power of the Protectorship, and this was denied him. A month after Edward's coronation, Somerset consolidated his own unassailable position by assuming this post for himself. Furious, Sudeley, determined to thwart any further advance by his brother, decided to increase his own power by raising his profile within the royal family. Dorset's wife, Frances, was the King's first cousin. Her daughters were in the line of succession. Sudeley knew Dorset was feeling alienated and embittered, his nose having been put out of joint by Somerset: when Catherine Parr's brother had been created Marquis of Northampton, many surmised that this had been a calculated snub to Dorset, who had until then been the only Marquis in England. This appeared to be confirmed in March, when Northampton was promoted to the Privy Council and Dorset was not. Sudeley set his sights on Dorset.

From January, the young Grey sisters noticed a new and increasingly regular visitor to Dorset House on the Strand. Jane, who had seen him about court, recognised Sudeley's gentleman servant, John Harington. Sudeley had sent Harington, a subtle negotiator, to pave the way for a friendship with the Dorsets, being himself occupied hunting other prey: aware that Catherine Parr had always loved him, even before her marriage to the King, he was vigorously wooing the widowed Queen. Paragon of virtue and religious sentiment though she was, Catherine, married off to two older men, found Sudeley irresistible. Within weeks of the King's death the handsome Admiral had his way with her 'under the plummet' (duvet) at her Chelsea manor, and in May 1547, just after the Princess Elizabeth had been placed in Catherine's care, the couple married.

Sudeley noted the influence his new bride exerted over the young princess; he realised that the wardship of Lady Jane Grey, next in line to the throne after Elizabeth, might prove invaluable. Watching Jane around court with newly kindled interest, especially in her interaction with the young King, it struck him that she might make Edward a suitable bride. He also suspected that his brother Somerset intended to see Jane married to his own son, 8-year-old Edward Seymour, Earl of Hertford, in due course. If Sudeley could persuade the Dorsets to sign their oldest daughter over to him as his ward, he could foil his brother's ambitions.

At 10, Jane was young to 'put out'. Moreover, the precise date of Sudeley's proposition is unclear. If it took place before Sudeley's marriage to Catherine Parr had been made public, Sudeley was asking Dorset to send Jane to the house of an unmarried man. If it occurred later, then it was to a household tainted by the breath of scandal. It was generally believed that females were lustful daughters of Eve, and that Catherine's marriage so soon after her widowhood was shameful. Were she to become pregnant it might even be uncertain whose child she carried, thus representing a threat to the stability of the country. Sudeley might have been condemned for treason. Harington was prepared for Dorset's objections and countered them with his own trump card. Sudeley, he assured Dorset, would ensure Jane made a most advantageous marriage.

'Marriage with whom?' Dorset demanded.

Harington then described how Sudeley, having observed Jane at court, found her 'as handsome as any lady in Christendom'. 'I doubt not,' Harington said, 'but you shall see him marry her to the King; and fear you not but he will bring it to pass.'[12]

Within the week, Dorset was at Seymour Place on the Strand, chatting earnestly with Sudeley himself in the private garden, struggling to make themselves heard over the crashing cacophony of the workmen next door. The Protector was demolishing the local parish church of St Mary and the Holy Innocents to make way for an immense palace in the Italian style, the first of its kind in the country, a monument to his increasing status as king in all but name. Sudeley assured Dorset Jane would make the ideal queen for Edward; as proof of friendship he offered a down payment of £200 towards an end payment of £2,000 for her wardship. Dorset compared the 'fair promises'[13] and friendliness of Sudeley with his cool treatment by the Protector, and sent for his daughter immediately.

Frances took more persuading. Her friend and stepmother Catherine Suffolk disapproved of Sudeley and had been appalled by his hasty marriage to their friend the Queen Dowager. Frances, often unfairly described as a 'dreadful mother',[14] wanted to keep Jane at home out of Sudeley's clutches, but she felt bound to obey her husband. Dorset had resolved that his daughter should be Queen of England. Accordingly, 10-year-old Jane was sent off on the short boat ride from Dorset House to Seymour Place.

Despite her mother's reservations, Jane, a highly intelligent, confident child, relished the greater independence of her new life. Sudeley proved an indulgent guardian. When not at Seymour Place, Jane attended the Queen Dowager's household. In Catherine's former home, the bustling royal manor of Chelsea, nestling amid its fragrant orchards and herb gardens, Jane observed 35-year-old Catherine's endeavours to remain physically attractive to her handsome husband. Jane herself acquired an inclination for finery, to the irritation of her learned tutor John Aylmer, who valued her intellectual gifts. She also developed a love of music under the tutelage of the Queen Dowager. Catherine and her cultured brother, Northampton, were the greatest patrons of musicians at court. Catherine also set Jane an example in religious matters. She had advocated church reform, supervising the best-selling translation of Erasmus's *Paraphrases of the New Testament* and writing *The Lamentation of a Sinner*, an account of her own search for salvation. She had not dared to publish it while her husband the King lived because of its Lutheran overtones, Henry having denounced Luther as a heretic.

Dorset noted impatiently that Sudeley, despite his promises, did not appear to be actively promoting Jane's relationship with the King. Somerset had banned Sudeley and Catherine from Edward's presence, despite the young King's distress – Catherine, whom he rather pathetically called *Mater Carissima*, occupied, he said, 'the chiefest place'[15] in his heart. But Somerset had had enough of his brother's manipulations: he felt the impressionable young King was best kept away from Sudeley. Who knew what ambitions that dangerous and charismatic man entertained?

In the household of the Queen Dowager and Sudeley, Jane and Princess Elizabeth were thrown together, although they never became close. Elizabeth had the teenager's intolerance of younger children and resented the fact that Jane was proving a better scholar than either Elizabeth or the boy king, both of whom enjoyed a reputation for brilliance. Her precarious station in life had made Elizabeth reserved to the point of psychosis. From being her father's heir and the child of the wife with whom he was scandalously besotted, she had become the bastard of a traitorous adulteress. Restored in 1544 to the line of succession, in law she remained illegitimate. Orphaned, she was dependent on the goodwill of others. Her feelings towards Catherine Parr were ambivalent. Catherine showed her kindness and affection, yet Catherine's hasty remarriage filled Elizabeth with moral outrage.

One day, Elizabeth would hold the destiny of Jane's sister Katherine in her nervous white hands. Her half-sister Mary would decide Jane's own fate.

For Sudeley, married to a king's widow, the only possible advancement would be to wed a king's daughter. The relationship between 14-year-old Elizabeth and Sudeley had already begun to raise eyebrows. Sudeley and his wife enjoyed a passionate, if volatile, relationship. At 36, after three infertile marriages, Catherine found herself pregnant for the first time. Her excitement was tempered by anxiety: she was old for a first-time mother. She pictured herself dying in childbirth, and her adored husband quickly replacing her with the fascinating young red-haired princess with her mother's dancing black sardonic eyes.

There had been a certain amount of jovial romping. Sudeley sent suggestive schoolboy messages to Elizabeth, asking 'if her great buttocks were grown any less or no'.[16] Kate Astley, the girls' governess, had warned Sudeley it was unseemly to visit a young woman's bedchamber 'barelegged',[17] and was causing gossip. For Catherine, six months pregnant, the last straw was to discover Elizabeth and Sudeley locked in each other's arms. After a fiery exchange with Sudeley, Catherine explained to Elizabeth that she should be more careful; her mother's example was held before her. Elizabeth, shocked and chastened, was sent to stay with Astley's sister, Joan Denny. Sudeley blustered that his behaviour had been merely 'sporting'. He was, he declared, a man of spotless life, and a nobleman to boot. All his attention was focused on Catherine's baby; he had certainly made lavish preparations.

Both Sudeley and Catherine were losing interest in theology. Catherine Suffolk's spiritual adviser, Hugh Latimer, complained that Sudeley avoided prayer meetings 'like a mole digging in the dirt'.[18] In August, Dorset visited Sudeley, who told him his brother the Protector had begun to make enemies. Sudeley painted for Dorset a picture where, having come of age, the King rejected the unpopular Protector. Knowing Somerset would not relinquish power without a fight, Sudeley said they must be prepared for a struggle. Dorset must canvas the support of the yeomanry, calling on them at home, taking with him 'a flagon or two of wine and a pasty of venison',[19] chatting with them in an unassuming, affable manner, to win their confidence. Dorset returned to Bradgate deep in thought.

Catherine Parr was delivered on 30 August 1548 of a baby girl, but she quickly succumbed to delirium, the first sign of puerperal fever, and on 5 September she died, leaving everything she possessed to her husband, and expressing the wish that it was a thousand times more in value. The care of baby Mary Seymour was bequeathed to Catherine Suffolk, who would resent the expense and inconvenience, but not for long. Within the year baby Mary would be dead.

Jane Grey returned home to Bradgate, after performing her first public role with a composure remarkable in an 11-year-old, walking in Catherine's funeral procession from the house to the chapel at Sudeley. After the greater freedom of Seymour Place, Jane resented the restrictions at Bradgate. In the year away from home she had grown self-assured and begun to question authority in a way that shocked her mother. Tudor society functioned on principles of obedience. Frances felt that Jane's wilfulness should be disciplined into becoming a force for good, and was disappointed that Sudeley had apparently neglected to provide better guidance. She was taken aback when, less than a fortnight after Jane returned home, Sudeley requested that she be returned to Seymour Place.

Sudeley's wife's wealth was reverting to the crown. He could not afford to let slip Jane's wardship. Anticipating Frances's objections, he assured Dorset that he would be keeping on all Catherine Parr's ladies, including the unmarried maids of honour. He would take the best possible care of Jane, and his own mother, old Lady Seymour, would be in charge of the household. She would treat Jane as if she were her own daughter.

He then wrote to Jane in the tone of a strict but loving father. Jane replied, assuring him that she would always be 'most ready to obey your godly monitions and good instructions'.[20] The tug of war over Jane continued. Dorset, aware that with Catherine's death Sudeley had lost status, wrote reminding him of Jane's youth. Jane needed a mother, and with the best will in the world, Sudeley could not be a mother to her. Jane, on the brink of adolescence, was at an age where the mind must be addressed 'to humility, sobriety and obedience'.[21]

Dorset added brightly that he still intended to seek Sudeley's advice about finding a suitable husband for his daughter.

Frances then wrote her own letter to Sudeley. She agreed that naturally Sudeley's advice would be sought when the time came for Jane to marry, but emphasised this was not imminent. She concluded by hoping that she could keep her daughter by her with his 'goodwill'.[22]

Sudeley hastened to Leicestershire, determined to convince the Dorsets to let him have Jane back. He brought with him to Bradgate Sir William Sharington, Under Treasurer of the Royal Mint. Handsome Sharington deployed all his powers of persuasion. Sharington was bankrolling Sudeley out of obligation: he had abused his position at the Mint to perpetrate massive frauds, which Sudeley had discovered. This was the price of Sudeley's silence. At Bradgate, Sudeley again trotted out his trump card, his intention of engineering a royal marriage for Jane. His ambitions had received a massive boost recently when Jane's principal rival for the King's hand, the infant Mary, Queen of Scots, had been sent to France to become betrothed to the Dauphin. A few moments alone with the King, Sudeley insisted, meaning away from his brother Somerset, and he would have Edward betrothed to Jane Grey in an inkling.

At last, after 'long debating and much sticking',[23] Frances conceded. Jane would be returned to Sudeley's care. Another £500 changed hands. Sudeley said he needed no bond in return. The seal on the contract was Lady Jane herself.

This decision sealed Jane's fate.

Lady Jane Grey

In autumn 1548, when Jane returned to Seymour Place, she found the household had changed radically since she had left a few weeks ago, before the death of Catherine Parr, her mother's friend and her own kindly mentor. Jane was feeling increasing pressure. Next May, she would be 12, able under canon law to make a binding marriage contract. Already she was attracting interest. Sudeley suspected that his brother Somerset planned to marry her to his son, Lord Hertford, who was descended from Edward III through his mother. Sudeley's enemies whispered that Sudeley himself secretly planned to marry Jane; others suspected him of even bolder plans, aspiring to marry the Princess Mary or the Princess Elizabeth. These rumours alarmed Elizabeth; conscious that her every move was under scrutiny and that she could not marry without the consent of the King, her half-brother and the Privy Council, she refused to receive Sudeley. But then her cofferer, Thomas Parry, who was in charge of her finances, began to appear at Seymour Place. Away from prying eyes and eavesdroppers, Parry and Sudeley strolled in the gallery, chatting confidentially, discussing the financial details of a possible marriage between Sudeley and Princess Elizabeth.

Sudeley's foolhardy flirtation with explosive matters of high state appalled the more experienced members of the Sudeley household. Roger Ascham, tutor to both the princess and Jane Grey, fearing the fallout, requested permission to absent himself, spending the whole Christmas season at Cambridge. Kate Astley and her husband John were overheard arguing furiously; later, Elizabeth noticed bruising on her governess's arms.

Sudeley's friends and confidants, including members of the Privy Council, strove to deflect him from his reckless course. They could all remember men who had died for seeking royal alliances. Wriothesely warned Sudeley: 'It were better for you if you had never been born, nay, that you were burnt to the quick alive than that you should attempt it.'[1]

Dorset, as usual enthusiastically backing the wrong horse, promised Sudeley his allegiance, declaring he would 'defend him against all men, except the King'.[2] Heedless of the danger he was placing his daughter Jane in, in pursuit of his own ambitions, Dorset hurried night after night to Seymour Place.

Sudeley was finally trapped when the luck of the devious fraudster Sharington ran out. On the orders of the Privy Council, Sharington's home, Lacock Abbey in Wiltshire, was ransacked and incriminating evidence of the rackets he had run while employed at the Royal Mint was revealed. Desperate to save his own skin, Sharington betrayed all he knew about Sudeley's ambitions to marry Elizabeth. Sudeley, with his customary arrogance, imagined he could face down his accusers. The next day, after attending Parliament as usual, he and Dorset dined at the London home of Dorset's Leicestershire neighbour, Francis Hastings, Earl of Huntingdon. They returned to Seymour Place with a group of friends, including Jane's youngest uncle, Lord Thomas. Thomas took Sudeley aside and advised him to throw himself on the mercy of his brother the Protector.

Sudeley scornfully rejected the suggestion. Instead he made another reckless move. Accompanied by two servants, he burst into the royal bedchamber through the Privy Garden, brandishing a pistol, possibly intending to kidnap the King. The King's little pet dog started yapping in alarm. Sudeley shot it. The report roused the household.

Next door in his palace, Somerset had heeded the warning of his advisers that he would only be safe when his brother was dead. That night Sir Thomas Smith, Clerk of the Privy Council, and Sir John Baker, Privy Councillor and lawyer, arrived at Seymour Place with orders for Sudeley's arrest. Baker, an uncompromising grey-haired 50-year-old, would come to be known as Butcher Baker. During the reign of Mary Tudor, he would renounce his own evangelical past and send his former co-religionists in droves to the fires of Smithfield.

Sudeley was condemned for high treason. He left last messages for the Princesses Elizabeth and Mary, allegedly urging them to 'conspire against my Lord Protector', written in orange juice with a 'hook plucked from his hose'.[3] He hid these secret missives in the soles of his velvet shoes. He still had them with him on the morning of 20 March 1549 when he was taken to Tower Hill to die.

Public executions followed a formal ritual, featuring a penitent last speech and a wish that the sovereign would reign long and happily.

Sudeley departed from the script. The messages to the princesses were discovered, and there was a scuffle before he was wrestled to the block and beheaded. He was said to 'die most unwillingly'.[4] Latimer, directed by the Council to preach a sermon denouncing Sudeley, proclaimed from the pulpit that Sudeley was 'a man the farthest from the fear of God that ever I knew or heard of in England'. He had died 'most irksomely, strangely, horribly'.[5]

Princess Elizabeth's comment has entered into history: she said Sudeley died 'a man with much wit and very little judgement'.

Dorset had escaped the consequences of his embroilment with Sudeley. He and his three daughters would soon occupy the centre stage. After Sudeley's downfall, Jane returned again to the bosom of her family at Bradgate. Having spent two years away from home, Jane and her family were strangers to one another; her return was a culture shock.

In one respect, Sudeley's surmise had been correct: his powerful brother Somerset had hoped to see Jane married to his son, Edward, Earl of Hertford. Now, on 5 October 1549, 10-year-old Hertford was engaged on a more thrilling assignment than matrimony. Westward he galloped through the quiet autumn roads towards Wiltshire on a life-or-death mission, leaving the forest of turrets and gilded weathervanes of Hampton Court behind, the countryside but a colourful blur as he speeded to take his father's vital message to Sir William Herbert, who commanded the royal army.

Somerset was still the most important of the three noblemen, the 'Mighty Tres Viri', who made up the triumvirate of the Protector. The other two were John Dudley, Earl of Warwick, and Sir William Herbert. Somerset had lost credibility, tainted by association through his brother's execution and by his own arrogant mishandling of the rebellions that had racked the country that summer. Triggered by the forced introduction of the new Prayer Book, written in English, protests had developed into a widespread revolt against the ruling elite. The wealthy nobility had bought up farms and enclosed the common land, causing hardship and even starvation among landless peasants.

By the end of May, rebellious mobs had been looting the estates of unpopular landlords near Bradgate, tearing down fences and slaughtering deer in the parks. Somerset, aware that big landowners were greedy, had flown in the face of advice from colleagues on the Privy Council and negotiated with the rebels, instead of sending out troops and crushing them by force, as Henry VIII would have done. His enemies had interpreted this as weakness. England teetered on the brink of civil war. The King of France, Henri II, seized the opportunity to exploit England's domestic crisis to declare war. Calais was about to be lost.

Somerset was forced to abandon his policy of negotiation and pardon and deal with the crisis at home as brutally as any of his predecessors. The government had imported foreign mercenaries to put down the rebellion in a bloodbath. Two and a half thousand men fell valiantly in Devon. Warwick led an army of 12,000 professional soldiers and German mercenaries against Norfolk farmboys who hoped only for 'an equal share of things'.[6] At Dussindale outside Norwich 3,000 died on 27 August.

The night after Somerset sent his son off on his wild ride to Wiltshire, he informed the 11-year-old King that he must leave Hampton Court for the greater security of Windsor Castle, because Somerset's enemies might seek him out and murder him. Edward carried a little sword to defend himself, but his deadliest enemy was the chilly autumn night; he was soon shivering with cold. At gloomy, unwelcoming Windsor they found few provisions.

Young Hertford was not having an easy time of it, either. He had reached the army in Wiltshire, and recognised Sir William Herbert by his lofty manner and red hair. Ambassadors had sneered that Herbert, whose first language was Welsh, knew no English or any other civilised language. He had a reputation for violence and was said to have murdered a man in Bristol in his youth. It was also said that when rebellious peasants overran his estate at Wilton in the summer, he had personally attacked them and hacked some people to pieces. But Herbert was cunning and ambitious. He had managed to secure the hand of Queen Catherine's Parr's elegant sister, Anne Parr, in marriage. By extension he was thus a member of the royal family.

Herbert also had a long memory: it was his wife's brother, William Parr, who had been kicked off the Privy Council by Hertford's father for divorcing his wife. Herbert made it plain to the messenger that he had no intention of bringing the royal army to assist Somerset. Herbert and his co-commander, Lord Russell, told Somerset to resign 'rather than any blood be shed'.[7]

Somerset had no option but to step aside. He threw himself on the mercy of the Council. Two days after his twelfth birthday, King Edward was obliged to order his uncle's arrest. On 14 October 1549 Somerset was taken to the Tower. It was less than seven months since his brother, Sudeley, had been executed.

Jane and her sisters had sat through sermons deploring the wickedness of the rebels. To attempt to overturn the preordained social order, which reflected the Divine Chain of Being, was sinful and could lead only to chaos. Fighting rebels under Warwick, the Greys' uncle, Sir Henry Willoughby, got his death wound. His wife had died 18 months earlier. Thomas, their eldest child, was taken to Bradgate to live as Dorset's ward.

He was the same age as Katherine. Nine-year-old Thomas Willoughby was then sent to Cambridge on 16 November to join Catherine Suffolk's two sons. The younger siblings, Margaret and Francis, now came into the lives of the Grey sisters. Sometimes that winter they were at Bradgate, sometimes at Wotton, the Willoughby seat. At the end of November 1549 they set off for George Medley's house, Tilty in Essex, Mary and Katherine on horseback, sitting in front of a servant who held them when they tired to make sure they didn't fall off, and Jane, like a grown-up lady, riding side-saddle. Their train included nurses, grooms and gentlemen servants. Bells rang in the village churches to announce the arrival of the procession and crowds poured out of the farmsteads and hovels to line the route and gaze at the celebrities, offering fresh horses, refreshments or places to rest.

After a few days with their cousins at Tilty, where little Mary Grey, tiny but indomitable, played happily with bossy Margaret, the sisters took the road for Beaulieu, the Princess Mary's house. Their mother travelled with them to the great turreted palace with its stone gateway carved with Henry VIII's initials. Frances remembered serving in Mary's household when Jane was a baby; her mother, Mary Rose, and Katherine of Aragon had been friends as well as sisters-in-law. Princess Mary, at 33, was still, astoundingly for a woman of her rank, single. Her father had had men killed for aspiring to obtain her hand for their sons. He wanted no dangerous rivals to threaten his son Edward. Now Edward's Privy Council screened potential applicants for Mary's hand. They could exercise a legal veto on any choice she made. Mary watched her youth ebb away, devoting her affection to God. Small and delicate, the princess had long been a martyr to menstrual problems, depression and tooth-ache. She was regularly bled for these ailments without effect. But her voice was strong, almost mannish, and she had piercing eyes and an independent spirit. She treated the Grey girls kindly, giving them gifts of clothing and beads, gambled at card games with their mother and played her lute for them. Like all the Tudors, she was a skilled musician. The only jarring note was her devotion to the Catholic mass, which the sisters, raised in the evangelical tradition, had been taught to despise. Despite their differences over religion, Frances remained close to Mary. This kind of subtle networking was one of the inconspicuous but essential functions of female courtiers. They managed to sustain links across religious and political divisions and warring factions. But things were about to become more complicated.

By February 1550, the Grey sisters and their Willoughby cousins were settled at Dorset House on the Strand. Honours were being heaped on

Dorset; he had been made Steward of the King's Honours and Constable of Leicester Castle, and had been granted extensive lands in five counties. This good fortune meant that Frances and her daughters could attend court functions in considerable finery.

The court was now dominated by the ruthless warrior Warwick, the new Lord President. Warwick's icy control was as intimidating as his potential violence. Warwick treated Edward as a maturing monarch, training him for matters of state. The young King followed a rigorous daily programme of exercise, prayer, study and occasional diversion, interspersed with meetings. Access to the monarch was limited. The Grey sisters, whose father was constantly at the King's side and who knew or were related to all the key figures at court, saw more of him than most people. Warwick had tightened security. The King's Privy Chamber had a new guard of security men and armed yeomen, and twelve bands of cavalry, 100 members of whom were commanded by Dorset. He even hoped to work with Somerset, now released from the Tower, and invited him on to the Privy Council. Warwick agreed with Somerset that dynastic marriages bound allies most effectively. He suggested that Somerset's daughter Anne might be married to Jane's 14-year-old uncle, Henry Brandon, the Duke of Suffolk, who was the King's study companion. Catherine Suffolk refused, saying she deplored forcing children into marriages that might prove unsuitable. Warwick promptly married Anne Seymour to his own oldest son, John Dudley, Lord Lisle.

Somerset still wanted Jane Grey for his son, young Hertford. Well educated, accomplished and pious, Jane was a major prize. The rediscovery of the New Testament through Greek seemed to the evangelicals to break a religious code though which the Vatican had suppressed religious truth. Dorset's two ruling passions were his zeal for religious reform and his ambitions for his brilliant daughter. Dorset still cherished higher ambitions for Jane than Hertford.

Jane was beginning to go her own way. It was in the autumn of 1550 when the Princess Elizabeth's former tutor Roger Ascham arrived at Bradgate and, upon encountering Jane Grey there, had with her the famous conversation that he reported twenty years later in his posthumously published book *The Schoolmaster*. This incident has formed the cornerstone of later analyses of Jane's temperament and historians' notion of the unpleasant characters of her parents. 'It was the last time I ever beheld that sweet and noble lady,' Ascham noted.[8]

Thirty-five year old Ascham had made his name in Protestant and intellectual circles five years earlier with the publication of his book *Toxophilos*. He had now been appointed as secretary to King Edward's

ambassador to the Low Countries at the court of Charles V, and had
been invited to stay at Bradgate to bid farewell to his wife Alice and the
Astleys, all based at Bradgate since Princess Elizabeth's household had
broken up with the arrest of Sudeley. He also hoped to see Jane, who had
sent a reference for him to his new employer. When Ascham arrived at
Bradgate he was informed that the Dorsets and their household were all
out hunting, except for Jane, who was reading in her chamber. Ushered
into her presence, he found her looking 'young and lovely'. He was
astounded to find she had been reading Plato's *Phaedo*, which describes
Socrates' courage in the face of death, 'with as much delight as gentlemen read a merry tale in Boccacio'. Ascham asked why she was not
out in the park disporting herself with everyone else. Jane smiled, and
remarked rather smugly that all their sport in the park was but a shadow
to the delight she found in Plato. 'Alas! Good folk, they never felt what
true pleasure meant!' She seized the opportunity of a sympathetic lis-
tener to pour out her grievances against her parents.

> I will tell you, and tell ye a truth which perchance ye will marvel at.
> One of the greatest benefits that ever God gave me is that he sent me so
> sharp and severe parents and so gentle a schoolmaster. For when I am
> in presence of either father or mother, whether I speak, keep silent,
> sit, stand or go, eat, drink, be merry or sad, be sewing, playing, dancing
> or doing anything else, I must do it, as it were, in such weight, meas-
> ure and number, even so perfectly as God made the world, or else I am
> so sharply taunted, so cruelly threatened, yea, presently sometimes
> with pinches, nips and bobs, and other ways (which shall not name, for
> the honour I bear them), so without measure misordered, that I think
> myself in hell till time come that I must go to Mr Aylmer, who teaches
> me so gently, so pleasantly, with such fair allurements to learning,
> that I think all the time nothing whilst I am with him. And when I am
> called from him, I fall on weeping, because whatever I do else but learn-
> ing is full of grief, trouble, fear and wholly misliking unto me. And thus
> my book hath been so much my pleasure, and brings daily to me more
> pleasure and more that in respect of it, all other pleasures, in very deed,
> be but troubles and trifles unto me.[9]

Although these remarks of Jane's have been used to demonise her parents, especially Frances, in reality, Ascham was either less impressed by
Jane's complaints about her parents than about her scholarship, or chose
to ignore them. When he wrote to her a few months later, he told her that
he had as yet met nobody on his travels who inspired such admiration

as she had done. But he had nothing but good to say of her parents, who also delighted in her achievements. Having no sons, their ambitions centred on their brilliant oldest daughter and the regime imposed on her was perhaps more rigorous than generally imposed on female children.

A major bone of contention was the Dorsets' love of gambling. Haddon, their chaplain, and Aylmer, their daughters' tutor, found themselves on the opposite side of the fence over this vice, regarded as vicious papist laxity by the strict evangelicals. The fanatically Protestant Jane added her disapproval to theirs. The servants at Suffolk Place were forbidden to play cards, but Frances and Dorset continued to play in private, for money. Haddon put down their addiction to gambling as 'force of habit, and a desire not to appear stupid, and not good fellows, as they call it'.[10] If the evangelical divines were disappointed in the Dorsets and perceived in young Katherine a taste for frivolity, Jane was their consolation. Jane eagerly followed the Princess Elizabeth's plain style of dress; she even snubbed the Princess Mary, who had sent her wonderful gowns of 'tinsel cloth of gold and velvet, laid over with parchment lace of gold'. Jane demanded scornfully 'What shall I do with it?'

'Marry,' her gentlewoman replied, 'wear it.'

'Nay,' snapped Jane, 'that would be a shame to follow my Lady Mary against God's word, and leave my Lady Elizabeth who followeth God's word.'

Dorset shared his daughter's fervour for the New Religion. A man of some learning and huge self-importance, he was, however, even more obsessed with his royal connections than his wife (he was descended from Edward IV's stepson). He told the exiled German divine John of Ulm, whom he supported financially, that he had the rank of a prince. Dorset would soon acquire a new title, courtesy of the mysterious sweating sickness. In the summer of 1551, both Frances Grey's half-brothers, Henry and Charles, Brandon's sons by Catherine Suffolk, suffered the first symptoms of the killer disease. Catherine hurried to their bedside at Buckden, the former palace of the Bishop of Lincoln, from her estates at Grimsthorpe. Fifteen-year-old Henry, Duke of Suffolk, was already dead when she arrived, and his brother died early the next morning. Catherine, in shock, retired into seclusion.

For Dorset, the deaths of the two young Suffolk boys meant promotion: he was elevated to his father-in-law's title as Duke of Suffolk. Frances and her husband now took up permanent positions at court and occupied a suite of rooms in Richmond Palace. Dorset owed his promotion to his support of Warwick (created Duke of Northumberland in 1551). Northumberland, determined to encompass the downfall of Somerset, had him accused of plotting to murder Northampton and

Northumberland himself. Dorset, now Duke of Suffolk, gladly signed the warrant for Somerset's arrest. He had learned that Somerset hoped to promote his daughter Lady Jane Seymour as a bride for the King, thus threatening Jane Grey's claim. Jane Seymour would become Katherine Grey's friend and confidante.

Somerset was tried for the trumped-up murder charges and condemned by his judges, the two new dukes. Somerset was in the middle of his dignified last speech when two horsemen came clattering over the cobbled street. There was a cry of 'A pardon! A pardon! God save the Duke!' Somerset's supporters threw their hats in the air for joy. But Somerset himself realised that the newcomers had merely hurried to the scaffold to spectate, and he asked for silence, so that he could prepare himself for death. Just before 8 a.m. he tied his own handkerchief over his eyes and admitted that he was afraid. His head was struck off with one blow and his body was tossed upon a cart.

Jane, who turned 15 in May 1552, now had no serious rivals as a prospective bride for the young King, her mother's cousin. Lady Jane Seymour, as the daughter of an executed criminal, was now out of the picture. Plans for Edward to marry the daughter of the French King Henri II had fallen through. Jane Grey was now regarded as the leading lady of evangelism in England. Brilliant, committed, like her cousin the King, to Protestantism, of considerable personal courage, thoroughly self-willed, she was more determined and less malleable than those about her supposed. She was of the stuff of martyrs.

In August, cheering crowds in the southern towns of Southampton, Salisbury and Portsmouth turned out to greet their teenage King. Small and slight, the bejewelled figure exuded the assurance and presence of a Tudor monarch. He appeared in good health. Frances Suffolk, however, was taken ill with an ague which saw her husband summoned to her side. Her physicians feared for her life. Frances was to recover; it was her cousin the teenage King who would succumb.

Edward was well enough, despite a distressing cough, to celebrate New Year 1553 at Greenwich Palace with 'sports and pastimes for the King's diversion; which were in as great variety and pomp, as scarcely ever had been seen before'.[11] Frances gave him a knitted purse of silver and gold containing £40 in half sovereigns, and he gave her three covered gilt bowls. A little later that month the young King expressed his affection for Frances and her family by bestowing upon them yet another great estate, The Minories, a former abbey near the Tower.

But the boy was ailing. He was probably suffering from tuberculosis, contracted in summer 1551 and reactivated when he caught measles in

April 1552. On 6 February his half-sister Mary, fully aware that under the terms of her father's will, and the last Act of Succession of 1544, confirmed in Edward's Treasons Act of 1547, she was Edward's heir, arrived in London with 200 attendants to visit the King. Frances and the Duchess of Northumberland rode through the capital in her train. Edward was still pallid and sickly but as the weather grew warmer he rallied sufficiently to be able to write a will in his own hand. His 'My Device for the Succession', only one sheet, excluded his half-sisters Mary and Elizabeth. Mary would dismantle his evangelical religious programme, and Elizabeth's mother had died a traitor and adulteress. Edward also bypassed the Stuart line of his aunt Margaret, on nationalist grounds. As the senior member of the Suffolk clan, that left Frances. But Edward, like his father, believed that only a male hand was capable of wielding the sceptre. Edward therefore bequeathed the throne, not to Frances, but to any sons she might bear. His will left the throne empty, by his naming only female vessels who might carry heirs. Of these only Frances was married. But this was soon to change. Northumberland, convinced that the young King could not long survive, announced the betrothal of his fourth son Guilford to Lady Jane Grey.

Jane at first refused, pointing out that, having been contracted to Lord Hertford, son of the ill-fated Somerset, she was not free. No written records of this contract have survived, possibly because they were destroyed on the orders of the Suffolks. Historians claim that the reaction of the thwarted Suffolks was violent: the Duke swore, Frances struck Jane repeatedly. Between them they persuaded her. Frances would later claim, however, that she had vigorously opposed the match. Certainly, it is on record that she had previously stated that she did not wish Jane to marry too young. Northumberland enlisted the help of the sickly young King. Jane's father was promised that the marriage would win him a 'scarcely imaginable haul of immense wealth and great honour to his house'.[12]

Meanwhile, 13-year-old Hertford, whom Frances still called 'son', continued to visit the Greys. Perhaps the boy was already attracted to Jane's pretty sister Katherine. Northumberland, however, had other plans for her. For all three Grey sisters, their cousin Margaret Clifford, Suffolk's niece Margaret Audley and Northumberland's own daughter Catherine Dudley, he had planned dynastic unions calculated to reinforce his power base, and to ensure the survival of the evangelical elite as the ruling force in England. The priority was the hasty betrothal of Jane and Guilford Dudley. This raised eyebrows, especially in the light of the King's obviously deteriorating condition, both in court circles and in the streets. The King was dying. The imperial ambassador noted that 'the matter he ejects from his mouth is sometimes coloured a greenish-yellow and black, sometimes pink, like the colour of blood'.[13] The physicians were at a loss. The ambassador noted also that Northumberland was now hedging his bets by insisting on the Princess Mary's rights to full arms as a 'Princess of England'. 'This all seems to point to his desire to conciliate the said Lady and earn her favour, and to show that he does not aspire to the crown.'[14] He added that the betrothal of Jane and Guilford looked suspicious, and was causing loose talk in the taverns. Several people of both sexes had their ears cut off for spreading rumours.

On 25 May 1553, a triple wedding was celebrated at Durham House, Northumberland's London residence. The young couples, robed in silver and gold fabrics forfeited to the King by the Duke of Somerset, were Guilford and Jane; the sickly young Lord Herbert and pretty 12-year-old Katherine; and Guilford's sister, 12-year-old Catherine Dudley, and Henry Hastings, son of the Grey's neighbour, the Earl of Huntingdon. The King, too ill to attend, sent rich gifts of ornaments and jewels. There were games, jousts and masques. Three days later the doctors confirmed that the King had only months to live. He was in agony, his swollen body covered with ulcers, unable to sleep without opiates. He now began making changes to details in his will. He crossed out the provision that Frances should rule as governor if he died before any male heirs were born. Above the line he inserted the stipulation that the throne should pass to Frances's male heirs, but in the absence of any such issue 'before my death', the throne should pass to Lady Jane Grey 'and her' heirs male.[15] Edward, like his father, had virtually excluded Frances, who was not pregnant and had no sons. She could therefore neither become governor nor claim the throne, which would pass directly to Jane as queen regnant.

The news that Jane was now Edward's heir upset both Jane and her father. Jane was stunned and horrified. She asked permission to make a quick visit home to see her mother, another indication that Frances was not the bullying parent depicted by later historians. This was refused by the Duchess of Northumberland, who reminded Jane that she needed to be near at hand at the moment of the King's death. Jane stole out of Durham House, took a boat and hastened down river to Suffolk Place, where her mother comforted her. Discovering Jane's disobedience, the Duchess of Northumberland sent a furious message to Suffolk Place threatening to keep Guilford with her if Jane did not return to the marital home. This would have caused a public scandal which none of the parties could afford, so an accommodation was reached, and the young couple moved into Catherine Parr's old house in Chelsea. Here they entertained their friends, and all seemed well, until they and several of their guests were struck down by a bout of food poisoning. The source was believed to be a salad made by a cook who had inadvertently picked the wrong leaf. But, as Edward's decision to name her his heir was at that very moment being sealed at Greenwich, Jane suspected her mother-in-law was behind it.

The dying King summoned senior judges to his bedside to ratify his will. He explained why he had disinherited his half-sisters in favour of Jane Grey, and instructed them to prepare the necessary documents. The judges had qualms. Some anxiously expressed concern before the Council that the will could not be enforced before the Act of Succession of 1544 was rescinded. Northumberland, furious at the potential thwarting of his ambitions, threatened to strip to his shirt and physically challenge anyone who opposed the King's wishes. He persuaded fourteen of the judges, but several refused. Frances was then summoned to meet with Edward to ensure she agreed to being passed over in favour of her daughter. On 21 June the nobility and chief officers of the Crown were commanded to sign the legal document: Edward had considered the question of the succession for a long time, both in sickness and in health. His sisters were only his 'half-blood', they were illegitimate and there was the dire possibility that they would marry foreigners. By contrast, his married and betrothed cousins, the Grey daughters, were legitimate, had been honourably brought up and 'exercised in good and Godly learning, and other noble virtues'.[16]

Suffolk was furious that Frances had been passed over, and convinced that Northumberland planned to see his own son crowned as Jane's co-ruler.

Edward was now desperately ill. In a last-ditch effort to keep the King alive until Parliament could be called in September, an old crone who enjoyed a reputation as a healer was summoned. She dosed him with potions including arsenic, which only aggravated his suffering. The country was in turmoil, groaning under the boot of Northumberland. It was rumoured that he was poisoning the King and intended to hand the realm over to the French. Edward made his last public appearance on 27 June, showing himself at a window, his pale wasted figure scarcely reassuring to the watching crowd. That same night, Northumberland was seen visiting the residence of the new French ambassador, Antoine de Noailles. When the people got wind of it gossip spread like wildfire and two citizens were chained to a post and whipped for uttering 'opprobrious and seditious words'[17] about Northumberland and his allies.

On 6 July Edward died. The next morning the Mayor of London and City Magistrates, along with the guard, swore an oath of allegiance to Queen Jane at Greenwich. Jane was brought by river to Sion, Northumberland's house at Richmond, where she was joined on 8 July by her father-in-law, Pembroke (Sir William Herbert), Northampton, Huntingdon and the Earl of Arundel, widower of her father's sister, Katherine Fitzalan. The noblemen knelt to pay homage to the 16-year-old Jane, who seemed overwhelmed by the stupendous change in her fortunes and the responsibility suddenly thrust upon her. Seeing her confusion, they agreed to ask Frances to join them, and she arrived accompanied by Northampton's wife and the Duchess of Northumberland. Together they managed to persuade Jane that she was Edward's rightful heir. Next day, Northumberland, as President of the Council, informed her officially that the King was dead and that she was Queen. The assembled company, including the Duke and Duchess of Northumberland and her own parents, then fell to their knees and swore to defend her with their blood. At this point, Jane, brilliant, rational, highly trained and committed evangelical as she was, collapsed. She fell to the ground, weeping inconsolably. This dramatic collapse generated the notion of Jane as unwilling victim of the manipulations of others. But Jane soon recovered, stood up and delivered a speech in which she modestly accepted her kingdom, expressing the hope that God would 'grant her the grace to enable her to govern ... with His approbation and to His glory'.[18]

At the celebratory banquet Jane sat in state on a raised platform under a canopy. A proclamation was read out declaring Mary and Elizabeth illegitimate, and reiterating the fear that they might reintroduce the Roman religion or marry foreigners. At Paul's Cross that morning, Nicholas Ridley, the Bishop of London, had preached the rightness of Jane's cause and declared Mary and Elizabeth bastards. His words were ill-received by the public. Clearly, Henry VIII's daughters still had the support of the people, if not of the evangelical elite.

Early on Monday 10 July, Jane travelled by barge along the river from Richmond to Westminster, where, as tradition demanded, she would take possession of the Tower. Having donned the formal royal robes laid out in readiness, she returned to her covered barge and was rowed on to Durham House to dine at noon.

At the subsequent meeting of the Privy Council, the bombshell fell: Northumberland had been convinced that Princess Mary would never have the audacity to mount a challenge without the support of the Emperor Charles V, and equally sure that Charles would not be willing to confront France and England. Her opponents had forgotten, seeing the frail, ageing figure of the deeply religious Mary, her Spanish pride, and that she was the granddaughter of the warlike Ferdinand and the indomitable Queen Isabella. Mary had sent a letter marked with royal seal, asserting that she, not Jane, was the rightful heir to the throne, and demanding their allegiance. The Council were shocked. Both Frances and the Duchess of Northumberland, when they learned of the letter, burst into tears. Jane alone was composed. She would defend England against the papist threat posed by Mary.

After lunch, at 2 o'clock, Jane, Guilford, their mothers, Jane's father Suffolk and ladies of the court arrived aboard the royal barges at the Tower. Here Jane was welcomed by Northumberland and the other members of the Council, and the company processed to the Tower gates. Guilford walked beside Jane, cap in hand, and Frances carried her train, a striking visual symbol of how the natural order had been overturned. The procession entered the Tower to the thunderous salute of cannon. As the great gates swung shut behind them, the crowd were called to attention by a fanfare of trumpets, and two heralds read out the proclamation declaring Jane Queen and the daughters of Henry VIII excluded from the succession as illegitimate. When the proclamation was read out at Cheapside and Fleet Street, few cried 'God save her', and at Cheapside a boy called Gilbert Potter shouted that Mary was the rightful Queen. His master, a gunner at the Tower, reported him, and he was arrested and put in the pillory. At 8 the next morning, to another blast of trumpets, he had his ears cut off, while a herald in royal livery read out his offence. There was general sympathy for the boy, and the sense that Jane's reign had begun inauspiciously.

Mary's defiance continued. The Tudor name was a rallying point, and hatred of Northumberland motivated others. On 12 July the Lord Treasurer, William Paulet, Marquess of Winchester, brought Jane the Crown Jewels, although she had not requested them. She had stated that she would not be crowned for at least a fortnight. Paulet suggested that she should try on the crown 'to see if it did become me',[19] and when she hesitated, he added that another crown would be made for her husband, to crown him as King. Jane had been signing herself 'Jane the Quene'; now she faced the possibility that she would be sharing her throne with her husband, and a row flared up between them. Jane eventually agreed with Guilford that he would be 'made King by me and by Act of Parliament'[20] in September. But moments later Jane thought better of it and called for the Earl of Arundel and her sister Katherine's father-in-law the Earl of Pembroke. She told them she was content to make her husband a duke, but not a king. Another report claimed that the title she had in mind was 'Duke of Clarence'. Meanwhile, the imperial ambassadors, Scheyfve and Renard, added fuel to the flames of suspicion surrounding Northumberland, claiming that he had made a secret deal with the

French to place the French King Henri II's ward, Mary, Queen of Scots, aged 11, on the throne of England if Jane proved unco-operative.

As Jane's forces were mobilised against Princess Mary, carts bearing troops and ammunition began to trundle into the Tower under the wondering gaze of Londoners. Guns, bows and arrows, spears, pikes, armour, gunpowder, tents and victuals were gathered. Jane confirmed her father as her chosen commander of her army: 'saying with great boldness that she could have no safer defence for her Majesty than her own loving father'.[21] Suffolk, however, under all the stress, was a broken reed, suffering from fainting fits, colic and the 'stone'. Realising that he was in no fit condition to lead an army, Jane asked the Council to select someone else. The Council picked the obvious candidate, Northumberland, whose crushing of the rebellion in 1549 made him uniquely qualified.

Northumberland, who feared his back-stabbing political enemies more than any foe, was reluctant to leave the capital but could not refuse. After a last interview with Jane, he and his army set out on 14 July for East Anglia, watched in icy silence by the crowds. As they passed through Shoreditch, Northumberland noted, 'The people press to see us, but not one sayeth God speed us.'[22]

Jane ordered a guard for the city gates and a curfew was imposed. News of the hostile mood in London encouraged popular support for rebellious country nobles to the west in the Thames Valley. Jane learned that in Buckinghamshire Mary had been proclaimed Queen, while she herself had been described as 'Queen of a new and petty invention'.[23] The East Anglian towns had been quick a few days before to proclaim Jane Queen, but now even evangelicals were rallying to Mary's cause. As Northumberland and Northampton made for Bury St Edmunds to cut off Mary's support from the Midlands, Mary herself rode out before her troops at Framlingham Castle in Suffolk on a white horse. When the horse spooked at the flashing steel and fluttering banners, she dismounted and walked along the ranks. Each soldier knelt, and she spoke to many, displaying the common touch. Many of the men loathed Northumberland, who had ridden roughshod over them so long.

In the Tower, Jane learned that five royal ships' crews had mutinied and forced their officers to defect to Mary's side. Jane remained undeterred, but her councillors were terrified by the wave of popular anger that was threatening to submerge them all, so 'each man began to pluck in his horns'.[24] Jane, aware now that she could not rely even on her own Council, ordered a strong guard to be mounted round the Tower. The gates were shut at 7 o'clock and the keys carried up to Jane in person. On 18 July she began raising new troops to be led into rebel Buckinghamshire. Even as she attempted to mount her defences, her generals had betrayed or abandoned her. Northampton and Northumberland, receiving letters from the Council warning that all was lost, fled Bury St Edmunds after nightfall, making for Cambridge, the focal point of the evangelical revolution.

Amid these ominous events, Jane stood godmother to the infant son of Edward Underhill, a radical evangelical cleric. Although too busy to attend the ceremony in the church on Tower Hill, she chose the names as tradition dictated. The baby was called after her husband Guilford and her father, Harry Suffolk. Her co-godparent, Pembroke, her sister Katherine's father-in-law, was already preparing to betray her. Gathering a large number of aldermen at his grim fortress, Baynard's Castle, he announced that they were riding to Cheapside to proclaim Mary Queen. Many of those present wept openly, rejoicing that the civil war was now over.

Mary was duly proclaimed as Queen, bonfires were lighted, church bells rang, men ran through the streets shouting the news. When the Council's soldiers reached the Tower, Jane's father realised all cause was lost. Threatened with arrest if he did not sign the proclamation, he complied, and on Tower Hill read it out declaring that Mary was Queen. He then went to find his daughter to break the news to her that she was Queen no longer. Jane received the news with composure, reminding him that he had encouraged her to accept the crown. Suffolk then dismantled her canopy of estate with his own hands. Jane retired with her mother and ladies to an inner chamber, 'with deep sorrow, but bearing the ill fate with great valour and endurance'.[25]

Jane and her husband were now subjected to mockery from the Tower guards. They were divested of all their valuables, even their petty cash. Every day, more of their connections were brought in as prisoners. When Northumberland and two of his sons, Ambrose and Henry, arrived in London on the morning of 25 July 1553, Arundel, in charge of the prisoners, noted the ugly mood of the crowd. Fearing that Northumberland might be lynched, he urged him to remove his distinctive red cloak, which he did. As the prisoners with their cavalry escort rode up the hill towards the Tower they were pelted with rocks amid cries of 'Traitor'. Sixteen-year-old Henry Dudley began to weep in terror. A boy around his own age burst through the ranks of men at arms lining the route and ran about, brandishing a sword and yelling. He had no ears. It was Gilbert Potter, the first victim of Jane's reign, but not the last.

On 27 July, Suffolk was brought to the Tower, to Jane's distress.

Frances rode immediately to Mary, now at Beaulieu in Essex. She arrived at 2 in the morning, shortly after the arrival of the imperial ambassadors. Later that morning, after her prayers, Mary received her. Frances pleaded that the Greys were pawns of the ambitious Northumberland, whom she also accused of poisoning her husband, Suffolk. She contended that, having poisoned Edward (widely believed), Northumberland was determined to kill Suffolk too, as Jane's protector. In that case, either Guilford would have become co-ruler, or, in collusion with the French, Northumberland would have placed 11-year old Mary Queen of Scots on the throne.

Mary's instinct was to pardon both Suffolk and Jane. She recalled how Frances's mother Mary Rose had abhorred Anne Boleyn and treasured the friendship of Katherine of Aragon, even attempting to persuade her brother Henry VIII that it was madness to think of forsaking her in favour of Anne Boleyn. But Scheyfve and Renard insisted that releasing Jane would risk 'scandal and danger'.[26] Reluctantly, Mary decided to detain Jane, but pardoned Suffolk the next day. He remained in the Tower for a fortnight, too ill to be moved. Jane was charged with treason. The usual penalty was death.

On 3 August, Mary entered London in a formal procession of nobles and courtiers to claim the Tower. Her purple velvet gown, heavily embroidered in gold, swamped her slight figure. She was described by one eyewitness as 'more than middling fair',[27] but she was ginger-haired, 37 years old, and looked middle-aged. Her half-brother's coffin was still watched over by twelve gentlemen, but no papist candle flickered in the gloom. On 8 August his funeral took place according to the reformed religion. Mary had wanted a full requiem mass, but was persuaded by the imperial ambassadors that this would cause confrontation, so she had a mass said for him in private.

Then the trials of the traitors began. Northumberland recanted his evangelical views and re-embraced Catholicism in an effort to appease the Queen. He scribbled a desperate letter to Arundel at the last hour, in which he entreated him to beg the Queen to spare him and grant him 'the life of a dog, that I might but live and kiss her feet'.[28] No pardon came. Northumberland and several others were beheaded. It was still common knowledge that Mary intended to pardon Jane. When she heard, while dining with friends, of her father-in-law's eleventh-hour conversion in hopes of a pardon, Jane was scandalised: 'Pardon?' she cried. 'Woe worth him! He hath brought me and our stock in most miserable calamity and misery by his exceeding ambition.' She wondered how he dared ask for a pardon when he had taken the field against Mary's forces. But his life was 'odious to all men, and as his life had been wicked and full of dissimulation, so was his end'. Jane declared she herself would die rather than renounce her faith, young though she was. She quoted the Scriptures, concluding that Northumberland was damned.[29]

This outburst crystallises Jane's intellectual position. While, like her mother, she blamed Northumberland for the lethal situation the Greys had become involved in, she intended to make a personal stand against the reintroduction of the mass, and die defending the new religion if it came to it. In her trial on 13 November she had the opportunity to display her commitment.

She was led from the Tower with her husband Guilford, his brothers Ambrose and Henry, and Thomas Cranmer, the Archbishop of Canterbury. With Cranmer in the lead, the little group of prisoners proceeded on foot to the Guildhall, led by a man carrying an axe, indicating to all who saw the procession that the accused were charged with a capital offence. Guilford wore black velvet slashed with white satin. Jane too was all in black, symbolising penitence, her black cape lined in black, her French hood trimmed in black. She held a prayer book in her hands, symbolising her piety. Another, covered in black velvet, hung from her waist. The lexicographer Michel Angelo Florio, who had dedicated his Tuscan dictionary to her earlier that year, recorded that Jane remained cool and composed throughout the proceedings until the sentence was read out. Jane was to be burned alive, the usual fate of a female convicted of treason. The procession retraced its footsteps. The axe was now turned inward as a sign that the death sentence had been passed. Many in the crowd wept in pity for Jane.

Mary did not want Jane to die. To present her as less dangerous, it was claimed the Grey sisters were illegitimate since Suffolk had previously been betrothed to the Earl of Arundel's daughter before he married Frances.[30] Suffolk back-pedalled furiously, swearing undying fealty to Mary, retracting his attacks on the repeal of Protestant legislation, and declaring that Mary should be free to marry whomever she chose, even if her choice were Philip of Spain, the son of Charles V. But when it became known that Mary had secretly accepted Philip's proposal, alarm bells rang. Would England now be subsumed into the Habsburg Empire?

Evangelical noblemen from the Greys' circle began to plot to prevent the Spanish marriage and the reconciliation with Rome, through replacing Mary with Elizabeth. Suffolk saw that his daughter's cause was now hopeless. He knew that if the plot failed, Jane risked execution.

The rebels finalised their plans just before Christmas. Suffolk was to raise support in Leicestershire; others were to recruit in Kent, Herefordshire and Devon. But through incautious boasting the plot became known. Jane's uncle, Lord Thomas Grey, urged Suffolk, still sick in bed suffering from the stone, to bring the rising in Leicestershire forward. Panicked and in agony, Suffolk relied upon his brother's judgement.

The Queen offered him the chance to prove his loyalty and gave him the opportunity to lead her troops against the rising in Kent led by his co-conspirator Thomas Wyatt. Suffolk fobbed the messenger off, saying, 'I was coming to her Grace. Ye may see I am booted and spurred,' ordered the messenger to be plied with ale and given a tip.[31]

When he and his brothers Lord Thomas and Lord John failed to arrive at court they were declared traitors. The next day Suffolk's Leicestershire neighbour and former long-term political ally, the Earl of Huntingdon, offered to pursue and arrest them. His son was Jane's brother-in-law, having married Catherine Dudley in the famous triple wedding of May 1553. Capturing Suffolk would both ingratiate him with the new regime and would also ensure that his family achieved a long-held ambition, total dominance in Leicestershire.

Suffolk sped northward over 'foul and deep' roads, planning to meet his brother at St Albans. They missed each other and eventually caught up with each other at Lutterworth. Their recruitment drive was ineffectual: Suffolk was tainted by his former association with the unpopular Northumberland. He also naively announced his lack of money. He found the city gates of Coventry closed in his face, and learned that Huntingdon had betrayed him. He and his company fled to his nearby castle at Astley, where they stripped off their armour. His brothers borrowed woollen coats from their servants to disguise their rank. Suffolk distributed his remaining cash to his followers and told them to escape as best they could. His keeper Nicholas Laurence helped him hide in a hollow oak tree, but only the next day Huntingdon's men forced Laurence to reveal the hiding place, and Suffolk was run to ground with dogs. Lord John was found hiding in the hay, while Lord Thomas reached Wales before he too was captured.

The Kentish rebels marched into London, looting and burning. Although their intention was to place Elizabeth on the throne, Jane and Guilford had already been convicted of treason and represented a potential danger. As the rebels advanced, Mary agreed to sign their death warrants, burning for Jane, hanging, drawing and quartering for her husband, both sentences commuted to beheading. The sentences were to be carried out on 7 February, within the week. The executions were delayed by further rebel advances. The battle in London continued all day until at last the rebels were defeated. In the early evening Jane heard the clang and clatter as rebel leaders were brought into the Tower. Mary was still unwilling to sign her death warrant. But the imperial ambassadors and the Privy Council, who had proclaimed Jane in the summer, combined forces to persuade her. The date was set for Friday 9 February.

Mary sent her own personal chaplain, John Feckenham, to the Tower to help Jane prepare for death and to cleanse her soul of heresy. Jane told the friendly former Benedictine monk that she was expecting him, but the time had passed for a theological debate. The priest returned to Mary and pleaded for a few more days of life so that Jane could receive instruction. Mary agreed. Jane was to die on Monday 12 February. Jane was resolute. Among her writings in the Tower is her prayer for courage: 'Lord, thou God and father of my life hear me poor and desolate woman. Arm me, I beseech Thee, with thy armour, that I may stand fast.'[32] Feckenham found her cool and composed as ever. He complimented her on bearing her pain 'with a constant and patient mind'. Jane replied that far from regretting her situation, she regarded it as a 'manifest declaration of God's favour towards me'. She welcomed the occasion to repent of her sins. The two now engaged in a lengthy discussion of the path to salvation and the Real Presence of Christ in the Host and the wine. Jane attacked the Catholic Church as the 'spouse of the Devil, for its idolatrous interpretations'.

Jane was left to compose her last letters, two of which survive, although the first is suspicious. It did not surface until 1570; perhaps the family may merely have wished to suppress the unflattering portrayal of Suffolk. In it she reminds him how she was pressed to take the crown. No letters to Frances or Mary Grey survive. But to Katherine Jane wrote that she must not attempt to save herself by accepting the Catholic faith. Guilford begged to have one last meeting with his bride, 'before dying he wished to embrace and kiss her for the last time'.[33] Jane replied that this would only increase their misery and pain; they should postpone it until they met elsewhere.

At daybreak the Tower rang to the sound of hammering as the scaffold for Jane was erected by the White Tower. As a royal princess Jane would have the privilege of dying in the privacy of the Tower grounds. Hammering echoed throughout the city as gallows were erected at every gate and on Tower Hill, where Guilford was to die. Just before 10, Jane watched as he was led out from the Beauchamp Tower. As Jane emerged for the last walk of her life, Guilford's body was carried into the Tower chapel, his head wrapped in a bloody cloth. Jane, who showed no emotion, followed the lieutenant of the Tower to the scaffold. She wore the same black gown and carried an open prayer book. Her ladies were in tears but Jane read her prayers with a dry eye. She mounted the steps, approached the rail and addressed a select audience.

She admitted her guilt in the traditional format, but the admission was qualified:

Good people, I am come hither to die, and by a law I am condemned to the same. The fact, indeed, against the Queen's Highness was unlawful, and the consenting thereunto by me: but touching the procurement and desire thereof by me or on my behalf, I do wash my hands thereof in innocence, before God, and in the face of you, good Christian people, this day.

Still gripping her prayer book, she wrung her hands, continuing:

I pray you all, good Christian people, to bear me witness that I die a true Christian woman, and that I look to be saved by none other means, but only but the mercy of God in the merits of his only son, Jesus Christ: and I confess, when I did know the word of God I neglected the same, loved myself and the world, and therefore this plague or punishment is happily and worthily happened unto me for my sins; and ye I thank God of his goodness that he has thus given me time and respect to repent.[34]

She asked them to assist her with their prayers while she still lived. She wanted no papist prayers for the dead. As she knelt down she turned to Feckenham and asked him: 'Shall I say this psalm?'

'Yea', he said.

She recited the *Misere mei Deus* in English, then rose to her feet, handed over her gloves and handkerchief to her gentlewoman Elizabeth Tilney, and her prayer book to Thomas Bridges, the brother of the Lieutenant of the Tower. She had inscribed it inside for his brother:

Good Master Lieutenant ... Live still to die, that by death you may purchase eternal life ... For as the Preacher says, there is a time to be born, and a time to die; and the day of death is better than the day of our birth. Yours, as the Lord knows, Jane Dudley.[35]

She began to untie her gown. The headsman stepped forward to assist her, but, horrified, she brushed him away and turned to her two ladies, who took her gown and helped her remove her headdress and kerchief. The executioner knelt and begged her forgiveness, which she willingly gave. He asked her to stand on the straw, and at that moment her eye fell upon the block, a rough beam of unhewn wood. 'I pray you dispatch me quickly,' she said.

As she knelt, she was struck by the thought that perhaps he would misinterpret her request and strike before she was ready. 'Will you take [my head] before I lay me down?' 'No, Madam,' replied the executioner.

Jane tied her own handkerchief about her eyes and stretched out a hand, groping blindly for the block. Panicked, she demanded: 'What shall I do? Where is it?'

Appalled, someone guided her to the block. She laid her head upon the beam, stretched out and said: 'Lord, into thy hands I commend my spirit.'[36]

Blood spurted everywhere. A French diplomat, surveying the gory scene on the scaffold, was amazed that that slight body could have produced so much blood. Jane's head was cast into the same pit in the Tower chapel as that of Guilford.

Lady Eleanor and the Derby Claim

After Mary Rose's second daughter, Eleanor, married Lord Clifford, eldest son of the Earl of Cumberland, Brandon endeavoured to help the young couple by enlisting Cromwell's support. But he felt Cumberland underestimated the real cost of maintaining his son at court, and was unimpressed with Eleanor's country residence, fearing it was unhealthy. In 1540, he succeeded in increasing the Cliffords' fortunes by winning a major lease for them.

Both Eleanor's sons died in infancy, but through her daughter, the head-strong Lady Margaret Clifford, her descendants continued as possible claimants to the throne of England long after Eleanor's death, and after her sister Frances's line had died out. The ambitious Northumberland had intended to marry Margaret, then aged 15, to his son, Lord Guilford Dudley, in 1552. Margaret was the heiress to her father's vast northern estates, where Northumberland cherished aspirations of establishing himself as a magnate. But Clifford was reluctant to see his only sur-viving child married to a fourth son, and fobbed Northumberland off. Northumberland urged the young King to intervene on his behalf. Other members of the court were appalled that, while Northumberland was leading the army against rebels in the Northern Marches, the King consented to act as his marriage broker: Edward sent an extraordinary letter to Cumberland on 4 July, desiring him to 'grow to some good end forthwith in the matter of marriage between the Lord Guilford and his daughter; with the licence to the said earl and all others that shall tra-vail therein to do their best to the conducement of it.'[1] The suspicion arose that Northumberland was pressing for the marriage because he harboured designs on the throne for himself and his family.

Having rejected Guilford Dudley as a suitor for Margaret's hand, Cumberland, rather strangely, now consented to marry her to

Northumberland's ageing older brother, Sir Andrew Dudley, in 1553. Possibly he felt pressured into this unlikely match, fearing Northumberland's ruthlessness and increasing power; but at the last minute Cumberland reneged on the marriage contract – fortunately for Margaret, who thereby escaped the fate of her cousin Jane Grey, a sacrificial victim on the altar of her father-in-law's ambition and her own father's vanity.

Although neither projected marriage to members of Northumberland's family had taken place, Margaret retained the sumptuous cloth Sir Andrew had sent for her bridal gown. She wore it for her wedding to Henry Stanley, Lord Strange, the future 4th Earl of Derby. With a legitimate claim to the succession not only by virtue of her descent from Mary Rose, but by the written testament of King Henry VIII, Margaret would never escape the spotlight, often through her own fault.

For Margaret's spectacular wedding, Queen Mary laid on a full programme of feasting, jousting and a tournament on horseback with swords, in which three of the Dudley brothers performed, and a contest of the Spanish *jeu de cannes* favoured by Queen Mary's husband, Philip of Spain. In this competition, combatants carried targets and hurled rods at one another. Although to English spectators the gallant entertainment appeared tame compared with the thrills and spills of tilting on horseback, King Philip participated so enthusiastically that the Queen begged him to desist.

Margaret's wedding took place in a country still reeling from the shock of the first of the notorious burnings that would earn the Queen the epithet Bloody Mary. John Rogers, a prebendary of St Paul's, had been executed at the stake only three days previously.

Margaret bore Derby five sons; three survived to continue the line. As Queen Mary declined, debilitated by age and depression, becoming a pale, shrivelled figure, Margaret hoped Mary would nominate her as her heir. Margaret's claim to the throne was inferior to that of her cousin Lady Jane Grey, since Margaret was descended from the younger sister. However, her mother Eleanor having died in 1547, it had the advantage of directness. If Princess Elizabeth were excluded on the grounds of illegitimacy, the same must apply to Lady Margaret Douglas, the Countess of Lennox, daughter of Henry VIII's older sister. Lady Margaret's father had had a wife living at the time of his 'marriage' to her mother. Mary, Queen of Scots, as the bride of the Dauphin, was clearly out of the running. That left the heirs of the French Queen, Mary Rose. The two surviving Grey sisters, Margaret's first cousins, although the daughters of Mary Rose's older daughter, were ineligible, tainted by the treason and execution of their sister Jane Grey and their father, Suffolk. Margaret, who feared and loathed the Grey sisters, never failed to point this out.

The question of the succession preoccupied the minds of not only the potential claimants and their adherents, but all the leading families and factions in the realm. Margaret's husband Lord Derby wisely never advanced his wife's claims; their sons displayed comparable discretion. The Earls of Derby were immensely rich and influential. The basis of the power of the great nobles was their ability to raise and maintain armed retainers, and their readiness to employ them in disputes. At times of crisis Elizabeth, Mary's successor, was forced, however reluctantly, to seek their assistance, although she and her advisers, the Cecils, strove to develop some strategy that would reduce the power of the nobility and also forestall any Catholic insurrection. Accordingly, Lord Derby was commanded to send his heir Ferdinando to court 'to be fashioned in good manners', a euphemism for intense indoctrination in Protestantism and unquestioning loyalty to Queen Elizabeth. (So successful was this training process that, when Ferdinando acceded to the Lordship of Man in 1594, legislation was swiftly passed in the Island against the 'reliques of popish superstition'.)

However, after his father's death in 1593, Ferdinando, now 5th Earl, briefly became the unwilling focus of a Catholic scheme to revive the family's pretension to the throne. The fact that Derby was one of the richest peers in England raised the hopes of exiled English Jesuits. The formal grounds advanced were that 'through propinquity of blood' the Stanleys were next in line to Queen Elizabeth. In the Derby heartlands in the north and west, Catholicism had survived, presumably with the connivance of Ferdinando's father and grandfather. The Cecils reported that Ferdinando was, in the view of leading Catholics, 'the fourth competitor in the road [i.e., claimant to the throne], *but if he be a Catholic, the first'.*[2]

The exiled Jesuits' agent on English soil was Richard Hesketh, an English adventurer who, having sought refuge in Spain, was sent back to operate in England on the promise of Spanish aid. When Ferdinando learned of the Catholic plot, Hesketh was captured and executed. Perhaps Ferdinando hoped to deflect suspicion: under the terms of Henry VIII's will, Ferdinando had been appointed Queen Elizabeth's successor. The throne was then to pass to Ferdinando's oldest daughter, Lady Anne Stanley. But Ferdinando died in mysterious circumstances after a violent fit of vomiting. It was rumoured that he had been poisoned by his Master of the Horse, possibly on the orders of the Cecils, or even the Queen herself.

Seacombe gives a vivid account of this event:

His [Ferdinando's] royal mistress, the Queen, had at that time many seditious and rebellious subjects, who, to avoid the punishment due to their crimes, fled to foreign countries. Amongst whom was one Richard Hackett, who was sent by these fugitives to prevail upon this noble and loyal Peer, to asume and set up a title and claim to the Crown of England, in right of his descent from Mary, the second daughter of Henry VII, and younger sister to King Henry VIII, and at that time Queen dowager of France, whose grandmother [granddaughter] was this Earl's mother; threatening, that unless he undertook this projected enterprize, and withal conceal him, the messenger and instigator of it, he should shortly die in a most wretched manner; but if he complied therewith, he might be assured of powerful assistance.

But this dutiful and loyal Earl, having no design or intention of claim against her Majesty, nor inclination to disturb her peaceable possesson at the hazard of his own life, honour, and opulent fortune; considered the proposition made to him as a snare laid for his destruston, and therefore rejected it with scorn and indignation.

However, these villainous menaces; proved not altogether vain, for within four months after, this noble Earl died a very miserable and surprizing death being seized and tormented by vomiting matter of a dark rusty colour, insomuch that he was supposed by the learned in the practice of physic and others to be poisoned, or else bewitched.

For there was found in his chamber, a little image made of wax, with hairs of the colour of his in the belly of it, which occasioned many and various speculations, conjectures, and constructions concerning the nature, meaning and effects thereof; but I have met with no remarks from the curious of that age, touching the real being, existence or power of witches and wizards, then or at any time in the world, nor of any observations made by them upon this extraordinary event, therefore submit so critical and obtruse a point to be discussed by the learned of our own times; and proceed to inform the reader, that his gentleman of horse was greatly suspected to have had a large share in this wicked scene and removal of his noble and indulgent master out of this world; for the same day the Earl took his bed, he fled away with one of his best horses, and was heard of no more.

His vomit was so violent and corroding, that it stained the silver and irons in the chimney of his room, upon which he had vomited; and when dead, though his body was wrapped in searcloth, and covered with lead, yet it so corrupted and putrified, that for a long time after, none could endure to come near the place it was laid in, till his burial.[3]

Ferdinando predeceased Queen Elizabeth by nine years. He was succeeded as Earl of Derby by his brother William, a less colourful character who knew better than to emphasise his claim to the throne. His mother, however, was less cautious. Although Margaret Clifford had been permitted to marry, she had been kept under close surveillance; retribution for any indiscretions she committed would be immediate and severe. With all three Grey sisters dead, Margaret became Elizabeth's heir under the terms of Henry VIII's will, a claim she trumpeted, with serious consequences. In her youth, Margaret's pretensions were dismissed as the vapourings of a fanciful chit of a girl. But when she continued to air her ill-advised aspirations after Elizabeth had succeeded to the throne, Margaret found herself in deep trouble. Her boasting that, in the eyes of many people, she was the heir presumptive to the crown, twice landed her in the Tower in 1579. Unrepentant, she was then accused of seeking by means of sorcery to discover when Queen Elizabeth would die, allegedly employing a magician, Dr Randall, a well-known physician, to cast spells to harm the Queen and to predict her death, a capital offence. Randall was convicted and hanged. Margaret was imprisoned until her death in 1596.[4]

After the failure of the Lady Jane Grey plot, it became clear that the Suffolk claims were doomed to failure. It was even questionable whether Henry VIII had had the right to bequeath the crown as he pleased, even with the authorisation of Parliament. Moreover, the will had not been signed by his own hand, as required by statute, but merely by dry stamp. There was much quibbling over the phrase 'and if it so happen that the said Lady Eleanor die without issue, then we will that the said Imperial Crown shall come to our next rightful heirs', not 'right heirs', as stated in the first Act of Succession.

Under Elizabeth, the legality of Mary Rose's marriage to Brandon and the legitimacy of their children was thrown into question. With each succeeding generation their connection with the throne grew increasingly remote.

Doomed and Secret Love

For 13-year-old Katherine and 9-year-old Mary Grey, life had become a nightmare. The horror did not stop with their sister's execution: across London rebels hung screaming in chains; prisoners were hung, drawn and quartered. Five days after Jane died, their father was escorted under heavy guard from the Tower to Westminster Hall. Suffolk faced his accusers courageously. His judges, however, found that Protestantism rather than patriotism had motivated him; he was found guilty of war-mongering, opposing the entry into England of Queen Mary's betrothed Philip of Spain, unsettling the crown and compassing the death of the Queen. He was taken by barge to the Watergate at the Tower, where he disembarked looking 'very heavy and pensive', and asked the bystanders to pray for him.

In a piece of Tudor theatre, rebels brought before the Queen, bound, with nooses about their necks, had been pardoned. But Frances knew her husband was doomed. She set about salvaging what she could from the wreckage to safeguard the future of her remaining two daughters. Bradgate and other Suffolk possessions were forfeited to the Crown. Frances implored the Queen to forgive Suffolk, if she could not pardon him, thus opening the possibility of eventual rehabilitation at court and the restoration of some of the attainted estates. Frances advised her daughters to exercise caution and resist the temptation to parade Protestant beliefs, as their father and sister had done.

Frances's worst fears were realised on 23 February 1554. Suffolk left the Tower under guard for Tower Hill, accompanied by Hugh Weston, the Queen's chaplain, who preached a sermon attacking Suffolk's religious beliefs. Suffolk was so angry that, when Weston began to follow him up the steps to the scaffold, he shoved him. The priest grabbed at Suffolk, and the two scuffling men tumbled indecorously to the foot of the scaffold.

Weston shouted that he was present on the Queen's orders; Suffolk relin-
quished his hold and recovered his dignity. He addressed the crowd, saying
he had offended the Queen and was justly condemned. He asked for the
Queen's forgiveness. Weston replied: 'My Lord, Her Grace has already forgiven you.' Suffolk reiterated his Protestant faith and recited the psalm of
the persecuted, *In te Domine speravi*. After Suffolk handed his cap and
scarf to the executioner and formally forgave him, a man stepped forward,
shouting that the Duke owed him money, demanding: 'My Lord, how
shall I do for the money that you do owe me?'[1] Suffolk told him to apply to
his officers. The execution then proceeded without further interruption.

On 24 April, Suffolk's brother Lord Thomas Grey, sentenced to death
in early March, was executed, and his head left on public display. But the
killing had begun to sicken people.

Frances now threw herself into rehabilitating her family fortunes.
In April several of the Grey manors in Leicestershire were restored to
her, including the lease of Beaumanor, near Bradgate, 'with free warren
and chase of deer and wild beast'. She hung up portraits of Catherine
Parr and her own mother, Mary Rose, the French Queen. In July 1554,
Frances was invited to join the Queen's Privy Chamber. Only six months
after their sister's traitor's death, Katherine and Mary found themselves
back at court. Gradually they settled into the routine of court life, and
started to feel increasingly secure. Physically, the sisters were a contrast:
pretty Katherine, sparkling with easy charm, had resisted the efforts of
her studious older sister and tutors to turn her into a scholar: Katherine
preferred pets to book-learning. Mary was stunted and plain, but intelligent and warm-hearted. At 8, she had been betrothed to a middle-aged
kinsman, Lord Grey of Wilton, a terrifying bridegroom for a child; Lord
Grey, a valiant warrior, was hideously disfigured, having had a Scottish
pike thrust through the roof of his mouth at the Battle of Pinkie in 1547.

At 12, only just old enough under canon law, Katherine had been married to Henry, Lord Herbert, son of the Earl of Pembroke, on the same day
as Jane married Guilford Dudley. Katherine knew and liked her 15-year-
old bridegroom. After the celebrations, Henry and Katherine repaired to
Baynard's Castle on the Thames. During the turbulent weeks that followed, the young couple grew close. When Henry's father announced
that they were to be divorced, they insisted that their marriage had been
consummated, desperate to prevent an annulment. But Pembroke, who
had yet to live down excluding Queen Mary from the succession, could
not risk Katherine becoming pregnant. Katherine was sent home to her
mother. The betrothal between Mary Grey and the battle-scarred Wilton
was also dissolved.

Katherine romanticised the union that had been blighted by politics, but her new duties absorbed her attention. Queen Mary rose early. Her ladies, impeccable in russet or black liveries, reported for duty at 9. Katherine followed the Queen to mass on Sundays. Her mother, Frances, attended the Queen as she dined under her canopy of estate, indulging her taste for highly flavoured food. The Queen's spirits were buoyant. She ordered new gowns in vibrant jewel colours and rich fabrics. Elated at the prospect of marriage to the Emperor's son, she hoped she would soon be blessed with heirs to secure the throne and the future of her religion in her father's realm. The Queen's mood infected everyone with a new sense of optimism.

On 20 July Philip arrived in England. Already dissatisfied with the marriage treaty, which gave him no authority in England, he was shocked when, by the light of the setting sun, he first beheld his bride. Ten years Mary's junior, he had been prepared for the age difference but not for her careworn appearance. So fair that she seemed to have no eyebrows, Mary wore a black velvet gown in the French fashion, embroidered with pearls and girdled with diamonds. Philip's Spanish entourage found it unflattering. The English, on the other hand, were delighted with Philip's youth, good looks and confident swagger.

The royal wedding was celebrated at Winchester Cathedral on 25 July 1554. At the banquet, Lord Herbert, Katherine's former husband, now a Gentleman of Philip's Privy Chamber, sat with the honoured guests. The Greys' friend Edward Underhill, whose son was christened Guilford on the last day of Jane's reign, gatecrashed the party. Having dodged the chief usher's attempts to bar him from the banqueting hall, Underhill blended in, waiting on the guests, bearing golden platters of meat and game. He noted the embellishments of the Hall and the fact that the Queen was seated in the place of precedence. After the feast, observing the dancing, he relished the annoyance of the Spaniards at being surpassed by the English. When the party broke up, Underhill made off with a huge venison pie, which he sent to London for his friends to enjoy.

By mid-September the court was buzzing with the news that the Queen was pregnant, but the bitter rivalry between the English and Spanish attendants was causing frequent clashes. As a distraction, Philip encouraged the Queen to hold spectacular masques and diversions. Also, intending to win over the flower of the English aristocracy so young nobles might later be persuaded to enlist in his father's wars, he achieved pardons even for the four Dudley brothers still imprisoned in the Beauchamp Tower. The youngest, Henry, was still married to the

Greys' cousin and childhood friend, Margaret Audley. Behind them they left the name Jane carved in the stonework.

Now, after losing her husband to the headsman's axe, Frances took an unprecedented step. Members of the Privy Council had suggested a possible marriage between Frances and Edward Courtney. At 12, Courtney, a great-grandson of Edward IV, had been imprisoned in the Tower in 1538. His father, accused of plotting to marry Courtney to Princess Mary, was executed. Courtney was only released on Mary's accession. Perhaps the idea was that, if Elizabeth, still considered illegitimate, were excluded, Mary might consider making Frances her heir. Mary had spitefully insinuated to her ladies that Elizabeth was not Henry VIII's daughter but bore a strong resemblance to handsome Mark Smeton, the young musician Anne Boleyn was reputed to have kept in a 'sweetmeat cupboard', calling for 'marmalade' whenever she required his personal services.[2] Mary had indicated that, despite the doubts about the Countess's legitimacy, her preferred heir would be her Catholic cousin Margaret Douglas, Countess of Lennox. She snubbed Frances by giving Margaret a prominent role at her wedding.

Neither Frances nor Courtney had any wish to marry each other. Frances recognised Courtney's instability. Courtney unchivalrously told the Queen he would rather emigrate than marry Frances. He might have saved himself the trouble. By the time he left England in May, Frances had married another.

Frances wanted to save her remaining daughters from danger, and refused to jeopardise the position of Elizabeth. Her former gentlewoman, Bess of Hardwick, and her husband, Sir William Cavendish, had asked Katherine to stand godmother to their infant daughter in March. She chose the name Elizabeth for the child – apparently innocently enough, since the mother's name was Elizabeth, but a tacit hint that the Greys supported the evangelical Elizabeth.

Frances had seen the peaceful domestic bliss achieved by her step-mother and friend Catherine Suffolk. After losing her husband, Brandon, and both her young sons, Catherine had scandalised the gossips by wedding a social inferior, her gentleman usher, Sir Richard Bertie. Frances, too, decided to choose a man whose station in life would for ever preclude her from any aspirations to the throne: she married her Master of the Horse, Adrian Stokes. Stokes was a year her junior, a former soldier and a highly educated Protestant. After their marriage, Frances largely retired from court. Her health problems increased; some may have occasioned, or been caused by, failed pregnancies. Her daughter Mary, now aged 10, remained in her care.[3]

Katherine, as the daughter of the Queen's first cousin, had her own rooms and attendants, and her pampered pet dogs and monkeys. She enjoyed court life, the games, gossip and dancing, despite the gathering clouds of intrigue and paranoia. The Queen, demoralised by her failure to produce an heir, now cut a woebegone, shrunken figure, washed out from being bled to cure her depression. Philip had flounced off, refusing to return unless his wife granted him a full coronation, something Mary knew Parliament would never agree to. He then demanded that Elizabeth, as Mary's heir, should be married off to an imperial ally. Upon reading this letter, Mary hurled her mirror across the room in a fury.

In March 1556, Mary was shaken by the revelation of a plot to invade England from France and replace her with Elizabeth, who was to be married to Courtney. In the wake of this disclosure, ten leading nobles lost their heads. Courtney himself escaped to France, only to die there later the same year, poisoned, it was said, by Philip's agents. Mary's religious fanaticism and her obsession with heretics and their intrigues deepened. Smithfield's grisly fires smouldered where Protestants had burned to death. An Italian Catholic described watching a man of 70 hobbling to the stake that year 'willingly, angrily and pertinaciously'.[4] He was followed by a young blind boy, who was also burned to death.

Katherine, like her mother and sister, maintained her friendships with her old Protestant friends, although they all disguised their true beliefs. That summer, Jane's writings were republished in Geneva. Fourteen-year-old Katherine's chief confidante was her childhood friend Lady Jane Seymour, the clever 16-year-old daughter of the Protector Somerset. The two girls had much in common: both were the daughters of noblemen executed for treason, both had been proposed as brides for King Edward. Sometimes they shared a bed, chattering till the small hours. Katherine poured out her affection for her former husband, Lord Herbert, and her dream that the Queen might someday permit them to remarry.

In March 1557, Philip returned to England. Hopes of a return to the glamorous days of masques and feasts were soon dashed when a second plot came to light. Protestant exiles backed by the French 'invaded' Scarborough from a French vessel. The exiles, led by the imaginative but bungling Thomas Stafford, were quickly rounded up, and the ringleaders, including Stafford, executed. Katherine and Mary Grey knew Stafford well. He had supported their father's rising in the Midlands in 1554, and his sister Dorothy would remain Mary Grey's lifelong friend.

This invasion, possibly engineered by an agent provocateur, destroyed the peace between France and England. Queen Mary now formally aligned herself with the imperial cause. In June, England declared war on

France. Many of Katherine's friends, including her former husband Lord Herbert, went off to war. In January 1558, Calais fell to the French. The English, debilitated by war and a succession of poor harvests, succumbed in their thousands to an influenza epidemic, which swept through the countryside, eventually reaching the court. Philip had left again, and the Queen, now a pathetic huddled figure, draped in black, hugged her swollen belly, which she now knew was not great with child but with disease. Elizabeth and her faithful William Cecil, surveyor of her estates, were already planning their next move in the event of Mary's death.

Katherine accompanied her friend Jane Seymour, sick with influenza, in a horse-drawn litter to Jane's mother's house, Hanworth in Middlesex, and spent a wonderful summer there with the Seymours while Jane recuperated. Katherine, at almost 18, slender, blue-eyed and blonde, caught the eye of Jane Seymour's brother, 19-year-old Edward, Earl of Hertford. The attraction was mutual: Katherine forgot her first husband. Hertford had the finely drawn, aquiline good looks of his haughty mother, a descendant of Edward III; he was attractive to women, and he knew it. He had an old score to settle with Katherine's former father-in-law, Pembroke. Hertford remembered how, at age 10, he had galloped across country to entreat Pembroke's help with the coup being mounted against his own father, Somerset. Pembroke refused.

The romance between Katherine and 'Ned' Seymour was perhaps inevitable; it was also political dynamite. Ned was of royal blood, too, on the maternal side, yet had no solid claim to the throne: if Katherine married the heir of the Protector who brought the 'true religion' to England, she would become a desirable alternative to the unmarried Elizabeth. If she bore a son, the threat to Elizabeth would increase a thousandfold. The Protestant view that female rule was contrary to the will of God was rapidly gaining credence.

The young couple's attachment soon became serious. Hertford asked his sister Jane, who passed secret messages between the lovers, 'to break with the Lady Katherine touching marriage'.[5] Before Katherine could reply, Ned's mother found out. Anne Somerset had endured enough terror to last a lifetime. She had recently remarried, and, like Frances and Catherine Suffolk, had chosen a man inferior to her in rank, her Steward, Francis Newdigate. This removed her from the perilous position of being perceived as a threat. Aware of the mortal danger a royal marriage would place him in, Anne begged Hertford to forget any notion of an alliance with Katherine. The 19-year-old Earl retorted that he intended to see Katherine when and where he pleased, 'both in that house and also in the court',[6] so long as the Queen did not expressly forbid him to see her.

The couple's opportunities to meet were curtailed after the summer, when Katherine returned to court. By October 1558, it was clear the Queen was in poor health. On 17 November, she died. Katherine and her ladies laid out the body. The Queen's embalmed remains lay in the chapel at St James's for almost a month. Katherine and the Queen's ladies took turns at keeping vigil and mass was said round the clock. Elizabeth, determined that there should be no lack of honour accorded to a Tudor monarch, threatened to punish anyone who neglected to pay their last respects. Requiem mass was said for Mary and for her Catholic kingdom. Once the mourning drapery was removed, the images would go, and the walls, newly whitewashed, would resound no more to the chanting of the rosary.

If Katherine expected honours to be heaped upon her as the next Protestant heir, she misjudged Elizabeth. Elizabeth had not forgotten that Katherine was the daughter of a traitor and the sister of Jane Grey, who had usurped her throne. Katherine was demoted from the Privy Chamber to the Presence Chamber, a public space to which all the major notables had access. On Saturday, from the humbler place allocated to her at the Tower, Katherine witnessed Elizabeth's state entry into London. Elizabeth, a true Tudor, understood the power of pageantry. The snow-laden murk was brightened by the courtiers' flashing gems and gold collars. Trumpeters in scarlet liveries and heralds in coat armour preceded the litter of white cloth of gold litter lined with pink satin in which the Queen reclined. Beneath her jewel-studded crown her red hair flowed loose – a symbol of chastity – over Queen Mary's coronation mantle of white cloth of silver and gold. Footmen in silver-decorated crimson velvet jerkins and Gentlemen Pensioners clad in scarlet walked beside the Queen's litter. The sight of the darkly handsome nobleman who rode directly behind the Queen set tongues wagging. Elizabeth's Master of the Horse, Sir Robert Dudley, the son, grandson and brother of executed traitors, now appeared quite unabashed by the weight of his disgraceful legacy. Mounted on a magnificent destrier, he led the Queen's white palfrey.

Katherine, perched on a crimson hassock in a chariot upholstered in striped scarlet and gold satin, studded with golden nails, surveyed the gorgeously draped and decorated streets and the cheering crowds. Next day, splendidly gowned, crowned with a coronet, almost deafened by the church bells and the fanfare of organs, fifes, trumpets and drums, she processed into Westminster Abbey after the Queen. Katherine's cousin Margaret Audley, the newly wed Duchess of Norfolk, bore the Queen's train. Teenaged Margaret was already once widowed: her first husband,

Henry, the youngest Dudley brother, had been killed in the imperial war in France. Hertford, Katherine's beloved, had had his titles restored by the Queen the previous day. Had she been aware of the Earl's reckless love affair with Katherine, Elizabeth might have been less generous.

Already the question of the Queen's marriage was paramount. Only a royal heir could ensure political stability. The husbands of the two previous female monarchs had been bad news: Guilford Dudley, son of ambitious, ruthless Northumberland; Philip of Spain, the foreigner who embroiled England in his father's military campaigns. Elizabeth was scandalously infatuated with the dashing Robert Dudley, a married man. She tried to reassure the Council by saying that if she did not marry, she would select a worthy successor. But this merely triggered rumours that she was barren and, inevitably, focused attention on Katherine Grey.

Elizabeth sought to diminish Katherine's potential power base by slighting her. Courtiers sycophantically followed suit. Katherine felt cold-shouldered. She complained to the Count of Feria, Philip's anglo-phile Captain of the Guard, that the Queen disliked her. On one occasion Katherine was so irritated that she lost her temper in the Presence Chamber, using 'very arrogant and unseemly words in the presence of the Queen'.[7]

Feria reported these snippets of gossip to his master, feeling they might prove useful. Elizabeth had quickly disengaged her country from involvement in the imperial war with France. Neither Feria nor Philip trusted her. She had rejected Philip's offer of marriage. He feared she might contract an alliance with Henri II of France. Feria had married the Catholic Jane Dormer, Queen Mary's favourite, who had served in her Privy Chamber with Katherine. He detested Elizabeth, but found Katherine a sweet girl, a refreshing contrast to the 'vain and clever'[8] Elizabeth. Katherine had confided to him that she was a Catholic, and that her Protestant family hated her. Katherine was spinning him a yarn, but Feria swallowed it. Feria had also gleaned that she no longer mooned over Lord Herbert. But Katherine never mentioned Hertford: Feria, assuming she was free of romantic entanglements, suggested she might consider marrying a Habsburg. Katherine, charming and manipulative, was merely exploiting the opportunity to make Hertford jealous. Warned off by his mother, he had ignored her for months.

But in Spain the notion took root; plans were made to get Katherine out of the kingdom. After Feria was recalled, his wife took over the role of go-between. Spanish ships were to drop anchor in the Thames and Katherine was to be smuggled aboard. On 30 June 1559, however, another dramatic incident scotched these romantic schemes. Henri II was riding against his young Scots Captain of the Guard, the Comte de Montmorency, when his opponent's lance pierced his helmet and shattered, one piece of wood penetrating through the King's right eye to the temple. A similar accident had occurred in 1524, when Katherine's grandfather, Charles Brandon, almost killed Henry VIII in a jousting accident. King Henri swayed but managed to stay on his horse until spectators rushed forward to assist him as he swooned. He lay fighting for his life for eleven days. His wife, Catherine de Medici, had several prisoners executed and splinters thrust into their decapitated heads to investigate possible remedies, but in vain.

Henri II's throne passed to his heir, the sickly Francis, who seemed unlikely to embark on any invasion of England. The plot to smuggle Katherine Grey to the Continent fizzled out. Katherine prepared to accompany the Queen on her summer progress, hoping this would provide an opportunity to meet up with Ned Hertford; but Hertford claimed he had been advised by his physician and his mother that he was too weak to join the Queen's progress. Probably his mother was still concerned about the potentially disastrous consequences of his relationship with Katherine.

Queen Elizabeth, clever, diplomatic and superficially conciliatory, never forgot a grievance. When her progress reached Eltham, where Katherine's grandmother Mary Rose had spent much of her childhood, Jane Dormer, Countess of Feria, arrived with a train of Spanish nobles to take her leave of the Queen before travelling to Spain to join her husband. Elizabeth had not forgotten that Jane's grandfather had sat on the jury that sent Anne Boleyn to the scaffold. Jane's father, Sir William Dormer, had been Elizabeth's jailer when Mary placed her under house arrest in 1554. Elizabeth deliberately kept Jane, now seven months pregnant, waiting, standing in the heat. The Spanish attendants, anxious about the countess's well-being, urged her to sit down, but she refused, although she appeared about to faint.

Katherine, who had witnessed the scene in amazement, was soon exhilarated by the arrival at Eltham of her beloved Hertford. Now everyone began to whisper about the 'great love between them'. Katherine's friends suspected that Hertford's ardour was motivated by personal ambition, and that it would all end in tears. But for Hertford and Katherine, this was their magical summer of love. They spent the heady August days together in the intimacy of the royal inner circle, housed in the turreted royal palace of Nonsuch in Surrey, enjoying a constant round of entertainment. The keeper of the castle, Katherine's uncle Arundel (widower of her father's sister Katherine) organised banquets, masques and hunts in the park to entertain the royal party. The trellised groves and ornamental fountains created the perfect fairy-tale setting for romance. Even the Queen, her eyes dazzled by handsome Robert Dudley, succumbed to its charms.

Speculation was rife. The Queen's governess Kate Astley begged Elizabeth to take a husband quickly, to quash the rumours that she had entered into an inappropriate relationship with a married subject. The Queen snapped that since she was never alone, that her ladies of the bedchamber were always nearby, she had little opportunity to behave incorrectly. And, if she did so desire, she added, who could stop her? Who had the authority to tell the Queen of England what to do? Kate Astley, shocked by this high-handed retort, reminded her former pupil that even the hint of scandal could trigger a civil war. Elizabeth recovered her composure, and mumbled, rather pathetically, that she needed Dudley around because 'she had so little joy'.[9]

When the royal party left Nonsuch on 10 August, Dudley remained close to the Queen's side at Hampton Court. Hertford consoled his beloved when Katherine's cousin Thomas Willoughby died from 'overheating'[10] while out hunting, and again two months later, when the publication of John Foxe's *Rerum in Ecclesia Gentarum* rekindled agonising memories of Katherine's sister Jane. Besides several new verses celebrating Jane's piety and steadfastness, the *Rerum* contained Jane's last letter to Katherine, and a detailed description of her death.

In early October 1559, Hertford rode from Hampton Court to Sheen to ask Frances for permission to marry Katherine. Frances received him with relief and pleasure. He had been her father's godson, and she was fond of him. Now Katherine's future was assured. Frances, although only 42, had been ailing for more than seven years. In 1552 she was described as having a constant burning ague and stopping of the spleen. She told her husband Adrian Stokes that she thought Hertford 'very fit'[11] as a match for Katherine, but she feared it might be difficult to persuade the Queen to grant permission for the marriage. Stokes agreed, and advised Hertford to gain friends on the Privy Council before approaching the Queen.

Towards the end of November Frances died. Everything she had not already passed to her daughters she left to Stokes, with whom she had been happy. Four years later, he erected a monument to her, surmounted by her image. Crowned, wearing the robes of a duchess, she bears in her hand a prayer book similar to the one Jane carried to the scaffold. Queen Elizabeth, mollified by the fact that Frances's second marriage had eliminated her from the ranks of potential pretenders to the Crown, showed her appreciation by awarding Frances in death an augmentation to her arms of the royal quartering as 'an apparent declaration of her consanguinity unto us'[12] and promised to pay for the funeral of her ' beloved cousin'.

Her mother's death set Katherine's wedding plans back. She was still in mourning when Hertford wrote a poem comparing his feelings to those of the Greek hero Troilus, separated from his beloved Cressida by political imperatives. Perhaps Hertford was uneasily aware that the Spanish had Katherine in their sights once again. The Queen's obsession with Dudley was damaging her reputation. If the Queen lost her throne, the Spanish ambassador advised Philip to instruct the Archduke Charles, when he came to England to press his suit to the Queen, at the same time to check out the lady Katherine, who was next in line.

Elizabeth, alert to potential threats, had learned of the Spanish plot to spirit Katherine away, and responded by drawing Katherine closer. In 1560, Katherine found herself transported into the Queen's inner circle. Nonetheless, she and Hertford pursued their romance, using his siblings Henry and Jane as intermediaries. The Queen's able Secretary, William Cecil, was driven demented by these court amours, principally the Queen's disgraceful relationship with Robert Dudley. The smouldering scandal erupted into volcanic proportions when Dudley's wife Amy Robsart was discovered dead at the foot of a flight of eight stairs. Amid rumours of foul play, Cecil extracted a promise from the Queen that she would never marry Dudley. The Queen had planned to ennoble Dudley. When she realised that she could not fly in the face of the opinion of her great nobles, Elizabeth, trembling with rage, slashed the patent for Dudley's earldom with a knife.

Cecil now reinforced to Hertford the admonitions of his mother and friends about the growing rumours about Hertford and Katherine, and the potentially destabilising effects. Katherine, unaware that her beloved had been warned off by Cecil, heard that he had been flirting with a girl called Frances Mewtas and sent him a furious letter. Hertford immediately declared that to avoid all suspicion he would marry her, the next time the Queen came to London.[13] When the court reached Westminster the lovebirds held a romantic tryst in Jane Seymour's private closet in the chambers of the maids of honour. With Jane as witness, they plighted their troth, swearing to marry at Hertford's London home the moment the Queen left the palace. Their promise was sealed, Hertford recalled, with kissing, embracing and joining their hands together. He gave Katherine a pointed diamond ring, which she would keep all her life.

Their opportunity came in the late autumn. The Queen was leaving Whitehall for a few days' hunting. Katherine, pleading toothache, was permitted to remain behind, with Jane Seymour for company. Hertford

himself left court that night. They planned to meet at his house at
Cannon Row the next day. Hertford rose early and dismissed his servants. Katherine and Jane Seymour left Whitehall by the orchard stairs and
walked along the sandy riverbank to Cannon Row in the chilly autumn
breeze. Hertford's second groom, John Jenkin, saw them arrive at the
house from the Watergate direction, and rushed to the kitchen to tell the
cook, who gawked at the two ladies. Hertford greeted them warmly, and
Jane hurried off to fetch the priest, who had been waiting nearby. Satisfied
that the couple were free to marry, the service proceeded. Hertford gave
Katherine the gold-linked wedding ring he had commissioned. Each link
was engraved with a line of a verse he had composed.

Hertford then thanked the priest, giving him an enormous tip of £10.
A few delicacies had been prepared, but, 'perceiving them ready to go
to bed,'[14] Jane left them to it. In later depositions, both Hertford and
Katherine described how, overcome by desire, as soon as the door was
shut they stripped off and threw themselves on the bed, both naked but
Katherine still wearing her headdress. He thought it was a fashionable
caul, but in reality it was a veil Katherine had brought with her especially in the pocket of her gown, which she put on as a symbol of her
new status as a married woman. For two hours the young couple gave
free rein to their passion, 'sometimes on one side of the bed, sometimes
on the other,'[15] until the time came for Katherine to return to court for
a dinner engagement. They dressed hastily and joined Jane. Hertford
accompanied his sister and his bride to the steps at the Watergate.

Katherine and Hertford now embarked on a new intrigue: how to
indulge their passion for each other as frequently as possible, while keeping the news of their marriage from the Queen. The political landscape
was in disarray. For the Protestant heir to the throne to be discovered in
an unsanctioned relationship was unthinkable. Jane Seymour remained
their cover story and confidante. Then, in March 1561, Katherine sustained three blows: Jane Seymour, her rock, fell ill and it was soon clear
that she was dying; Hertford was appointed overseas; and Katherine
thought she was pregnant. She asked Jane what she should do. Jane said
there was nothing for it but to confess all to the Queen, and trust in her
mercy. On 29 March, Jane, aged only 19, died. A few days later, Hertford
and Katherine had an urgent meeting in the courtyard at Westminster.
He was under enormous pressure to undertake the European trip, and
also attracted by the idea of the adventure. He told Katherine that if
she expressly told him she was with child, he would stay, but otherwise he was going. Katherine, inexperienced and anxious, said she was
still unsure.

Hertford decided to go. Before he left he wrote his will, bequeathing lands worth £1,000 a year to Katherine. He gave her a signed parchment and some money, and said if she really was pregnant he would come back as soon as he could. After Hertford left, Cecil sought Katherine out and reminded her of the folly of engaging in a close friendship with Hertford without the Queen's consent.

Hertford arrived in Paris on 13 May and plunged into a ferment of activity. Cecil sent his own 19-year-old son Thomas to join him. Thomas brought with him a long memorial from his father with instructions about prayer, Bible study and confession. The two young men visited various French cities, hunting, partying and spending money like water. When Cecil found out, he was furious. But Hertford was winning friends and making a good impression on the French King and his court.

Katherine, now in her eighth month, dreaded facing the Queen. Since Hertford had left, she had sensed that the Queen was showing 'a great misliking with her'. She had sent numerous letters to France, addressed to 'my loving husband', but had no reply.[16] She had no idea whether his love had cooled or whether he had been warned against communicating with her. The only witness to their marriage was Jane Seymour, who was dead. The priest was probably a Protestant exile whom it would be almost impossible to trace. Katherine, frantic, conceived a desperate plan.

Her former father-in-law, Pembroke, had approached her in June suggesting a remarriage to his son, Lord Herbert. Now Katherine was Elizabeth's heir, she was again highly eligible. Katherine had dismissed Pembroke's suggestion. Now, however, as a last resort, she wrote to Lord Herbert saying that she considered they were still married. Herbert began the courtship ritual, sending portraits of himself and items of jewellery. But Katherine still hoped Hertford would return to claim her. She sent Jane Seymour's former manservant, Glynne, to Hertford, with an urgent message that she was 'quick with child'.[17] Herbert suddenly realised that Katherine had been using him. Humiliated and enraged, he demanded his gifts returned. When Katherine did not reply, he sent her a bitter letter in July: he said he saw she intended to keep his presents, 'but if I cannot have them at your hands, I will seek them at that companion's hands ... by whose practise to cover your whoredom and his own knavery and adultery you went about to abuse me ...'.[18] He added that, having hitherto led a virtuous life, he was not about to compromise his honourable reputation by leading the rest of his life 'with a whore that almost everyman had'. He pointed out that they had been legally divorced years ago, and if Katherine sought to entrap him 'with some poisoned bait under the colour of sugared friendship', all he had lost was

a few tokens which she had tricked him out of 'both to cover your abom-
ination and his likewise'.

Katherine was exhausted. She had been up until after midnight the
night before attending a dinner given by Cecil for the Queen. Next day,
at long last, she received a package from Hertford, brought by his brother
Henry Seymour, but it contained only a pair of bracelets from Paris.
To her disappointment, it was not even a personal gift. The Queen had
instructed Hertford to commission chains and bracelets for herself and
her ladies from a French goldsmith.

By the time the royal progress reached Ipswich, Katherine recognised that she was the subject of common gossip and needed someone
to intercede for her with the Queen. In desperation, she turned to the
Queen's favourite, Robert Dudley, once her sister Jane's brother-in-law.
If anyone could soften the Queen's fury, Katherine reasoned, it was he.
But when Dudley broke the news to Elizabeth the next day, she flew
into a rage. Katherine was arrested and taken to the Tower under armed
guard. The Queen ordered the Lieutenant of the Tower, Sir Edward
Warner, to interrogate Katherine rigorously about the relationship with
Hertford and who knew about it. Elizabeth, remembering how her own
mother had lost her life through slander and intrigue, abhorred plots
and conspiracies. On 2 August 1561 Katherine was grilled relentlessly
by professionals. She was friendless, due to give birth imminently and
terrified that her husband had deserted her. Yet she showed something
of her sister Jane's resolute and courageous spirit. Warner reported that
'as to the love practises between her and the Earl of Hertford [,] She will
confess nothing'.[19]

The Queen sent to Paris ordering Hertford to return immediately. At
first he whined that he was sick in bed with fever, and told Nicholas
Throckmorton, the ambassador, that he had no idea why the Queen had
summoned him. This was a lie. He knew Katherine was about to give
birth, and that she had been arrested and imprisoned in the Tower. When
Hertford got back to England he sent Katherine posies and made efforts
to co-ordinate their stories. On 24 September Katherine gave birth to a
son, Edward Seymour, Viscount Beauchamp, heir to Elizabeth under the
will of Henry VIII, following his mother in the line of succession. The
male Protestant succession was secure. Cecil was delighted. The Queen
was incandescent.

Katherine continued her lying-in in the mansion house of the Tower
Lieutenant, surrounded by familiar furnishings and her pet animals. Her
husband's rooms were only a few doors away, and they were allowed
to send each other messages. Outside the Tower, efforts went on to

promote Katherine and her son as Elizabeth's legal heirs. If they succeeded in persuading the Queen, Hertford, Katherine and their baby son
would soon be free. Elizabeth ignored the propaganda and threatened
to have Katherine's son declared a bastard. She ordered a church commission to examine the 'infamous conversation and pretended marriage
betwixt the Lady Katherine Grey and the Earl of Hertford'.[20] The young
couple were rowed up and down the Thames from the Tower to the
Archbishop's Palace at Lambeth for questioning day after day.

There were irregularities in their marriage: the banns had not been
read out for three Sundays in a row; nobody had given the bride away;
the couple had not taken Holy Communion. But according to canon
law, a marriage was valid if vows were exchanged in the presence of
witnesses. The problem was that Jane Seymour was dead and the priest
had vanished.

Hertford was determined to appeal. Meanwhile, he bribed two of his
guards to allow him to spent time with his wife. On 25 May, late at night,
Katherine welcomed him into her fine silk-hung bed where for a precious
half hour they made love 'with joyful heart'.[21] Four days later Hertford
managed another tryst with romance, but the third time the guards panicked and Hertford found the door to his wife's room bolted. She heard
him cursing and struggled to get the door open but failed, to her distress,
longing to be with her 'sweet bedfellow',[22] her 'naughty Lord',[23] again.

Katherine knew she had fallen pregnant again. When Hertford got
her message, he was overjoyed. Elizabeth's commissioners had declared
their son Edward a bastard. They would not get away with the same
trick twice: Katherine and Hertford had declared their marriage before
the Archbishop of Canterbury and other dignitaries, during their lengthy
and repeated interrogations.

Katherine and her children were still in the Tower in summer 1563
when the plague ravaged London, killing a thousand people a week.
Eventually, the Queen agreed that they should be moved to protect them
from the disease. However, they were to be separated and their relatives
were to foot the bill. Katherine's older son, Edward, was to be sent to her
mother-in-law the Duchess of Somerset at Hanworth, with his father.
Katherine and baby Thomas were to be sent to her uncle, Lord John
Grey, at Pirgo in Essex. Elizabeth informed John that he was now his
niece's jailer and that Katherine was not being released, simply moved
for her own protection. She was forbidden to contact her husband or
her sister Mary, who remained at court. Katherine left her rooms in the
Tower wrecked, the bed of changeable damask and the furniture 'torn
and tattered by her monkeys and dogs'.[24]

She arrived at Pirgo with her baby, his nurse, three ladies and two manservants. At first she played happily, dressing up her baby in tiny jackets of russet velvet, with hats to match, and ordering new furs for herself, but when the novelty wore off she sank into depression and lost her appetite. Lord John became concerned about her, and wrote to Cecil. Cecil suggested Katherine could keep on petitioning the Queen, suggesting what she might say and offering to read the drafted message, which would then be entrusted to Lord Robert Dudley, the one person who could deliver it without risking the Queen's displeasure. Katherine cast herself on the Queen's mercy, admitted that she did not deserve it 'for my most disobedient and rash matching of myself, without your highness's consent'.[25]

Katherine naively believed the petition would do the trick; she wrote passionately to Hertford about their imminent reunion. She longed to be merry with him, as they were when their two sweet little boys were gotten in the Tower, leaving no shadow of misunderstanding over her meaning. But her hopes were dashed. Elizabeth was unbending. Katherine wept and took to her bed. Her uncle even began to fear she might harm herself.

Hertford's stepfather, Francis Newdigate, blamed Lord John Grey, who reacted by cataloguing all the expenses he had had since having Katherine and her household billeted upon him. Cecil passed the account to Hertford and it was paid. He had been currying favour with the Queen through small gifts, and trying to move Dudley to obtain a pardon for Katherine, but Dudley said the Queen was in no mood to hear it. Lord John boldly declared that it was Lent, and the Queen's confessor ought to exhort her to forgive and forget if she herself sought forgiveness. He was clapped up in the Tower. Efforts to promote Katherine as her rightful heir enraged Elizabeth. Katherine and baby Thomas were bundled out of Pirgo and placed under close arrest, first at Ingatstone and later at Gosfield Hall, the house of Sir Owen Hopton, a former Lieutenant of the Tower. Katherine kept up her desperate efforts to contact her husband and older son. Hertford replied with gifts and trinkets. His mother, Lady Somerset, complained to Cecil that it was 'unmeet … that this young couple should thus wax old in prison', but Cecil sadly replied that he himself was now 'somewhat in disgrace' for the 'part he had taken as their advocate with the Queen'.[26]

Katherine and her beloved husband, whom she had adored so passionately in defiance of the Queen and at huge risk, would never meet again. In January 1568, Katherine knew she was dying. She may well have starved herself to death. She had two last requests. The first was a message to the Queen, begging her forgiveness for marrying without the royal consent. Katherine's mother Frances had successfully entreated Queen Mary to forgive Katherine's father for his treason, just before his execution, and this had saved the family from ruin. Katherine pleaded with the Queen for her own children and for her husband, Hertford. Katherine hoped that he would now be freed, 'to glad his sorrowful heart withal'.[27]

She then asked for her ladies to bring her jewellery box. Inside were the pointed diamond that Hertford had given her when they were betrothed in his sister's chamber at Whitehall, and the wedding ring with its five gold links, and a *memento mori* ring mounted with a death's head. As she handed the last of the rings to Sir Owen, Katherine said: 'This shall be the last token unto my Lord that I shall ever send him. It is the picture of myself.' The ring was engraved for her husband: 'While I lived, yours.'[28]

Elizabeth never truly forgave Katherine for marrying Hertford. She ordered Hopton to make the funeral arrangements for 'our cousin the Lady Katherine, lately deceased, daughter of our entirely beloved cousin, the Lady Frances, Duchess of Suffolk'.[29] Katherine had been too dangerous to be 'entirely beloved'. Elizabeth put on the expected public show of mourning, but the Spanish ambassador, for one, felt her grief was feigned. 'She was afraid of her,' he added.[30]

Katherine's funeral was packed and was carried out with the pomp and circumstance due to a Tudor princess. On banners, escutcheons, bannerolls and paper hangings adorning the house and the church, Katherine's arms were represented, symbols of her position as Elizabeth's Protestant heir. A local legend claims that one of Katherine's pet dogs pined to death upon her grave, as the Skye terrier of Mary Queen of Scots would also be reputed to do.[31]

Her son Thomas was placed in the care of his paternal grandmother, the Duchess of Somerset, who was already caring for his brother Edward, and brought up in state; the 6-year-old Viscount Beauchamp being considered heir presumptive by the Council. Six years later, both boys were declared illegitimate, although the Protestant party still supported their claim. Their father remained a widower for twenty-eight years, working behind the scenes to establish his sons' legitimacy and to re-establish himself in the Queen's favour. In 1596 he married Frances Howard. When she died in 1600 he married another member of the Howard family, another Frances. Three years later Queen Elizabeth herself was dying, and her counsellors implored her to name her successor. Beauchamp's name was mentioned. Immediately the old flames of hatred were rekindled.

'I will have no rascal's son in my seat, but one worthy to be a king,' the dying Queen snarled.[32] They were her last coherent words.

The following year, Hertford won the battle for his sons' rights. Beauchamp was proclaimed heir by Parliamentary statute. In 1606 the clergyman who had married Hertford and Katherine emerged from the shadows, gave his account of the ceremony and vouched for its validity. Once, this would have been inflammatory stuff. Now, it occasioned hardly a ripple. King James lost no sleep over the descendants of Mary Rose. The Grey girls were gone: Lady Jane on the scaffold, Lady Katherine dead, Lady Mary too, widowed, childless and obscure.

But secret and unsuitable marriages were a family trait: first Mary Rose and Brandon, then Katherine and Hertford: in 1611, Hertford's grandson, Lord William Seymour, secretly wed and attempted to elope with Lady Arbella Stuart, great-granddaughter of Margaret Tudor, Queen of Scotland, and the granddaughter of Lady Margaret Lennox, whom Henry VIII had imprisoned for marrying. Henry VIII's niece, Lady Margaret Douglas, later Countess of Lennox, was imprisoned for falling in love with Thomas Howard, a younger brother of the Duke of Norfolk, and exchanging gifts with him in a secret marriage contract. In July 1536, Lord Thomas was sent to the Tower. He was attained by Act of Parliament and died in prison, and Lady Margaret Douglas was also sent to the Tower.[33]

'The Least of all the Court ...'

In the Tudor world order, royalty needed to look the part; Mary Grey, stunted and misshapen, did not. She further disqualified herself by falling in love with a commoner, a widower twice her age. Thomas Keyes was a former soldier who, as Sergeant Porter, was in charge of palace security, a post of huge responsibility, which testified to his loyalty and integrity, as well as his imposing physique. Keyes, the biggest man at court, was capable of dealing with drunken brawlers and other threats. Mary Grey saw him daily at the palace gates, with the guard. Despite the almost comical difference in their physiques, the discrepancy in their status and the risk of the Queen's displeasure, Keyes courted lively little Mary traditionally with tokens and gifts – a ruby ring, a gold chain with a little hanging bottle of mother of pearl. With one sister dead and the other under house arrest, Mary and her admirer had to await the psychological moment before progressing their relationship.

In the autumn of 1564, the Queen had more pressing concerns than Mary Grey's romance with the Sergeant Porter. In one of her more far-fetched ploys, she had proposed her beloved Robert Dudley as a consort for Mary, Queen of Scots. She had elevated Dudley to the Earldom of Leicester, to make him a more fitting match. Mary indignantly rejected Elizabeth's cast-off lover and revealed her plan to marry her Catholic cousin, Henry, Lord Darnley. The announcement plunged Elizabeth's Council into a furore. Darnley would be able to raise an English army from the Catholic North, and to rely on the support of all Catholic Europe. The Queen's anger blazed. When the Council again raised the question of Katherine Grey's claim to the throne, it poured fuel on the flames.

Mary and Keyes could hardly have chosen a less propitious moment to decide to wed. But, recklessly, they went ahead and picked a date, 16 July 1565. They planned to marry in secret while the court was distracted, attending a huge wedding at Durham House on the Strand, between Henry Knollys, a grandson of Mary Boleyn, and the heiress Margaret Cave. The scheme nearly miscarried; the Queen almost missed the Durham House party because of the need to avert a diplomatic incident between the French and the Spanish ambassadors over a question of precedence. However, the matter was resolved, and the extravagant wedding feast, a tourney, two masques and a ball, kept the court occupied until the early hours, leaving ample time for Mary and Keyes and a handful of their friends, servants and three of Mary's cousins to hasten down the rush-strewn corridor to a room near the Council Chamber.

Here by candlelight the giant Sergeant Porter and the tiny Maid of Honour took their vows; he slipped on her finger a gold ring that would have fitted a child. Everyone knew how dangerous it was: Mary's cousin Margaret Willoughby, the orphan who had stayed with the Grey sisters in 1554 and was now married to Sir Matthew Arundell, was afraid to witness it, so she listened to the proceedings from outside the chamber door.

Mary knew that the risk would be much less for a servant than for someone of higher rank, and had accordingly sent for a sweet country girl, Frances Goldwell, in the service of Lady Knollys's sister, Lady Howard of Effingham, to be a witness. Mary had a soft spot for young Frances. The small gathering celebrated the clandestine nuptials with wine and festive fare, and then the guests departed and Thomas and Mary went to bed. Their happiness would be short-lived.

Less than two weeks later, on 29 July, Mary, Queen of Scots, married Henry Darnley in her private chapel in Edinburgh. Mary assured the Queen of England that she would do nothing to enforce the newly-weds' substantial joint dynastic claim or to overturn the laws of England. She and Darnley asked to have the succession settled in their favour by Act of Parliament.

Elizabeth, well aware that the Parliament she had prorogued would press Katherine's claim, was not in the mood for any more trouble from the Greys. On 21 August gossip reached her ears about Mary Grey's marriage. Cecil, appalled, denounced it as 'monstrous'. 'The Sergeant Porter, being the biggest gentleman of this court, has married secretly the Lady Mary Grey. The least of all the court ... the offence is very great.'[1]

Lady Howard interrogated her servant Frances Goldwell, but loyal Frances played dumb and pretended she had not understood what was going on, confirming Lady Howard's view that she was stupid. Frances risked dismissal, but Mary knew her friends would take her in. For Mary herself, and her new husband, things were more serious. Elizabeth, incensed, ordered them to be thrown into separate prisons, like Katherine and Hertford. Elizabeth's problem with the Greys was that Parliament's support of their claims as Protestant claimants to the throne threatened Elizabeth's absolutist belief in the divine right to rule and the authority of the monarch. Dynastic legitimacy was all; it must prevail over the secular power of parliamentary statute.

Mary's first jailor was kindly Sir William Hawtrey, High Sheriff of Buckinghamshire. He made life as pleasant for Mary as he could. But she was confined in a 12ft/sq room in his house at Chequers, overlooking trees and gardens where she was rarely permitted to stroll. She was forbidden to see anyone or go anywhere. She was allowed only one groom and one waiting woman, and her food, which the Queen was paying for, was far from lavish. Mary now began bombarding Cecil with letters, entreating him to plead for her with the Queen for forgiveness.

Keyes paid even more dearly for his love than his bride. He had enjoyed a position of trust, and his betrayal was adjudged the more abhorrent. Where Mary was confined in a country house, Keyes was thrown into the dreaded Fleet, the ill-reputed prison built in 1197 on the eastern bank of the Fleet River in Farringdon. He was placed in single confinement in a tiny, cramped cell, agonising for a man of his stature. He lingered on in the Fleet after Mary was moved to Buckinghamshire to the care of her step grandmother, Catherine Suffolk.

When she arrived on 7 August 1567, Catherine Suffolk could not believe how impoverished Mary was or the deplorable and dilapidated condition of her few possessions. She had an old feather bed, torn and patched, a couple of tattered hangings and a canopy of fine silk scant 'good enough to hang over some stool' (lavatory). The Duchess of Suffolk, who had lost many of her own possessions during her long exile under Queen Mary, was at a loss how to provide for the new member of her household. She was already reduced, she told Cecil, to borrowing from her friends. She hoped Cecil would persuade the Queen to send a few necessities to equip just one room, which Mary would share with her maid, 'some old silver pots to fetch her drink in, and two little cups ... one for beer another for wine'. She thought it might be too much to ask for a pitcher and bowl to wash in, although Mary needed these, too. She added that Mary was sad, and ate 'not so much as a chicken's leg in two days'.[2]

Mary was, under law, Elizabeth's heir. Katherine Grey's sons had again been declared illegitimate. In May 1568, four months after Katherine's untimely death, Mary, Queen of Scots, escaped her island prison in Scotland and arrived in England aboard a fishing boat. Cecil persuaded the Queen to imprison her Scottish cousin, but he could not convince her to release Mary Grey. Instead, in June 1569, Mary was moved from her step grandmother's house to a less congenial prison, in the London home of affluent merchant and former Lord Mayor Sir Thomas Gresham. This not only tightened up security on Mary, but meant that she was no longer a drain on Elizabeth's finances, as the wealthy Gresham took over Mary's expenses.

Gresham House in Bishopsgate had advantages, a garden where Mary could walk under supervision and a chapel where she could pray. But the household was an unhappy one; Gresham's ill health, the loss of the Greshams' only son and the constant carping and resentment of Lady Gresham soured the atmosphere. Mary had not been there long before the Greshams were actively petitioning the Queen to remove her. Mary spent most of her time locked in her room with her books in English, French and Italian. At last her husband was released from the Fleet and given a post at Sandgate Castle, in his home county of Kent. In May he plucked up the courage to ask Archbishop Parker to intercede for him with the Queen and beg that Mary might be released so they might live together. But no pardon for Mary was forthcoming from the Queen.

Gresham redoubled his efforts to get rid of his unwelcome house guest. A far-sighted entrepreneur, he had built the Exchange shopping centre, but its shops remained for the most part untenanted. He now realised that a royal visit would kill two birds with one stone: it would attract storekeepers to set up in the centre and it would at the same time present an occasion where he could ingratiate himself with the Queen and endeavour to get Mary relocated. Accordingly, he told the shopkeepers to put on a gala show, placing attractive goods on display and lighting candles. In return, he promised to charge no rent for that year. The Queen was delighted by a banquet and a play, which was mundane but full of flattery; she toured the arcades and set the seal on a successful day by calling for a herald and dubbing the Gresham shopping centre the Royal Exchange. The shopping precinct became an overnight success; milliners, haberdashers, armourers, apothecaries, booksellers, goldsmiths and glass-sellers flocked to tenant the mall, and Gresham was soon able to quadruple the rents he charged.

Meanwhile, Thomas Keyes, broken by the ill effects of his confinement in the Fleet and despairing of ever seeing Mary again, died. When the news was broken to Mary, she was distraught. She was sent to one of Gresham's country houses to recuperate, but it was a month before she could bring herself to write to Cecil, who had been created Baron Burghley by Queen Elizabeth on 25 February 1571, pleading again for her freedom and the Queen's pardon. Grief had inspired a new resolution in Mary, and a sting in her words. She wrote: 'God having now removed the occasion of her Majesty's justly conceived displeasure towards her':[3] for the first time, she signed herself Mary Keyes. A portrait of Mary dated 1571 shows her proudly displaying her wedding ring. With her new steadfastness, Gresham found Mary's presence even more of a trial. Determined to be rid of her, his efforts to get her removed became manic. He wrote to Burghley twice in one day in November 1571, and again in January he begged Burghley to bring about her removal because Mary and Lady Gresham quarrelled incessantly.

In May 1572, the Queen finally agreed to release the last Grey sister. But she did not release Mary's inheritance. Mary found herself penniless. Her stepfather Adrian Stokes had just remarried, to Anne Carew, widow of Sir Nicholas Throckmorton, who brought with her into the marriage six sons and a daughter. Gresham suggested Mary be sent to join the Stokes household. Mary knew she would be welcome there, but she was reluctant to add to her stepfather's financial burdens. Reluctantly Elizabeth agreed to pay her cousin a small allowance. A few days later Mary, to everyone's relief, left the Greshams', 'with all her books and rubbish', as Gresham recorded contemptuously.[4]

Mary was 27. After seven years as a prisoner, she enjoyed the welcome offered her in the lively household of her stepfather and his new wife. But Mary valued her independence and was loath to be beholden. By February 1573 she was running her own modest household in the London parish of St Botolph's Without Aldgate. She could now enjoy visiting her friends. The Queen's attitude towards her was perceptibly softening. At New Year 1574, Elizabeth accepted Mary's gift of a pair of bracelets. The following year, Mary's income from her mother's former estates was increased. She could now afford fashionable clothes and keenly followed the prevailing theological debate between the 'forward' Protestants, derisively known as Puritans, and the conservatives, favoured by the Queen. But she cleverly avoided avoid personal involvement either with religious matters or the succession. By the end of 1577, Mary, rehabilitated, was appointed Maid of Honour to the Queen. She spent Christmas at Hampton Court, the most splendid of Elizabeth's palaces, where the walls shone with gold and silver, and the paintings and furnishings were breathtaking.

This happiness was not to last. In 1578 the shadow of the plague fell once more upon the kingdom. By 17 April, Mary knew she was dying. She had not followed the flight of the court, who always headed for the country at the first sign on infection, perhaps hoping her 'mystic ruby' would protect her. This magical treasure was reputedly created from the crystallisation of the blood in very ancient wise unicorns, pooled at the base of their horn, a distillation of their mystic essence. Both Lady Jane Grey and Mary possessed one.

Mary drew up her will, calling herself Lady Mary Grey – the name she used at court – yet acknowledging her marriage to Keyes by writing 'widow'. She bequeathed her mystic ruby and her mother's jewels to her step grandmother, Catherine Suffolk, and her tankards, her horses, her bed and her money to friends and cousins; the bulk of her modest fortune went to her late husband's daughter and granddaughter. She was 33.

Queen Elizabeth ordered that Mary should be buried in Westminster Abbey on 14 May in her mother's tomb. Mary's grave has no personal marker or monument. But Mary, unlike her older sisters, died free, and perhaps found peace. With all three Grey sisters dead and Katherine's boys pronounced illegitimate, their cousin Margaret Clifford, now Countess of Derby, became Elizabeth's heir under the terms of Henry VIII's will.

Within weeks, partly thanks to her own rash behaviour, Margaret was placed in various people's houses as a prisoner. She died 18 years later, without ever tasting freedom again.

Alas!

Burghley continued to cherish the ambition that one day one of Katherine Grey's sons would reign. Both had at various times been declared illegitimate, but then, Elizabeth herself was illegitimate in law. However, the great statesman's hopes were blighted by the headstrong Tudors' proclivity for unsuitable romantic liaisons. In 1581, 19-year-old Lord Beauchamp became infatuated with his relation Honora Rogers. Beauchamp's father Hertford found her an unsuitable wife for a future King of England. He nicknamed Honora 'Onus Blowse', 'that tiresome tramp',[1] and ordered his son to drop her. Beauchamp promised, but secretly continued to bombard Honora with love letters, bewailing their separation. In August 1585, the exasperated Hertford had his son kidnapped and imprisoned in one of his houses. Beauchamp threatened suicide if he were forced to part from his beloved, and entreated Queen Elizabeth to intervene.

The wily Elizabeth seized the opportunity to destroy Beauchamp's claim to the throne by promoting an unsuitable alliance which would virtually disqualify him. When the Queen intervened, Hertford had no choice but to accept his son's marriage. Elizabeth cunningly pacified Hertford by finally granting him permission to marry his mistress of the past ten years, Frances Howard, daughter of Lord Howard of Effingham.

Hertford, now 46, had been a widower for twenty years or more by the time he and Frances married. (They may have been clandestinely married years before he was able to acknowledge her in public.) Hertford attempted to have this marriage set aside in 1595 (hoping to clear his still illegitimate sons' claims to the throne). He was arrested again, and Frances died in 1598.

In May 1601, now over 60, he secretly married once more; his new bride was Frances Prannell, confusingly also born Frances Howard, now a wealthy and beautiful 21-year-old widow. Frances was the daughter of

Thomas Howard, 1st Viscount of Bindon. She had many suitors, one of whom, Sir George Rodney, in despair at her marriage to Hertford, wrote her a sonnet in his own blood, threatening suicide. In her 'Answer', a witty verse-epistle of 160 lines, Frances drew on various literary sources, including Munday's *Hecatonphila* and Shakespeare's *As You Like It*, mocking Rodney's Petrarchan posturing:

> No, no, I never yet could hear one prove
> That there was ever any died for love.[2]

Upon receiving this, Rodney wrote a farewell note and slit his own throat. It was rumoured that the marriage was unhappy: the ageing Hertford was so jealous of his bride's allure and popularity at court that he kept her sequestered in the country, where her principal entertainment was hunting rabbits. (After Hertford died in 1621, at the unusual age, for the time, of 82, Frances married Ludvick Stuart, Duke of Richmond, and her life became more cheerful until her death in 1639.)

Burghley, now a white-bearded sage, but his acute faculties undiminished, quickly rallied from his disappointment and concentrated his energies on Katherine's younger son, Thomas Seymour, the boy conceived in the Tower when his amorous parents defied their jailors to be together. Burghley was buoyant: he was at last making progress with his plot for the destruction of Mary, Queen of Scots. The previous year, he and Walsingham had drafted the Bond of Association, whose members pledged to arrange Mary's murder in the event of any palpable threat to Elizabeth's life.

In February 1587 Mary was executed.

In 1589, 24-year-old Thomas Seymour appealed against the decision that rendered him illegitimate. Although the appeal was rejected, Thomas was undismayed, conscious that the veneration the older generation felt for the Queen was not shared by his compeers. Among younger people he sensed a restless longing for change. Society marginalised old women, and the Queen was visibly ageing. Moreover, resentment against female rule had long festered in the country. In 1591, Hertford scored an immense propaganda coup when he entertained the Queen during her summer progress at one of his manor houses, Elvetham in Hampshire. Hertford laid on a magnificent spectacle for the royal visit, including an artificial lake and an island crowned by a huge ruined fort. Upon her arrival, he welcomed the Queen attended by 300 mounted retainers, all resplendent in chains of gold, sporting black and yellow feathers in their hats, a princely display of power and status disguised as a mark of respect to the elderly monarch. The pageant's themes, winter and spring, were presented as the expression of adulation of the Queen, whose vanity had remained undiminished with her advancing years, but the subtext was that Gloriana was a childless old maid. The impressive show, fireworks and banquets presented by Hertford had been outshone within living memory only by the triumphant celebrations staged in 1575 at Kenilworth Castle, organised by the Queen's favourite, Robert Dudley, Earl of Leicester.

A few months after his father's extravaganza, Thomas Seymour reinforced his appeals about the validity of his parents' marriage and his own legitimacy. It was a dangerous game. In 1594, Thomas's cousin Margaret Clifford's only son, Ferdinando, Earl of Derby, would die in suspicious circumstances. In the autumn of 1595, Sir Michael Blount, Lieutenant of the Tower, was caught secretly stockpiling arms for Hertford. Hertford found himself once more a prisoner in the Tower. He was released on the intervention of Burghley and his son, Sir Robert Cecil. But Hertford's dynastic ambitions received another blow in 1600 when Thomas predeceased him, aged only 37.

Thomas was dead, Beauchamp's marriage had disqualified him as a claimant to the throne, yet Hertford, undaunted, still fancied his family's chances. He clung to the hope that the clan's aspirations could be revived by a brilliant match for his grandchild, Edward Seymour. This dynastic union would involve Arbella Stuart, granddaughter of the redoubtable Bess of Hardwick, now Countess of Shrewsbury. In 1574, Bess, a former lady-in-waiting to Hertford's mother-in-law Frances Grey, had married her daughter Elizabeth Cavendish – Katherine Grey's godchild – to Charles Stuart, younger son of the Countess of Lennox, brother to the murdered Henry, Lord Darnley, husband of Mary Queen of Scots. This match, arranged by the mothers, resulted in the birth in 1576 of Arbella Stuart. 'My jewel Arbell',[3] the darling of her ambitious grandmother Bess, was thus a great-granddaughter of Margaret Tudor, Queen of Scotland. Since Arbella and both her parents had been born in England, many considered her claim superior to that of James I.

Increasingly, however, her gender counted against her. People were convinced that all the social problems and political unrest of the decade had come about because the country was ruled by a woman; the weakness of character traditionally ascribed to females was reflected in England's ills. Hertford hoped that a marriage between Arbella and young Edward Seymour, uniting as it did the Tudor lines of Henry VIII's two sisters, could create a joint candidacy which would attract widespread support.

In 1602, a servant to the Countess of Shrewsbury appeared at Hertford's London house in Tottenham, asking to speak with the Earl alone. Hertford knew well enough what lay behind this unheard of request from a servant. The man was duly admitted to his presence. But when he heard the outrageous message he bore, Hertford's nerve failed.

Queen Elizabeth, suspicious to the point of paranoia, possibly with good reason, had ensured that Arbella had been kept well out of the public gaze throughout her entire adult life. From the age of 18 to 28, she had been sequestered in the country. Arbella, like Jane Grey, was highly educated, but she was trapped in dependence and maidenhood, with no prospects of marriage. In her enforced seclusion her imagination fed on stories of intrepid and unconventional marriages, like those of her parents and of her mother's godmother, Katherine Grey. Determined to spread her wings and break free of her enervating situation, the message she sent to Hertford through her grandmother's servant stated that Arbella's grand- mother would do nothing without the Queen's permission. However, Arbella, dizzy with notions of romance, had another suggestion: she pro- posed that young Edward Seymour should come to Hardwick in disguise, pretending to be a relative of some old man suing to sell land or borrow money. Arbella had never met Edward, so she instructed the servant to ask Hertford that his grandson should bring with him as identification either a picture of Lady Jane Grey or something in Jane's handwriting, both of which she was familiar with – ideally, Arbella suggested, the Greek testament that Jane had left to Katherine Grey on her death.

But Hertford scented danger. He had paid too high a price for his own secret unauthorised marriage into the Tudor dynasty. He listened to the servant's message, and then sent him under guard to Cecil. When the Queen learned of Arbella's scheme, the spectre of the fear which had consumed her 40 years before, when Hertford married Katherine, resur- faced. Elizabeth was already in poor health and in no state to deal with upsetting news.

Arbella was in an equally parlous condition. She stopped eating, waxed hysterical and spent much time penning frantic letters to the Queen, accusing Robert Cecil and Hertford of conspiring against her.

In 1603, the Queen died. She had repudiated the descendants of Mary Rose Tudor, her aunt. The way was clear for the Stuart succession. Representatives of the peers, gentry and councillors signed the proc- lamation of 25 March. The next year, laws were passed that set aside Henry VIII's will.

Arbella was invited back to court, but remained unmarried and with- out estate. She rallied her forces for one final desperate act of defiance, marrying Beauchamp's younger son, 22-year-old William Seymour, with- out royal permission. James I ordered Seymour flung into the Tower, but he escaped and fled to France. Arbella was on her way to join him when she was captured and sent to the Tower, where she died in 1615. It was said that she went mad, or possibly starved herself to death, as Katherine is said to have done in 1568.

Her bridegroom fared slightly better. William Seymour remained in exile until 1616, supported by his grandfather Hertford. Under Charles I, he was gradually rehabilitated at court. Now Earl of Hertford, his grandfather having died in 1621, after seeking out the clergyman who had married him to Katherine Grey and therefore legitimising their offspring, William set about re-establishing the family reputation. He had his grandmother Katherine disinterred from her grave in Yoxford, Suffolk, and brought to Salisbury Cathedral, where she was interred with her husband in a magnificent tomb in the corner of the south choir aisle. Katherine's reclining figure is slightly elevated above that of her spouse, as an indication of her royal status. The Latin inscription celebrates the lovers, united at last:

Incomparable Consorts,
Who, experienced in the vicissitudes of changing fortune
At length, in the concord which marked their lives,
Here rest together.

In January 1649 William witnessed the execution of Charles I, and was later given the task of helping entomb the monarch's decapitated body. With three other peers, William was seeking a suitable place where the King's body, its head crudely tacked back in place to lend it dignity, might be interred. Parliament had chosen St George's Chapel, Windsor, for the burial – sufficiently remote and fortified, and therefore unlikely to become a Royalist rallying point or shrine. The four men stamped the floor of the choir in their leathern boots and tapped with staves until they heard a hollow sound. When they opened the tomb they discovered it contained the coffins of William's great-great aunt, Queen Jane Seymour, and another huge coffin, which could only be that of Henry VIII himself, William's great-great uncle.

Under Henry VIII's will, backed by Henrician statute, William Hertford, grandson and heir of Katherine Grey, was the rightful monarch, rather than James Stuart's son Charles I. But the story of the Tudor succession was over, and the burden of their royal descent was lifted at last from Mary Rose Tudor's descendants.

Her niece, Queen Elizabeth I, a woman not given to sentimentality, would comment dismissively: 'You know them all: Alas! What power or force has any of them, poor souls!'

Notes

Chapter 1

1 Calendar of State Papers (CSP): Venetian
2 BL Cotton MS S TITUS
3 BL MS royal 2 AXVIII, f. 29 (Beaufort Hours)
4 Leland, John, *Antiquarii de Rebus Britannicus Collectanea*, vols IV and V (London: 1612; 6 vols ed. Thomas Hearne, Chetham Society, Oxford: 1715, London: 1770), p. 181; BL Cotton MS Julius B.XII, f. 61v–63
5 Allen, P.S. (ed.), *Opus Epistolarum Des. Erasmi Roterodami*, vol. 1 (Oxford: Oxford University Press, 1906), p. 193
6 Ibid., vol. 1, p. 6; Mynors, R.A.B., and Thomson, D.F.S. (trans), *The Complete Works of Erasmus* (CWE), vol. 2 (Toronto: University of Toronto, 1974), p. 216
7 CSP: Spanish, vol. 1, 176
8 Leland, *Antiquarii de Rebus Britannicus Collectanea*, vol. V, p. 353
9 Colvin, H.M., *The History of the King's Works*, vol. III, pt 1 (London: HMSO, 1975), p. 34
10 Leland, *Antiquarii de Rebus Britannicus Collectanea*, vol. V, p. 372
11 College of Arms MS, 1 M 13, f. 66r & v
12 Fisher, John, *The English Works of John Fisher* (ed. J.E.B. Mayor) (Early English Text Society, no 27, 1876), p. 306

Chapter 2

1 Balfour Paul, J. (ed.), *The Reference of the Great Seal of Scotland* (Edinburgh: 1882), 2602, p. 553
2 Ibid., 67v
3 Ibid., p. 271
4 Petrus Carmelianus, *Honorificia gesta solemnes cerimonii & triumphi habiti in suscipienda legatione pro sposalibus et matrimonio inter principem Karolum & Dominam Mariam* (London: 1509), translated into English London, 1509, printed in *Camden Miscellany* (ed. J. Gairdner), vol. 9

Chapter 3

1 CSP: Spanish
2 Letters and Papers Illustrative of the Reigns of Richard III and Henry VII, ed. J. Gairdner, Rolls Series, 2 vols (London: 1861–63) (L&P)

3 CSP: Spanish
4 Ibid.
5 Pegge, Samuel, *Curalia; or an Historical Account of some Branches of the Royal Household*, Part I (London: 1791), p. 89
6 Gunn, S.J., *Charles Brandon, Duke of Suffolk c.1485–1545* (Oxford: Oxford University Press, 1988), p. 5
7 Ibid.
8 Paston Letters. Letter LXXXV Sir John Paston to John Paston Esq. or Margery Paston his wife, 23 or 25 August 1478 (London: Charles Knight & Co.)
9 Deposition of Walter Devereux, Earl of Hereford, 1552, in *Rivals in Power: Lives and Letters of the Great Tudor Dynasties* (ed. D. Starkey) (London: Macmillan, 1990), p. 40
10 Gunn, *Charles Brandon, Duke of Suffolk c.1485–1545*, p. 28 and n.
11 Report of the Deputy Keeper of the Public Records, 36 (London, 1875), 146; L&P I.i. 604 (12), 682 (5); PRO E 36/214, fo. 261
12 Jones, M., and Underwood, M.G., *The King's Mother* (Cambridge: Cambridge University Press, 1992), p. 236
13 L&P Hen VIII, vol. 1, pt 1, p. 38
14 *The Great Chronicle of London* (ed. A.H. Thomas and I.D. Thorney, London: 1938)
15 Starkey, *Rivals in Power*, p. 29
16 Williams, Neville, *Henry VIII and his Court* (London: Macmillan, 1971)
17 Hall, Edward, *The Union of the Two Noble and Illustre Famelies of York & Lancaster*, ed. H. Ellis (London: 1809)
18 Ibid.
19 L&P
20 Plowden, Alison, *The House of Tudor* (Stroud: The History Press, 1970, repr. 2011)

Chapter 4

1 CSP: Spanish
2 Weir, Alison, *Henry VIII: King and Court* (London: Ballantine Books, 2001), p. 136
3 Cavendish, George, *The Life and Death of Cardinal Wolsey* (London: Folio Society edn, 1962), p. 13
4 L&P
5 CSP: Milanese
6 Ibid.
7 L&P Hen VIII, vol. 3, pt 2, p. 2958

Chapter 5

1 CSP: Venetian
2 Ibid.
3 Perry, Maria, *Sisters to the King: the Tumultuous Lives of Henry VIII's Sisters – Margaret of Scotland and Mary of France* (London: André Deutsch, 2002), p. 117
4 L&P Hen VIII, vol. 1, pt 2, p. 2656
5 Scarisbrick, J., *Henry VIII* (London: Yale University Press, 1968), p. 40
6 BL MS Cotton Vitellius CXI F52

7 L&P, Peter Martyr to Lud. F. Mendoza, 3 March, Epist. 537
8 L&P
9 L&P, vol. 1, pp. 4850–4851

Chapter 6
1 L&P Hen VIII, vol. 1, pt 2, p. 3139
2 Perry, *Sisters to the King*, p. 125
3 Calendar of State Papers relating to English Affairs existing in the Archives
   and Collections of Venice and in other Libraries of Northern Italy (ed. L.
   Rawdon-Brown, G. Cavendish-Bentinck, H.F. Brown and Allen B. Hinds,
   38 vols, London, 1864–1947) (hereafter Cal Ven), vol. II, p. 505
4 L&P
5 CSP: Venetian
6 Hall, *The Union of the Two Noble and Illustre Famelies*, p. 569
7 L&P Hen VIII, vol. 1, pt 2, p. 3334
8 Sanuto, Marino, *Diarii*, vol. XIX, (Forni Editori: 1890)
9 SP 1/10 f.84 1515

Chapter 7
1 L&P Hen VIII, vol. 1, pt 2, p. 3252
2 Cal Ven, vol. II, p. 500
3 Weir, *Henry VIII: King and Court*, p. 527: 'When Mary's body was
   exhumed in 1784, her hair was found to be reddish-gold and nearly two
   feet long. A lock has been preserved in Moyse's Hall Museum, Bury St
   Edmunds. It was probably the same colour as Henry VIII's hair.'
4 Cal Ven, vol. II, p. 500
5 L&P Hen VIII, vol. 1, 1509–1514
6 Moulton Mayer, Dorothy, *The Great Regent* (New York: University of
   California, 1966), p. 70; Du Bellay, M. and G., *Les Mémoires de Martin et
   Guillaume du Bellay avec les Mémoires du Maréchal de Fleuranges et le
   Journal de Louise de Savoye*, vol. VI (Paris: 1753), p. 183; Perry, *Sisters to
   the King*, p. 135
7 Hall, *The Union of the Two Noble and Illustre Famelies*, p. 570; Perry,
   p. 133
8 Du Bellay, *Les Mémoires de Martin et Guillaume du Bellay ...*, Vol. VII,
   p. 184; Perry, p. 136
9 Moulton Mayer, *The Great Regent*, p. 72
10 Cal Ven, vol. II, 511, p. 211
11 Du Bellay, *Les Mémoires de Martin et Guillaume du Bellay ...*, Vol. II,
   p. 187
12 Cal Ven, vol. II, pp. 496, 507, 535
13 Ibid., p. 500
14 BL MS Cotton Caligula DVI, f. 257
15 BL MS Cotton Caligula DVI, f. 146
16 L&P Hen VIII, vol. 1, pt 2, p. 3416
17 Ibid., p. 3387
18 Ibid.
19 Hall, *The Union of the Two Noble and Illustre Famelies*, p. 571
20 Quotes in L&P Hen VIII, vol. 1, pt 2, 3376
21 Cal Ven, 1515
22 BL MS Cotton Vespasian BII f. 10

23 L&P Hen VIII, vol. 1, pt 2, 3449 & 3461
24 L&P Hen VIII, vol. 1, pt 2, p. 15
25 Ibid., p. 3461; BL, MS Cotton Caligula DVI, f. 196v
26 Fleuranges, Robert de la Marck, *Histoire des Choses Mémorables en France,* printed in *Les Memoires de Martin et Guillaume du Bellay avec les Memoires du Marechal de Fleuranges et le Journal de Louise de Savoie,* 7 vols (Paris: 1753)
27 Cal Ven, vol. II, p. 553

Chapter 8

1 Journal of Louise of Savoy
2 BL, MS Cotton Vespasian FXIII, f. 281; L&P Hen VIII, vol. 2, pt 1, p. 16
3 Gunn, *Charles Brandon, Duke of Suffolk,* p. 35
4 L&P Hen VIII, vol. 2, pt 1, p. 222
5 Perry, *Sisters to the King,* p. 158
6 BL MS Cotton Caligula DVI, f. 186 r (LP II.i.80)
7 L&P Hen VIII, vol. 2, pt 1, p. 224
8 Perry, *Sisters to the King,* p. 156
9 L&P II.i., pp. 224–6, 256, 367.
10 Duke of Suffolk to Henry VIII, 22 April 1515, reprinted in Starkey, *Rivals in Power,* p. 49
11 Cal Ven, vol. II, p. 618
12 Ibid., p.224
13 Du Bellay, *Les Mémoires,* vol. VI, p. 185

Chapter 9

1 *Four Years at the Court of Henry VIII: Selections from Despatches written by Sebastian Giustiniano, Jan 12, 1515 to July 26, 1519* (2 vols, trans. and ed. L. Rawdon Brown, London: 1854); Weir, *Henry VIII: King and Court,* p. 201
2 Hall, *The Union of the Two Noble and Illustre Famelies,* p. 584
3 Cited in D. Starkey, *Henry VIII: A European Court in England* (London: Collins & Brown, 1991); Weir, *Henry VIII: King and Court,* p. 203
4 Perry, *Sisters to the King,* p. 189
5 BL MS Cotton Caligula BL, f. 275; L&P Hen VIII, vol. 3, pt 1, 1024
6 Hall, *The Union of the Two Noble and Illustre Famelies,* p. 586
7 Ibid., p. 591

Chapter 10

1 CSP: Venetian
2 Ibid.
3 L&P Hen VIII, vol. 2, pt 2, p. 4479
4 Ibid., p. 4481
5 Ibid., p. 4479
6 *Four Years at the Court of Henry VIII ...;* Weir, *Henry VIII: King and Court,* p. 215
7 Cavendish, George, *The Life and Death of Cardinal Wolsey* (London: Folio Society edn, 1962), p. 100
8 Cited in R. Lacey, *The Life and Times of Henry VIII* (London: 1972); Weir, *Henry VIII: King and Court,* p. 219

Chapter 11

1 *The English Works of John Fisher*; Weir, *Henry VIII: King and Court*, p. 227
2 CSP: Venetian
3 Cited in Dulcie M. Ashdown, *Ladies in Waiting* (London: 1976); L&P Hen VIII; Weir, *Henry VIII: King and Court*, p. 221
4 CSP: Venetian; Weir, *Henry VIII: King and Court*, p. 226
5 Fleuranges, *Histoire des Choses Mémorables en France*; Weir, *Henry VIII: King and Court*, p. 228
6 Richardson, Walter C., *Mary Tudor: The White Queen* (London: University of Washington, 1970); Weir, *Henry VIII: King and Court*, p. 227
7 Ibid.
8 CSP: Venetian
9 Vergil, Polydore, *Anglica Historia, AD 1485–1537* (Basel: 1543, 1546; Leyden, 1651; ed. Henry Ellis, London: 1846; trans. and ed. Denys Hay, Camden Society, 3rd Series, 74, Royal Historical Society, London: 1950); Weir, *Henry VIII: King and Court*, p. 228
10 CSP: Venetian
11 Fleuranges, *Histoire des Choses Mémorables en France*; Weir, *Henry VIII: King and Court*, p. 229
12 Ibid.
13 CSP: Venetian
14 Stow, John, *The Annals of England, or, a General Chronicle of England* (London: 1592; ed. E. Howes, London: 1631); Weir, *Henry VIII: King and Court*, p. 231

Chapter 12

1 Starkey, *Rivals in Power*, p. 64
2 Elis Gruffydd, *Chronicle*, November 1523; Starkey, *Rivals in Power*, p. 64
3 Starkey, *Rivals in Power*, p. 64
4 Weir, *Henry VIII: King and Court*, p. 246
5 Ibid., p. 249
6 Scarisbrick, *Henry VIII*, p. 136; Perry, *Sisters to the King*, p. 229
7 L&P, vol. 4, pt 1, pp. 1511, 2159
8 Cavendish, *Cardinal Wolsey*, p. 62.
9 *Hall's chronicle: containing the history of England, during the reign of Henry the Fourth, and the succeeding monarchs, to the end of the reign of Henry the Eighth, in which are particularly described the manners and customs of those periods. Carefully collated with the editions of 1548 and 1550* (London: 1809), p. 703
10 Childe-Pemberton, William S., *Elizabeth Blount and Henry the Eighth, with some account of her surroundings* (London: E. Nash, 1913), p. 138
11 Cited in Bradley M. Morton, *Elizabeth Blount of Kinlet* (Kidderminster: 1991); Weir, *Henry VIII: King and Court*, p. 220
12 *The Register or Chronicle of Butley Priory, 1510–1535*, pp. 51–55
13 Grafton, *Chronicle London* (1569), p. 393
14 Hall, *The Union of the Two Noble and Illustre Famelies*, p. 756
15 L&P Hen VIII, vol. 4, pt 3, p. 6738; Perry, *Sisters to the King*, p. 268

Chapter 13

1 Hall, *The Union of the Two Noble and Illustre Famelies*, p. 758; Cavendish, *Cardinal Wolsey*, p. 125

2 L&P Hen VIII, vol. 4, pt 3, p. 5859
3 Ibid., p. 6019
4 Cavendish, *Cardinal Wolsey*, p. 219
5 Hall, *The Union of the Two Noble and Illustre Famelies*; Cavendish, *Cardinal Wolsey*
6 CSP: Spanish; L&P Hen VIII; Weir, *Henry VIII: King and Court*, p. 327
7 Cal Ven, vol. IV, p. 761
8 Perry, *Sisters to the King*, p. 269
9 Cal Ven, vol. IV, p. 761

Chapter 14

1 Brewer, F.S. (ed.), *Calendar of Letters and Papers, Foreign and Domestic, of the Reign of Henry VIII*, vol. XIII (London: 1894–1910), p. 280
2 L&P Hen VIII, vol. 6, 1533 585
3 MS College of Arms I, 15, f. 124v; Green, M.A.E., *Lives of the Princesses of England* (London: 1849), vol. V, p. 140; Perry, *Sisters to the King*, p. 286
4 CSP: Spanish
5 *Crónica del Rey Enrico Ottavo de Inglaterra* (the Spanish Chronicle – sometimes attributed to Antonio de Guaras; written before 1552; ed. Marquis de Molins, Madrid: 1874; trans. Martin A.S. Hume as *The Chronicle of King Henry VIII of England, being a contemporary record of some of the principal events of the reigns of Henry VIII and Edward VI, written in Spanish by an unknown hand*, London: 1889); Weir, *Henry VIII: King and Court*, p. 349
6 *Chronicle of King Henry VIII*, p. 136
7 Wriothesley, Charles and Hamilton, William Douglas (eds), *A Chronicle of England During the Reign of the Tudors, 1485–1559*, vol. I (London: Camden Society, 1875), p. 160
8 Gunn, *Charles Brandon, Duke of Suffolk*, p. 221
9 De Lisle, Leanda, *The Sisters Who Would be Queen* (London: Harper Press, 2008), p. 19
10 Childs, Jessie, *Henry VIII's Last Victim: the Life and Times of Henry Howard, Earl of Surrey* (London: 2006), p. 260; De Lisle, *The Sisters Who Would be Queen*, p. 20
11 Strong, Roy, *Artists of the Tudor Court, The Portrait Miniature Rediscovered, 1520–1620* (London: 1978), pp. 201–3; Hoak, Dale, 'The Coronations of Edward VI, Mary I and Elizabeth I and the Transformation of the Tudor Monarchy' in C.S. Knighton and R. Mortimer (eds), *Westminster Abbey Reformed* (Aldershot: 2005), pp. 147–9; De Lisle, *The Sisters Who Would be Queen*, p. 25
12 Tytler, Patrick F. (ed.), *Edward VI and Mary*, vol. 1 (London: 1839), p. 138; Haynes, Samuel (ed.), *A Collection of State Papers Relating to Affairs in the Reigns of King Henry VIII, King Edward VI, Queen Mary and Queen Elizabeth From the Years 1542–70, Left by William Cecil Lord Burghley*, vol. VI (London: 1740), p. 838; De Lisle, *The Sisters Who Would be Queen*, p. 30
13 De Lisle, *The Sisters Who Would be Queen*, p. 31
14 Starkey, *Rivals in Power*, p. 134
15 De Lisle, *The Sisters Who Would be Queen*, p. 37
16 Haynes, *A Collection of State Papers ...*, vol. VI, p. 98
17 De Lisle, *The Sisters Who Would be Queen*, p. 38
18 Ibid., p. 41

19 Tytler, *Edward VI and Mary*, vol. 1, p. 140; De Lisle, *The Sisters Who Would be Queen*, p. 42
20 Tytler, *Edward VI and Mary*, vol. 1, p. 133; De Lisle, *The Sisters Who Would be Queen*, p. 46
21 Haynes, *A Collection of State Papers ...*, vol. VI, p. 78; De Lisle, *The Sisters Who Would be Queen*, p. 47
22 Haynes, *A Collection of State Papers ...*, vol. VI, p. 79; De Lisle, *The Sisters Who Would be Queen*, p. 47
23 Tytler, *Edward VI and Mary*, vol. 1, p. 140; De Lisle, *The Sisters Who Would be Queen*, p. 48

Chapter 15

 1 De Lisle, *The Sisters Who Would be Queen*, p. 49
 2 Ibid., p. 50
 3 Ibid., p. 53 and n.14, p. 325
 4 Ibid., p. 54
 5 Bernard, G.W., 'The Downfall of Sir Thomas Seymour' in G.W. Bernard (ed.), *The Tudor Nobility* (Manchester: 1992), p. 231; De Lisle, *The Sisters Who Would be Queen*, p. 54
 6 De Lisle, *The Sisters Who Would be Queen*, p. 58
 7 Ibid., p. 60
 8 Ascham, Roger, *The Whole Works*, ed. Revd Dr Giles, vol. III (London: John Russell Smith, 1864), pp. 118–9
 9 Ibid.
10 Robinson, Hastings, *Original Letters Relative to the English Reformation*, vol. I (Cambridge: Cambridge University Press, 1847), pp. 285, 286
11 Strype, John, *Ecclesiastical Memorials Relating Chiefly to Religion*, vol. II, pt 2 (Oxford: Clarendon Press, 1822), p. 30
12 Wingfield, R., *Vita Mariae Reginae*, trans. D. MacCulloch, Camden Miscellany XXVIII, 4th series, 29 (London: Camden Miscellany, 1984), p. 245
13 Loach, Jennifer, *Edward VI* (New Haven and London: 1999), p. 159
14 De Lisle, *The Sisters Who Would be Queen*, p. 100
15 Ibid., p. 104
16 Ibid., p. 106
17 Nichols, John G. (ed.), *The Diary of Henry Machyn* (London: 1848), p. 34; De Lisle, *The Sisters Who Would be Queen*, p. 107
18 De Lisle, *The Sisters Who Would be Queen*, n.22, p. 331
19 Ibid., pp. 115–6
20 Ibid., p. 116
21 Wingfield, *Vita Mariae Reginae*, p. 265
22 Nichols, John G. (ed.), *The Chronicle of Queen Jane and Two Years of Queen Mary* (London: Camden Society, 1850), p. 8
23 Bryson, Alan, 'The speciall men in every shere, 1547–1553', PhD thesis, University of St Andrews, 2001, p. 280; De Lisle, *The Sisters Who Would be Queen*, p. 119
24 De Lisle, *The Sisters Who Would be Queen*, p. 120
25 Malfatti, C.V. (trans.), *The Accession, Coronation and Marriage of Mary Tudor, as related in Four Manuscripts of the Escorial* (Barcelona: Malfatti, 1956), p. 19
26 Harbison, E.H., *Rival Ambassadors at the Court of Queen Mary* (London: 1940), p. 67

27 De Lisle, *The Sisters Who Would be Queen*, p. 127
28 Beer, Barrett L., *Northumberland, The Political Career of John Dudley, Earl of Warwick and Duke of Northumberland* (Kent, OH: Kent State University Press, 1974), p. 160
29 Nichols, *The Chronicle of Queen Jane and Two Years of Queen Mary*, pp. 25, 26
30 CSPS, vol. XI, pp. 334, 359
31 Nichols, *The Chronicle of Queen Jane and Two Years of Queen Mary*, p. 25
32 De Lisle, *The Sisters Who Would be Queen*, p. 146; Foxe, John, *Acts and Monuments*, ed. Revd Stephen Reed, vol. VI (London: 1838), pp. 415, 417
33 De Lisle, *The Sisters Who Would be Queen*, p. 149 and n.26, p. 335
34 Nichols, *The Chronicle of Queen Jane and Two Years of Queen Mary*
35 Ibid., pp. 56–7; Harris, Nicholas, *The Literary Remains of Lady Jane Grey* (London: Harding, Triphook and Lepard, 1825), cxvii, pp. 58–9; De Lisle, *The Sisters Who Would be Queen*, n. 28, 29, p. 335
36 Ibid.

Chapter 16

1 Nichols, John G. (ed.) *Literary Remains of King Edwards the Sixth* (J.B. Nichols & Sons: 1857), vol. 1, clxv
2 Hatfield House Papers, pt iv, p. 461ff
3 Seacombe, John, *History of the House of Stanley* (Preston: E. Sergent, 1793), section four, p. 1737
4 Peck, Francis, *Desiderata Curiosa* (London: T. Evans, 1732 and 1735), p. 141

Chapter 17

1 Nichols, *The Chronicle of Queen Jane and Two Years of Queen Mary*, pp. 63–4; De Lisle, *The Sisters Who Would be Queen*, pp. 157–8
2 De Lisle, *The Sisters Who Would be Queen*, p. 167
3 Ibid., p. 168, notes that since 1727 a portrait by Hans Eworth of the hard-faced Lady Dacre and her beardless 21-year-old son has been described as showing Frances and Stokes
4 Wyatt, Michael, *The Italian Encounter with Tudor England* (Cambridge: 2005), pp. 122–3; De Lisle, *The Sisters Who Would be Queen*, p. 172
5 BL Add MSS 33749, ff. 47, 66
6 Ibid., 47
7 CSPF vol. II, p. 45
8 Said by Count de Feria, Spanish Ambassador, to Philip of Spain, April 1559; De Lisle, *The Sisters Who Would be Queen*, p. 188
9 De Lisle, *The Sisters Who Would be Queen*, p. 192
10 Ibid.
11 Ibid., p. 194
12 Harris, *The Literary Remains of Lady Jane Grey*, cxvii
13 BL Add MSS 37749, ff. 58, 49
14 Ibid., f. 43
15 Ibid.
16 CSPF, vol. IV, p. 159; BL Add MSS 37749, f. 51
17 De Lisle, *The Sisters Who Would be Queen*, p. 212
18 Tanner MS 193 f. 224
19 CSPD vol. I, p. 184

20 Haynes (ed.), *State Papers*, vol. I, p. 378
21 Baker, J.H. (ed.), *Reports from the Lost Notebooks of Sir James Dyer*, vol. I (London: 1994), p. 82
22 Longleat MSS, Portland Papers, 1 ff. 92, 93, PO/1/93
23 De Lisle, *The Sisters Who Would be Queen*, p. 228
24 Strickland, Agnes, *Lives of the Tudor Princesses* (London: Longmans, Green, 1868), pp. 225–6
25 Ellis, Henry, *Original Letters Illustrative of English History*, First Series, vol. II (London: Harding, Triphook and Lepard, 1825), pp. 281–2
26 Ibid., p. 286; De Lisle, *The Sisters Who Would be Queen*, p. 258
27 Cotton Titus MS, no 107, ff. 124, 131
28 Ibid; De Lisle, *The Sisters Who Would be Queen*, pp. 268–71
29 Harris, *The Literary Remains of Lady Jane Grey*, cxx
30 Ibid.
31 Ibid.
32 Spencer Beesley, Edward, *Queen Elizabeth* (London: Macmillan, 1892), p. 238
33 Starkey, *Rivals in Power*, p. 89

Chapter 18

1 Ellis, *Original Letters*, vol. II, p. 229
2 Read, Evelyn, *Catherine, Duchess of Suffolk* (London: Cape, 1962), p. 144; CSPD, vol. I, pp. 294, 297; De Lisle, *The Sisters Who Would be Queen*, p. 274
3 CSPD vol. I, p. 425
4 De Lisle, *The Sisters Who Would be Queen*, p. 282

Chapter 19

1 HMC Bath, vol. IV, pp. 190–3; De Lisle notes (p. 350) that this is 'more literally, the burdensome female companion of a beggar'
2 F. Seymour, 'The answer of the countess of Hertford', Bodl. Oxf., MS Rawl. poet. 160 [lines 1–115 only], fols. 118v–119v
3 De Lisle, *The Sisters Who Would be Queen*, p. 287

Bibliography

Primary sources

Bodleian Library: Tanner MS, 193 ff. 224, 227

British Library, Cotton MSS, Augustus, Caligula, Cleopatra, Galba, Julius, Nero, Otho, Tiberius, Titus, Vespasian, Vitellius

College of Arms MS

Calendar of the Patent Rolls, Philip and Mary (CPR)

Calendar of State Papers (CSP)

Calendar of State Papers Domestic (CSPD)

Calendar of State Papers Foreign (CSPF)

Hatfield MSS (Hatfield House, Herts)

Letters and Papers Illustrative of the Reigns of Richard III and Henry VII (L&P), ed. J. Gairdner, Rolls Series, 2 vols (London: 1861–63)

Secondary sources

Ascham, Roger, *The Whole Works*, ed. Revd Dr Giles, vols I–III (London: John Russell Smith, 1864)

Balfour Paul, J. (ed.), *The Register of the Great Seal of Scotland* (Edinburgh: 1882)

Beaufort, Lady Margaret, *The Mirror of Golde for the Synfulle Soule* (London: William Pynson, 1506)

Beer, Barrett L., *Northumberland, The Political Career of John Dudley, Earl of Warwick and Duke of Northumberland* (Kent, OH: Kent State University Press, 1974)

Brewer, F.S. (ed.), *Calendar of Letters and Papers, Foreign and Domestic, of the Reign of Henry VIII* (London: HMSO, 1894–1910)

Carmelianus, Petrus, *Honorificia gesta solemnes cerimonii & triumphi habitiin suscipienda legatione pro sposalibus et matrimonial inter principem Karolum & Dominam Mariam* (London: 1508)

Cavendish, George, *The Life and Death of Cardinal Wolsey* (London: Folio Society edn, 1962)

Chapman, Hester W., *Lady Jane Grey* (London: Little, Brown, 1962)

——, *Two Tudor Portraits: Henry Howard, Earl of Surrey, and Lady Katherine Grey* (London: Little, Brown, 1960)

Childe-Pemberton, William S., *Elizabeth Blount and Henry the Eighth, with some account of her surroundings* (London: E. Nash, 1913)

Colvin, H.M., *The History of the King's Works* (London: HMSO, 1963–82)

Crónica del Rey Enrico Ottavo de Inglaterra (the Spanish Chronicle – sometimes attributed to Antonio de Guaras; written before 1552; ed. Marquis de Molins, Madrid: 1874; trans. Martin A.S. Hume as *The Chronicle of King Henry VIII of England, being a contemporary record of some of the principal events of the reigns of Henry VIII and Edward VI, written in Spanish by an unknown hand*, London: 1889)

De Lisle, Leanda, *The Sisters Who Would be Queen* (London: Harper Press, 2008)

Du Bellay, M. and G., *Les Mémoires de Martin et Guillaume du Bellay avec les Mémoires du Maréchal de Fleuranges et le Journal de Louise de Savoye*, 7 vols (Paris: 1753)

Ellis, Henry, *Original Letters Illustrative of English History*, First Series, vol. II (London: Harding, Triphook and Lepard, 1825); Second Series, vol. III (London: 1826)

Erasmus, Desiderius, *Adagiorum* (Basle, 1508), *Moriae Encomium Opus Epistolarum*, ed. P.S. and H.M. Allen (Oxford: Oxford University Press, 1906–58)

Fleuranges, Robert de la Marck, *Histoire des Choses Mémorables en France*, in du Bellay (above)

Fox, Julia, *Jane Boleyn: The Infamous Lady Rochford* (London: Phoenix, 2007)

Grafton, Richard, *A Chronicle at Large and Mere History*, vol. II, ed. H. Ellis (London: 1809)

——, *Chronicle London* (1569)

Gunn, S.J., *Charles Brandon, Duke of Suffolk c.1485–1545* (Oxford: Oxford University Press, 1988)

Hall, Edward, *The Union of the Two Noble and Illustre Famelies of York & Lancaster*, ed. H. Ellis (London: 1809)

Hall's chronicle: containing the history of England, during the reign of Henry the Fourth, and the succeeding monarchs, to the end of the reign of Henry the Eighth, in which are particularly described the manners and customs of those periods. Carefully collated with the editions of 1548 and 1550 (London: 1809)

Harris, Nicholas, *The Literary Remains of Lady Jane Grey* (London: Harding, Triphook and Lepard, 1825)

Haynes, Samuel (ed.), *A Collection of State Papers Relating to Affairs in the Reigns of King Henry VIII, King Edward VI, Queen Mary and Queen Elizabeth From the Years 1542–70, Left by William Cecil Lord Burghley*, vol. VI (London: 1740)

Jones, M., and Underwood, M.G., *The King's Mother* (Cambridge: Cambridge University Press, 1992)

Leland, John, *Antiquarii de Rebus Britannicus Collectanea*, vols IV and V (London: 1612; 6 vols ed. Thomas Hearne, Chetham Society, Oxford: 1715, London: 1770)

Malfatti, C.V. (trans.), *The Accession, Coronation and Marriage of Mary Tudor, as related in Four Manuscripts of the Escorial* (Barcelona: Malfatti, 1956)

Mynors, R.A.B., and Thomson, D.F.S. (trans), *The Complete Works of Erasmus*, vol. 2 (Toronto: 1974)

Moulton Mayer, Dorothy, *The Great Regent* (New York: University of California, 1966)

Nichols, John G. (ed.), *The Diary of Henry Machyn* (London: 1848)

——, *The Chronicle of Queen Jane and Two Years of Queen Mary* (London: Camden Society, 1850)

——, *Literary Remains of King Edward the Sixth*, vol. 1 (J.B. Nichols & Sons, 1857)

Palsgrave, John, *L'Eclaircissement de la Langue Francoyse* (London: 1530)

Peck, Francis, *Desiderata Curiosa*, (London: T. Evans, 1732 and 1735)

Perry, M., *Sisters to the King* (London: André Deutsch, 2002)

Plowden, Alison, *Lady Jane Grey* (Stroud: Sutton, 2003)

——, *The House of Tudor* (Stroud: The History Press, 1970, repr. 2011)

The Register or Chronicle of Butley Priory, 1510–1535

Richardson, Walter C., *Mary Tudor: The White Queen* (London: University of Washington, 1970)

Robinson, Hastings, *Original Letters Relative to the English Reformation* (Cambridge: Cambridge University Press, 1847)

Sanuto, Marino, *Diarii*, vol. XIX (Forni Editori: 1890)

Scarisbrick, J., *Henry VIII* (London: Yale University Press, 1968)

Seacombe, John, *History of the House of Stanley* (Preston: E. Sergent, 1793)

Starkey, D. (ed.), *Henry VIII: A European Court in England* (London: Collins & Brown, 1991)

—— (ed.), *Rivals in Power* (London: Macmillan, 1990)

Strickland, Agnes, *Lives of the Tudor Princesses* (London: Longmans, Green, 1868)

Strype, John, *Ecclesiastical Memorials Relating Chiefly to Religion*, vol. II pts 1 and 2 (Oxford: Clarendon Press, 1822)

Thomas, A.H. and Thorney, I.D. (eds), *The Great Chronicle of London* (London: 1938)

Vergil, Polydore, *Anglica Historia, AD 1485–1537* (Basel: 1543, 1546; Leyden, 1651; ed. Henry Ellis, London: 1846; trans. and ed. Denys Hay, Camden Society, 3rd Series, 74, Royal Historical Society, London: 1950)

Weir, Alison, *Henry VIII: King and Court* (London: Ballantine Books, 2001)

Williams, Neville, *Henry VIII and his Court* (London: Macmillan, 1971)

——, *The Cardinal and the Secretary* (London: Macmillan/McGraw Hill, 1975)

Wingfield, R., *Vita Mariae Reginae*, trans. D. MacCulloch, Camden Miscellany XXVIII, 4th series, 29 (London: Camden Miscellany, 1984)

Wriothesley, Charles and Hamilton, William Douglas (eds), *A Chronicle of England During the Reign of the Tudors, 1485–1559*, vols I and II (London: Camden Society, 1875)

Index